HEBRIDEAN JOURNEY

HEBRIDEAN JOURNEY

By

HALLIDAY SUTHERLAND

GEOFFREY BLES
52 DOUGHTY STREET, LONDON, W.C. 1.

PRINTED IN GREAT BRITAIN BY
J. AND J. GRAY
EDINBURGH

FIRST PUBLISHED 1939
REPRINTED   1940
REPRINTED   1942
REPRINTED   1944
REPRINTED   1946

TO THE MEMORY

OF

COMMANDER LIONEL G. PENNINGTON, R.N.

AND

HIS NINETY-EIGHT COMPANIONS

WHO PERISHED IN THE SUBMARINE *THETIS*

IN LIVERPOOL BAY

ON THURSDAY, 1ST JUNE 1939

CONTENTS

CHAPTER I

FELLOW TRAVELLERS

"NOW that man," said the S.S.C. (Solicitor in the Supreme Court), "has remarkable powers of observation."

"Indeed he has," I agreed, "and it shows how unobservant most of us are."

"It will be interesting to see the crosspieces changing as we cross the border," said the Head Clerk.

Our conversation referred to a well-informed Scotsman who had left the train at Carlisle and to what he had told us about telegraph poles, my fellow passengers now being an elderly Solicitor in the Supreme Court and his Head Clerk.

As the express was approaching Carlisle, I had commented on the similarity of scenery on the border and on the difficulty of knowing where England ended and Scotland began.

"Yes," said the well-informed Scot, "it's difficult to tell from the scenery, but there's one very simple way of knowing. Just look at the telegraph posts and the crosspiece to which the insulators are fixed. In England the crosspieces are attached to the south of the posts—facing London, as it were—but as soon as you're over the border the crosspieces are fixed to the north of the posts, facing Edinburgh."

"Most extraordinary!" I said.

"Not at all. It's very simple. Well, here we are at Carlisle. I get out here and motor to Dumfries. Good afternoon, gentlemen."

"Good afternoon," we answered cordially.

In a short time we were all peering like children through the windows. The telegraph posts on the left were being watched by the S.S.C. and myself, those on the right by the Head Clerk, who used the windows in the corridor. All of us wore glasses, and each man polished his glasses for the task in hand. Windows were wiped with newspapers. Now to watch telegraph posts passing at the speed of seventy miles an hour is no easy matter. You must look ahead, and then turn your head rapidly in order to see the post clearly for the fraction of a second. It is right to add that these ocular exercises are condemned by the majority of ophthalmic surgeons, especially in cases of myopia, astigmatism, pres-byopia, night-blindness, rheumatic irido-cyclitis, and squint. Not that we cared. Each wished to be the first to call "north."

"South—south," I called.

"South," called the S.S.C. "And what's it on your side, John?"

"South," called the Head Clerk.

At that moment the name of a station flashed past.

"Did you see what that was?" asked the S.S.C.

"Yes," I answered, "it was Springfield [a station in Scotland], and to-day is not the First of April!"

"South!" called the Head Clerk.

"Come in, John," said the S.S.C., "we've all been had."

We sat upright in our seats and sought to disguise our ruffled dignities. I was the first to break the silence by saying, "I wonder if that man always tells the same story on his way to Scotland."

2

"If he does," replied the S.S.C., "he has a good reason for leaving the train at Carlisle. Anyway, he's not a Scotsman."

"Of course he's a Scotsman."

"Well, he didn't speak like one," said the S.S.C., who had an Edinburgh accent, which may be detected by the pronunciation of the word "five" as "fiivf."

In England there are solicitors, but in Scotland in addition to solicitors there are Enrolled Law Agents and special societies or incorporations, namely "Solicitors before (or in) the Supreme Courts," "Writers to His Majesty's Signet," and "Members of the Society of Procurators," known in Glasgow as "Writers." Moreover, in Aberdeen there are "Members of the Society of Advocates," not to be confused with Advocates in Edinburgh who are members of the Bar of Scotland.

The man who left the train had a strong Glasgow accent, and although he was not a public benefactor he was certainly an entertainer, for he had also told us a story which illustrates the perils of overpunctuality. The story was about three Scotsmen who met at Euston Station at 7 p.m., which was three hours before the Edinburgh night express, stopping only at Carlisle, was due to leave. They dined in the station restaurant and then adjourned to the refreshment-room, where the rest of their time was occupied in drinking double whiskies. About 10 p.m. the barmaid, who had overheard some of their conversation, drew attention to the clock, and the trio hurried towards the platform. At first they walked rapidly, then trotted, and finally galloped in single file as the train began to move. An obliging porter opened a carriage door on the last coach, and the two leading runners fell into the train. The third man fell on the platform, from where the porter and a ticket-collector assisted him to rise. He was unhurt, for the anaesthetic had been well administered. "A pity you've missed the train, sir," said the collector, a sympathetic man.

"A pity!" exclaimed the Scotsman. "It's more than a pity; it's a disaster of the first magnitude."

"No, no, sir," said the collector. "There's another train in the morning."

"Another train be damned! The two fools who caught that train came here to see me off!"

This must have been the same Scotsman who, on another occasion, opened conversation with a fellow-countryman in a third-class compartment of an express travelling some-where in England during the night. The two had reached the stage of exchanging flasks in the approved manner, which consists of wiping the mouth of your neighbour's flask with your pocket handkerchief before partaking of its contents. Then did the first Scotsman, being a man who liked short drinks and long words, say to the second, "This new amalgamation of the railways is, in my opinion, the most miraculous advance in contemporary civilisation."

"Is that so?" said his companion, who had no wish to argue the point.

"Of course it is, and I'll prove it in a minute. You and I have got to face the facts however miraculous they may be. A few minutes ago you divulged that you're travelling to Glasgow. Is that a fact or is it not a fact?"

"Of course it's a fact."

"Well, there you are! And that proves my contention, because I'm travelling to London, and here we are, the two

4

of us, in the same carriage. Aye, the amalgamation is nothing short of miraculous."

I was going for the week-end to the Manse of Hopekirk before visiting the Western Isles, and travelling from London by the west coast route on which the train passes from England into Scotland across the River Sark. All frontiers should be visible, like the great barrier of the Pyrenees rising from the south-western plains of France, or the Rhine. Your invisible frontiers are dangerous, as witness those post-war frontiers of Central Europe where the kitchen of a house may be in one country and the dining-room in another. The mouth of the Tweed is a good frontier between England and Scotland, but from Berwick-on-Tweed the border line runs south-west, and so similar is the scenery on either side that without a map no traveller could tell whether he was in England or Scotland. The Fells of Cumberland are similar to the hills of Dumfries in their monotony and desolation. There is little arable land, and the contour of the hills is unrelieved by trees or crags.

All along these border lands are the dry dykes raised by generations of men, women, and children. These are stone walls built without mortar and therefore called dry. They run criss-cross over the hills and so divide the grazing. In the aggregate they must extend for hundreds of miles, and all the flat stones of which they are built were once picked from the surface of the land and then wedged together, each according to its shape. It was a fine art, this building of dykes, and is now almost lost, as now there is only one man left in Dumfriesshire who knows how to repair them. The modern farmer uses wire fencing, and that is not so good for the sheep, because the dry dykes give shelter against driven snow.

The well-informed Scotsman had told us of an American whom he entertained in Dumfriesshire and who, after a week of motoring, remarked, "I've seen the Pyramids, but in my opinion these stone dykes are as wonderful."

"How do you make that out?" asked his host.

"They run for hundreds of miles and yet there are no other stones to be seen. Where did all these stones come from? They must have been brought from a great distance."

"And did you enlighten him?" I asked.

"No, no, I thought it best to leave him wondering."

At the eastern side of the Scottish Lowlands the country is more fertile. There is arable land in the basin of the Tweed and in the vales of its tributaries—the Gala, Yarrow, Ettrick, and Teviot. Many of the hills are wooded, and in the towns of Galashiels, Jedburgh, and Hawick are the textile woollen industries. At Hawick station the Minister met me with his car, an ancient vehicle, in which he left me opposite the Town Hall whilst he entered shops to buy provisions.

The car smelt of petrol, and the smell of petrol reminded me of the murderer Rouse who lured an unknown tramp into his car, stunned his victim, and set the car on fire in the hope that the charred remains would be identified as those of Rouse, who had reasons for wishing to disappear. These morbid thoughts I kept to myself. For one thing I was not an unknown tramp; for another, the Minister, so far as I knew, had no wish to disappear; and lastly, he had already assured me that the car was perfectly safe and that all old cars smell of petrol.

On returning with the provisions, he asked me what I thought of the Town Hall.

6

"I would like to knock it down, especially the castellated tower."

"Yes," he agreed, "the longer you look at it, the more you dislike it."

Most shams are ugly, albeit I once saw one that was amusing. One of the speakers in a Union Debate at Edinburgh was nearing the end of a perfervid speech—"Mr. Speaker, sir, we must all loathe and detest a sham"—and to emphasise the words, he swung his right arm in order to point directly at his opponent on the other side of the house, but so violently did he swing the arm that a detached white starched cuff shot from his sleeve and slithered across the polished floor. That ended a promising peroration.

The hamlet of Hopekirk, lying, as its name implies,[1] in the shelter of hills, is seven miles south of Hawick, and in olden time was part of the wide battlefield on which Picts and Scots and Britons of Strathclyde, Angles and Saxons and Danes waged their wars, until in 1018 the whole region to the Tweed and the Cheviots was united with Scotland under Malcolm II. Then came another five centuries of battles, raids and forays between Scots and English, centuries whose spirit R. L. S. seized when he wrote:—

> "O they rade in the rain, in the days that are gane,
> In the rain and the wind and the lave,
> They shoutit in the ha' and they routit on the hill,
> But they're a' quaitit noo in the grave.
> Auld, auld Elliots, clay-cauld Elliots, dour, bauld Elliots of
> Auld!"

Hopekirk is now a peaceful place consisting of a church and manse, a schoolhouse, and a farm with its cottages.

[1] Hope in Celtic means a sheltered place in the hills.

The present church stands hard by the site where from the ninth century, through the vicissitudes of the years, a church was built and rebuilt, and carved stones from these buildings have been recovered from strange lodgings. By means of a hint in an old manuscript the most important stone was found in the rockery of a near-by mansion house. This stone, pronounced by two antiquaries to be " a revolutionary discovery," was once the top part of a pillar in an early "Saxon" church, its carving being that of the ninth century. In the year 854 a contemporary annalist wrote of two churches which Bishop Ecgred of Jedburgh built, and so possibly the first stone church at Hopekirk was one of them.

The builders of a later church used this stone for another purpose, and hollowed out the top so that it was converted into a *piscina*—the basin in which a priest washes his hands before and after Mass. And now, more than a thousand years after that stone was first rough hewn, it has been set up in the present church as a baptismal font backed by a wall in which other ancient stones are incorporated.

CHAPTER II

A NEGLECTED SAINT

THERE is something distinctive about the manses of
Scotland. Outwardly they are as substantial and un-
decorated as a large farmhouse, but lack the out-buildings
of a farm. Inwardly they possess the combined atmosphere
of old leather-bound volumes and fresh-cut flowers, and on
the Sabbath morning you can sense the preoccupied calm of
the man who is about to lead his neighbours in the public
worship of God.

There is also the manse garden. The monks of old and
of to-day have their gardens, and that may be why every
country manse has its garden and glebe. The glebe or
grazing is now usually let to a neighbouring farmer, but the
garden, unless the stipend be too meagre, is well kept. At
Hopekirk they had a beautiful garden of about one acre.
Three-quarters was well-tended lawn with apple trees, and
the rest was a vegetable garden surrounded by flowers and
paths, edged with summer-snow, aubretia, candytuft, and
wild thyme. It was an oblong garden, and at the corners were
delphiniums larger and bluer than any I had seen before.
In the beds beyond the border plants were pansies with
large faces and as multi-coloured as a collection of butter-
flies. Behind the pansies there stood clumps of lupins,
peonies, hollyhocks, coreopsis, ox-eye daisies, and poppies
against a background of sweet peas. There was also a pergola
of the rapid-growing American Pillar, and beyond the per-

gola crazy paving and an arbour of roses—Madame Bovary and Dorothy Perkins.

The Minister was proud of the vegetables in the centre of the plot, especially of his carrots, as these are most difficult to grow. When you pull carrots you bruise the stem, and from the bruise an odour ascends into the air and attracts the fly that ruins the crop. For that reason after you have pulled your carrots you dust the bed with naphthaline so that the fly will not know that carrots are growing there. This precaution ceases to be necessary after the middle of July when this particular insect retires from work. At the foot of this garden, just across the road, there runs the rapid trout stream that is called the Rule, and takes its name from a Celtic word which means "swift moving."

As we walked in the garden I told my friend that I was on my way to the Western Isles.

"Well," said he, "if you're going to write about the Isles I hope you won't perpetuate the St. Columba myth."

"Myth!"

"Yes, the myth that but for Columba there would have been no Christianity in Scotland in the sixth century, the truth being that St. Ninian founded his missionary settlement at Whithorn exactly one hundred and sixty-six years before Columba landed on Iona."

"Quite so," I said, "but that mission was a failure and Christianity in Scotland was dead when Columba came."

"That's part of the myth. If Christianity was dead, how do you explain the existence of Bishop Kentigern, St. Mungo, who lived on the banks of the Molendinar Burn in Columba's time? You can read in Adamnan how Columba came from Iona to 'rejoice in the light of Kentigern,' and how on parting they exchanged their pastoral staffs 'in pledge and testimony of their mutual love of Christ.'"

"Even so," I persisted, "Ninian's influence was confined to a very small part of Scotland."

"That's another part of the myth. Ninian founded forty churches or chapels, of which thirteen were in the North of Scotland, and he got as far north as Shetland."

"I never heard that before."

"The extent of Ninian's work is only now becoming known again."

"Is all this proved?"

"I think it is proved. We owe the proof to A. B. Scott. He's now minister at Helmsdale and one of the best scholars in the Church of Scotland. Why not read the evidence?"

"I'm not capable of writing Church history."

"No, but if you intend to mention St. Columba you might as well know the truth about his contemporaries and the early Pictish Church."

"Very well," said I, "lead on where danger threatens most."

So we went indoors; the drawing-room was loaned to me as a study, and my friend produced *Adamnan's Life of St. Columba*, together with the *Rise and Relations of the Church of Scotland* and *The Pictish Nation: its People and its Church*, both by A. B. Scott, D.D. On the Saturday and Sunday I read until midnight, and on the Sunday and Monday mornings I was up at 6 a.m. Hilaire Belloc, in his invaluable essay *On Getting Respected in Inns and Hotels*, advises that "a fourth way is to tell them to call you extremely early, and then to get up extremely late."[1] To this I would add, with great respect, that when staying with

---

[1] *On Nothing and Kindred Subjects*, p. 14.

friends a totally different method should be adopted. Do not ask to be called but make a practice of being up and about at 6 a.m. It is not difficult, especially if you are only doing it for a couple of days, and the results are well worth the reversal of your usual habits. You may be, as am I, a sluggard by nature, but in the opinion of your friends you will be regarded as one of the world's workers. Moreover, you will have set a good example, and on your second performance you will find the entire family following you downstairs at 6 a.m., protesting that it is also their almost invariable custom to be up and about for two hours before breakfast and before the servants. That is all to the good, because the first thing the family will do is to make tea. Here the family consisted of the Minister, his wife, and their daughter Joan, aged eighteen.

St. Andrew is not the rightful Patron Saint of Scotland, an honour which belongs to Ninian, the son of a British chief. Ninian was born in Galloway and, according to tradition, in the year 362. During his childhood, in the years 367-8 the unconquered Picts in the north invaded Roman Britain and came within sight of London. The invaders were driven back into Caledonia by Theodosius the General, who then established the northern Province of Valentia which included Galloway. Thereafter Ninian was sent to Rome, and probably was taken there as a hostage for his tribe's good behaviour.

From Rome Ninian went to Tours, where he stayed with St. Martin in his missionary monastic settlement of Locotegiacum or Little White House, and thereafter returned to Scotland with masons from Tours and built Candida Casa or White House, which the Anglo-Saxon translated Whitherne, whence the present name Isle of Whithorn in Wigtown. On hearing of the death of St. Martin when building Candida Casa, Ninian dedicated it in his honour, and that fixes the date of the first stone church in Scotland as 397. This church has long since disappeared, but the bell of St. Ringan (Ninian), of very rough workmanship, is in the Antiquarian Museum at Edinburgh.

The biographers of St. David tell of how when a child he was taken to see St. Paldy, then very old and blind, whose mission was in Wales but who once had worked with Ninian. They also say that David's father was warned in a dream to send on behalf of his son an offering of honey, fish, and the dressed carcase of a stag to "the Monastery of Manchan." Now Manchan was the "Master" of Candida Casa in the early part of the sixth century, and afterwards David stayed for a time at Whithorn.

This last fact was not known to his biographers for the simple reason that they knew no Celtic. They knew that David had stayed at "Rosnant," but not knowing what the word meant they invented the story that this was an old name for David's own monastery at St. David's, Pembroke. They did not know that Nan was Ninian's Britonic name, or that Rosnant was Celtic for Promontory of Ninian, and that such a word must mean a promontory of land into the sea or into a river. Moreover, they did not know of Ninian's school, for they speak of Whiteland instead of Whithorn and mistake Glasserton in Galloway for Glastonbury (Glaston) in Somerset. Yet in Ninian's school, at Candida Casa, were trained men such as Caranoc, by whom Patrick the Saint of Ireland was baptized, and Finbar the Irishman, who was one of the teachers of Columba.

13

To the time of the Reformation, Whithorn was the place of pilgrimages in honour of the first apostle of Christianity in Scotland, and this makes it all the more astonishing that Scotsmen, Catholic and Protestant alike, should have allowed so much of the story of their first great missionary to be forgotten. Many post-Reformation writers have contributed towards this national forgetfulness inasmuch as they misunderstood the following passage in Bede's *Ecclesiastical History*: "The Southern Picts received the true faith by the preaching of Bishop Ninias, a most reverend and holy man of the British Nation." This they took to mean that Ninian's influence was confined to the south of Scotland. Now the Venerable Bede (A.D. 672-735) was a trustworthy historian, but for geography he relied on Ptolemy's map of A.D. 150 in which Scotland is misdrawn so that it lies east and west instead of north and south. Therefore when Bede refers to southern Picts he really means the eastern Picts who inhabited the present eastern coast of Scotland. Many a professor has come to grief at that particular hurdle, because the existence of Ninianic settlements along the east coast has been proved, and the range of Ninian's work, once disputed, is now confirmed by the researches of A. B. Scott, who has shown that Columba owed his instruction to Ninianic sources, and that Ninian's foundations were active and flourishing in Columba's time and long after.

In south-western Shetland, in the parish of Dunrossness and about seven miles from Fitfull Head is a little peninsula called St. Ninian's Isle. Of this place the Rev. Mr. Brand wrote, in 1701: "To the north-west of the Ness lies St. Ninian's Isle, very pleasant; wherein there is a Chappel and ane Altar in it whereon some superstitious people do burn

Candles to this day. . . . If therefore, Celtic and Christian, we cannot suppose them to be earlier than the visit of the Celtic missionary Cormac, a contemporary of St. Columba, about the year A.D. 580, nor, unless a Christian remnant can have survived amid the exterminating paganism of the Norsemen, can they be assigned to a later date than the invasion of the latter in the year 872." Although the place was called St. Ninian's Isle, it never occurred to Mr. Brand that the chapel might date from Ninian's time. He probably regarded the name as dedicated, just as the present church of St. Peter in Birmingham is dedicated to that Saint and does not date from apostolic times. Yet in the twelfth century Aelred had written of Ninian: "In the distant isles they offer thanks to the most merciful God who had revealed his Name, sending to them a preacher of truth—a lamp of Salvation."

Wind, rain, sand, and waves demolished the little chapel, and when Mr. Gilbert Goudie visited the place in July 1876 he found "stones and builtwork which suggested a building of great antiquity." A few weeks later he returned and found that the sea had washed bare a new stratum of graves. On one of these he found the fragment of a sandstone slab with Ogham characters, the oldest form of writing in the Celtic language. Mr. Goudie now realised that he had discovered the site of a pre-Scandinavian Christian church which, from the name of the place, was probably one of St. Ninian's foundations. The stone was removed to the Museum of the Society of Antiquaries at Edinburgh, where it remains to this day, but the Edinburgh antiquaries flouted the suggestion that either the stone or the site was directly connected with Ninian. Being a modest man,

Mr. Goudie, in deference to the opinions of those whom he thought to be more learned than himself, did not press his views.

Now comes the climax. During the present century a photograph of that stone inscription was sent to the Rev. Archibald B. Scott. He was not told where the stone had been found, and was merely asked to decipher the Ogham writing. His reading was: "Establishment of the Community of Ninian the Baptiser." With a slight literal variation his translation has been approved by all Celtic scholars on the continent of Europe and in America.[1] So interested was I in this history that I visited the National Museum in Edinburgh and made a tracing of the Ogham characters on the stone, which are here reproduced.

Scale ⅙ linear.

Much Catholic tradition survived as superstition among the Scottish Protestant fisherfolk long after the Reformation, and the fishermen of Dunrossness when in danger at sea used to make a vow to St. Ninian, and if spared they fulfilled it in the following way. By night they went secretly to the old churchyard, left their shoes and stockings at the gate, and walked three times round the ruins. They then threw a piece of silver through the window of the chapel and returned to the gate without looking back lest they should see the skeleton of the Saint acknowledging the offering by

[1] *The Rise and Relations of the Church of Scotland*, p. 277.

16

raising its hand and sometimes its skull above the window-sill.[1] This custom must have been based on a tradition that St. Ninian was buried there, and this is by no means improbable, for having reached the Shetlands, he would know that according to Ptolemy's Map he had come to Thule, the farthest point of Britain.

[1] L. Roubaudi. *Nice et ses environs*, p. 342, quoted by Peter Anson in *Fishermen and Fishing Ways*, p. 70.

CHAPTER III

A WOMAN REMEMBERS

ON the Sunday afternoon at 3 p.m. my hostess entered the drawing-room and said: "David and Joan are going for a walk. Would you like to join them?"

"Yes, with pleasure. A walk is just what I would like," I answered brightly.

As the three of us crunched on the gravel path to the gate Joan looked back and called: "Mother! Where shall I take them?"

"My dear," came the devastating answer, "it does not matter where you take them. You might lead them round the house for the next two hours, and neither of them would be any the wiser. If you take them on the road just see that they are not run down by motor-cars. Wherever you take them they will see nothing, but Joan—if you listen to what they are saying you may learn something about the history of the Early Pictish Church."

Then did I, crunching the gravel under my heels, turn back and say: "What a memory you have—after all these years!"

Women have long memories and may remember far-off happenings long since erased from the tablets of your mind. When I had met my hostess a few weeks earlier at a small dinner party at Notting Hill Gate I would have sworn that it was our first meeting. Her husband was the brother of

my friend J. H. Cattanach who died in 1937, and having
known the brothers at Edinburgh University, I remarked
to the lady that it was strange she and I had never met in
the past.

"Oh, but we did meet!"

"Then I'm sorry to have forgotten."

"No need to be sorry. I never expected for a moment
that you would remember, although you saw me, or rather
didn't see me, for the best part of a day."

This was awkward, and the others were now as much
interested as I was in the duologue. I felt like a walker on
the shore when the sands begin to sink, but bravely I asked:
"When did this meeting take place?"

"In the fourth year of the War. You were in naval uniform and on leave. You were staying in Tain, and Joe was
with you. The two of you came over from Tain to the
manse at Golspie."

"What brought them over?" asked her husband.

"Oh, I suppose Joe thought it a kindness to see how I
was getting on when you were in Mesopotamia. So far as I
was concerned they might never have come. They shook
hands with me when they arrived and when they left—and
that was about all."

"Well," said I, "now that you remind me I remember
being on leave in Tain and that Joe was staying with us, but
it's most extraordinary that I've forgotten about the visit
to Golspie."

"Not in the least extraordinary," she continued. "You
and Joe had begun some argument in the train and continued
it all day."

"A discussion," I suggested.

"Call it a discussion if you like, but it went on all morning in the manse study." Turning from me she addressed the larger audience: "I left them both in peace till lunch. All through lunch their discussion continued. They never noticed what they were eating. After lunch they went back to the study. At three o'clock I suggested a walk in the grounds of Dunrobin. From one point you get a splendid view of the castle. Off we went, but although I walked in the middle it was impossible to change the subject. They saw nothing, and when we had gone round the Castle three times I lost patience and told them that if they did not look at the Castle I would leave them, go straight home and let them return to Tain without afternoon tea. That made them look, and Joe remarked that he had always believed in the existence of the Castle and was glad to see it was still there. They then resumed their discussion, and at tea he [indicating me] surpassed himself. Joe was anxious about the time of the train, though the train from the north was then often two hours late, but he [indicating me] was not in the least anxious—'There's no need to hurry, Joe. If we miss the train she can give us a couple of bedrooms for the night.' After that they shook hands with me and walked off to the station. But I forgive you [indicating me] and hope you'll come to the manse at Hopekirk."

"Well," said I, "my only apology must be the discussion. What was it all about?"

"I haven't the least idea. All that remains is the picture of two oddities striding along, talking incessantly, often with heat, and utterly oblivious of all surroundings. It was intensely funny."

Her admission made me sad. What are the lost books of

Livy in comparison with our lost discussion! A discussion
that began in a train and continued for the best part of a day,
on an even keel, steering a straight course between the
Scylla of lunch and the Charybdis of tea, not to mention the
towers, turrets, keep, and extinguisher roofs of Dunrobin
Castle—that, I say, was no ordinary discussion, and the
whole Earth must be poorer because it is lost. If only the
lady had listened—what undreamt-of happiness might now
be in store for my readers. Yet that is the way of the world
where all the best things get lost, perchance that we may find
them in Heaven.

For the most part the Minister and I talked of St. Ninian,
and of those "far-off unhappy days and battles long ago,"
about which the passions and prejudices of history have not
yet died, until my train was due to leave on the Monday.
Then, as the car approached the station, my friend remarked:
"Your train's in. We'll have to hurry." It may be that his
car was not very fast, that my watch was slow, or that our
time-tables were out of date. We hurried across the platform, and I entered the train having exactly thirty seconds in
which to bid my host good-bye. A well-timed parting,
because to me farewells at railway stations are irksome
affairs. The desire to make or to continue conversation is
overshadowed by the fact that it must be broken off by
the starting of the train. The inhibition is overwhelming,
and to overcome inhibitions we should seek the aid of
Ritual.

Ritual is a ceremony whereby the mind is enabled
to express its inmost thoughts with the greatest ease,
and thus mental energy is conserved, or ought to be conserved, for creative work. Without ritual the amenities

of civilisation would be lost, and a moment's thought will indicate what a world of trouble is saved by such simple words as "How do you do." For that reason I admire the kindly folk who have evolved a ritual of farewell at railway stations.

A large woman accompanied by two or more children and many parcels enters the carriage. Having placed her children and parcels on the seat, she blocks the corridor and leans out of the window. On the platform are her friends, and each is kissed. A small child is then lifted up so that it may also be kissed by the lady in the train, who is usually called Auntie. She is the priestess and the ritual that follows is antiphonal:

Priestess.   Give my love to Mum.
Response.   We'll tell her.
Priestess.   And to Dad.
Response.   We'll tell him.
Priestess.   And to Effie.
Response.   We'll tell her.

All relatives and friends are then recalled by their Christian names, and as each name is mentioned the response is made —"We'll tell him [or her]." When the list of names is ended, then, if the train has not yet started, the ritual proceeds—

Priestess.   Tell Mum I'll be seeing her soon.
Response.   We'll tell her.

The list of names is repeated as before, and then, if the train has not yet started, more messages are delivered for each and all, such as "Tell Mum I've enjoyed my holiday," the responses being the same.

As soon as the train starts those on the platform say in

unison, "Remember to send a post card," and begin to wave their hands. To this the lady in the train replies, "I won't forget," and waves her hand until the train is out of the station, when she waves a handkerchief until the station is out of sight. Then breathless but triumphant she enters the carriage and sits down among her children and parcels.

Let no one mock this homely ritual which springs from the heart, and happy are those who know so many to whom they may send their love. Neither let anyone seek to improve the ritual as did one minx who, on the platform at Victoria when the boat-train was leaving and the sending of a post card had been mentioned, shouted: "And remember to write Angle Tare after the address!" That tore the ritual.

CHAPTER IV

ON MY WAY TO THE ISLES

THE next week-end found me at Fort William on the eastern shore of Loch Linnhe and, according to the map, at the foot of Ben Nevis, although from no part of the town is it possible to see the highest mountain in Britain. The town is a centre for motor coach tours in the Western Highlands, and on the Saturday night the main street was filled with tourists. The shops selling sweets, cigarettes, souvenirs, fish and chips, and books were crowded, as were also the public houses before closing at 9 p.m. Itinerant musicians playing concertinas or bagpipes strolled amongst the crowds, and in a side street the Salvation Army was singing.

Not having booked rooms I was fortunate in finding an hotel where bed and breakfast cost 8s. There were no vacant beds in the hotel, but they gave me a bed in a neighbouring house, or rather in a wooden room attached to the side of the house. To reach this bedroom I passed through a large room with two beds, and asked what the procedure was in the event of the larger room being occupied. In that event the communicating door would be locked, and I would gain entrance to my wooden bedroom through a door which opened on to the garden. At 10 p.m. I learnt that the larger room had been taken by two ladies, and so I retired via the garden.

On Sunday morning Loch Linnhe looked its best, for the

sun was shining, and under a clear sky the water was blue. There was scarcely a breath of wind, merely a puff that here and there broke the mirror surface on which the sides, yellow masts, rigging, and funnels of anchored yachts and steamers were reflected. Across the loch white houses, green fields and hills were bathed in sunlight. At breakfast in the hotel, an Englishman asked if he might sit at my table, and to this request I readily agreed. Apart from his accent I knew that he was an Englishman because he sugared his porridge. It was a good breakfast, and Dr. Johnson's judgment stands: "If an epicure could remove by a wish, in search of sensual gratifications, wherever he had supped he would breakfast in Scotland."

Solitude and contemplation have their place in the scheme of things, but only those who travel alone know the craving for talk, and moreover there is no one in the world from whom we cannot learn. The Englishman had also the urge to talk. He was clean shaven, middle-aged, and wore a knicker-bocker suit of which the checks were somewhat large. "This is my first visit to Scotland," he said, "and, say what they like, this scenery beats anything in England. I'm a press photographer, and so I ought to know something about it."

"Yes, indeed," said I.

"Press photographers come across some very interesting things," he continued.

"I'm sure they do," I agreed, because it was now obvious that he had information which he wished to impart.

"Only last week I was at a place in Somerset where they are making glue out of human skulls shipped from Spain. The workman who told me about it said that the stench when they opened the cases made him sick. What do you think of that?"

"I think that if the story be true you should give it to your paper. It's the kind of scoop that is rewarded by a directorship."

"Yes, but there's always the difficulty that when it comes to proof the very people who told you will back out of it in case they lose their jobs."

"Quite so, but the real difficulty is that the story rings false. Neither side in Spain have had time to prepare skulls for export. Even if they had time our Customs would never allow such cargoes to be landed. What's more, being a doctor, I can tell you that glue is not made from skulls, even of animals, but from the long bones."

He looked disappointed, and so I continued: "That's the way false propaganda begins. In the Great War we told the world that Germany had a corpse factory for extracting fat from dead bodies. In war a lie may be good propaganda. Take the story about——"

At that moment, to my astonishment Joan Cattanach and one of her aunts from London crossed the breakfast-room to wish me good morning. They were on a motor tour and were leaving at once in Miss Mary Cattanach's car. These were the ladies who had occupied the room in the annexe next to mine. So I went outside to see them off.

"What a coincidence that you two should have stopped at this hotel and have had the room next to mine!"

"Yes, wasn't it?" agreed Miss Mary Cattanach.

Then, since it was a beautiful morning and I was in great good humour, I asked: "By the way, which of you two snores?"

26

"Neither of us snores, Halliday. You were awakened by the echo of your own snoring. It shook the annexe, but we were too polite to mention it this morning. So you see, your snores come home to roost." With that she let in the clutch and the car glided away before I had time to protest that I do not snore and that her metaphor was mixed. Thereafter I went for a short walk, and out of my musings on coincidences in general I evolved the Law of Coincidence, which is that the greater the mathematical odds against any two separate events occurring simultaneously and becoming correlated the greater is the coincidence. According to that law the greatest coincidence of which I have ever heard happened to the Lord Justice-Clerk of Scotland in the year 1937.

Staying at a well-known English spa, he was sitting in the lounge before dinner when a man, a total stranger, in immaculate evening dress, came in and sat down near him. After a time he said: "Do you come from Scotland?"

"Yes," said the Lord Justice-Clerk.

"Ah," continued the affable stranger, "I wonder if you happen to know my friend Lord Aitchison?"

Wondering if there might be a member of the peerage with the same name as himself, of whom he had not heard, the Lord Justice-Clerk replied: "Do you mean the judge?"

"Yes—the Scottish judge."

"Oh, yes," said Lord Aitchison, amazed at finding this new acquaintance, "I have met him. When did you see him last?"

"As a matter of fact I was shooting with him last week."

"Dear me! I didn't know he had a shoot."

27

"Oh, rather, he's got a very good shoot down in Ayrshire."

Shortly afterwards the dinner hour arrived and the two went into the dining-room to sit at separate tables. During dinner the Lord Justice-Clerk told the head waiter of the conversation in the lounge. The head waiter was a man of large experience of life who had met many strange characters in his day.

"Well, my lord, do you mind if I mention the matter to the manager?"

"I wouldn't bother. I'm making no complaint. He's probably just a boaster and quite harmless." Yet the Lord Justice-Clerk, from his knowledge of psychology and of criminals, reflected that if the man was a crook it was likely enough that he would know about judges and might pretend to have a friend on the Bench. So he said to the head waiter, "Well, just as you like—but remember, I make no complaint."

Next morning the affable stranger did not appear at breakfast, and on the previous night in the hotel events had moved with the rapidity of a film. The manager had telephoned to the police giving them a description of the man. The police had sent a plain-clothes officer to the hotel, who on seeing the stranger thought he answered the description of a wanted man, and had then telephoned Scotland Yard. In the early morning a car with two of the C.I.D. arrived from London, the suspected man was interviewed in his bed, confessed his identity and was then arrested. He was a well-known jewel thief, but on this occasion he was not arrested for theft, but, being a convict on licence, for failing to report to the police in accordance with his conditional liberation. He was leniently dealt with locally, a fine being imposed, and on the afternoon of the next day he returned rejoicing to London. If he ever learnt of the chain of circumstances that led to his arrest he would have the melancholy satisfaction of reflecting that the odds were many millions to one against his having spoken in an English hotel to the Scottish judge whom he claimed to know.

A coincidence also led to the detection of the man who devised "the perfect crime," whereby he was robbing the Post Office Savings Bank with such impunity that to the police of Britain he was known as the Phantom Forger, for there were no clues and no one could remember his appearance. His method was to enter a post office and open a Savings Bank Account with a deposit of five shillings, as do hundreds of people every day all over the country, but, unlike other depositors, he gave a false name, address, and occupation. Only once, and I think he must have been tempted to smile on that occasion, did he describe himself as an engraver.

He thus acquired savings books and proceeded to alter their serial numbers and the names of the post offices from which they had been issued. Even the false name and address was altered and also the date stamp of the issuing office. He had discovered a method of obliterating postmarks, but what that method was I do not know, and if I did know I would not tell you, for all knowledge is not strength and some is dangerous. Even more remarkable was his ability to draw postmarks with pen and ink, which meant that, like the late Lord Kelvin, he had the gift of drawing perfect freehand circles, and that is very rare. By this means he forged entries showing various deposits until the purported deposits amounted to well over £3. He could then present the book at any post office in Britain, except at the one where it was supposed to have been issued, and obtain £3, this being the maximum amount which may be withdrawn without notice to the Head Office.

When the book reached the Head Office, as do all savings books after money has been withdrawn, the account was at once found to be fictitious. Yet it was impossible to know from what post office the book was originally obtained, since the only genuine entry and postmark were those of the office which had paid the Phantom Forger. Now, in the large and busy post offices all over Britain, where he presented these books, it was impossible for the staff to remember the appearance of every person who withdrew £3 on a particular date. Nor was it feasible for every post office in the country to detain every person who wished to open an account with a deposit of five shillings, until the police had ascertained his or her identity.

Here then in real life was the perfect crime, and provided the Phantom Forger continued to play a lone hand, never employed a confederate, or told a friend, there seemed to be no reason why these forgeries should not continue until his hand had lost its cunning. To be immune from detection even the most clever criminal must play a lone hand, for as a friend of mine in the C.I.D. once said: "Believe me, doctor, if there was such a thing as honour among thieves Scotland Yard might as well close down."

Neither confederate nor friend but a slight slip and a coincidence led to the appearance of the Phantom Forger in the dock of the Central Criminal Court. As I have said, he presented the forged books at large post offices all over the country but, for some reason which I cannot fathom, he obtained the books at sub-post offices. Thus one morning according to plan he entered a sub-post office in a large store near the Elephant and Castle, deposited 5s, and on this occasion gave not only a false but also a non-existent address in Putney which is a considerable distance from the Elephant and Castle. As soon as he was out of the office the girl who had given him his savings book turned to her colleague and said:

"Look at that! I've lived in Putney for twenty years and I've never heard of such a terrace."

"Neither have I," said the other girl, who also lived in Putney. "Let's show it to the postmaster."

Now the postmaster also lived in Putney, and as soon as he saw the address he telephoned to Scotland Yard, for every indoor employee in the postal service had been warned about the Phantom Forger. From Scotland Yard a radio message was sent out, and within two minutes a police car was outside the store. The man had gone, but from the girls the two detectives learnt something about his appearance. To this clue the detectives added a brilliant example of deductive reasoning, for on the assumption that the man was obtaining savings books at sub-post offices they proceeded to the next nearest, and arrived in time to see a man coming out. His appearance was not incompatible with that given by the girls, and so one of the detectives accosted him: "I am a police officer and would like to know what you were doing in that post office."

Now if the man had answered, "I was buying a book of stamps, here it is," he might have been allowed to walk away, but he replied, "I was enquiring about a dog licence."

"Don't you know," said the detective, "that dog

31

licences cannot be obtained at sub-post offices? I'm not satisfied."

Whereupon the man bolted, was captured, confessed, and in due course was sentenced. To say that I have "a sneaking sympathy" for him would be to make use of a mean phrase, and on reading the trial I felt great sympathy for one who had used such exceptional gifts to so little purpose. Each forgery must have entailed hours and hours of laborious work, and all for a gross profit of £2, 15s., because travelling expenses must have been heavy. Yet as a more or less law-abiding citizen I should rejoice that three people who lived in Putney happened to be employed near the Elephant and Castle, and indeed I think that behind the Law of Coincidence is the Finger of Providence.

And now I was Sunday-bound in Fort William, by which I mean that on Sundays there are no steamer sailings, no trains running on branch lines, and no motor-coach excursions. That is all to the good, as the laxest Sabbatarian would admit if he studied the week-day schedules affecting hundreds of employees. Not until 8 a.m. on Monday did the *Loch Fyne* sail for Oban, my next port of call, and in the meantime I had to consider how the Sunday should be spent. At 11.30 a.m. I heard High Mass at the Church of the Immaculate Conception, and afterwards, greatly daring, I waylaid the Very Reverend Canon William Macmaster on his way from the Church to the Presbytery. I had never met him previously, and it needs courage to waylay a priest, still more a canon, who has said a late Mass, because the man is fasting and eager for his breakfast. Nevertheless, the Canon gave me a cordial welcome and invited me to supper at seven o'clock. That settled the evening, and in the afternoon I walked to a farm where once I had stayed. It was only six miles from Fort William, but in time it was over forty years away.

The road to Lundavra, six miles south of Fort William, is rough and hilly. There are four long steep hills over a mile apart to be climbed and descended on the way to the loch and farmhouse of that name. In the first mile the road rises from sea level to 487 feet, but from this height there is no view of Ben Nevis by reason of Cow Hill to the north-east. The road descends to the valley of the water of Kia-chruish, the river that runs from Lundavra into Loch Linnhe, and then rises to 432 feet. Here the view of the Ben is shut out by the hill called Bundbbaird g hall, but between this last and the mountain of Mullach nan Coirean is a valley running to the north-east. Where the road crosses the bottom of this valley, just beyond the small schoolhouse at Blarmachfoldach, Ben Nevis can be seen across this glen. The road then rises to 514 feet, descends and again rises to this height, but the Snow Mountain is now hidden behind Mullach nan Coirean. Ben Nevis is a gigantic mass of bare rock, but all the other mountains are heather-clad and in their valleys are streams and the grazing land of sheep farms.

At two places there is a gate across the road to prevent sheep from wandering, and farther on the grazing is divided by a long dry dyke beside the road. Best of all did I remember the long hills up which as a boy I had walked with my father, while my mother and sister stayed in the trap. In those days only ladies and girls remained in a vehicle when the horse was going uphill. Gentlemen always walked. All over Scotland public wagonettes and coaches stopped at

33

the foot of a long incline so that the male passengers might alight, and if any showed signs of keeping to their seats the driver would merely turn and say: "This is where the Prince got out and walked." This remark would bring the laziest and fattest men on to the road, and in emulating the example of the Prince they felt that, breathless though they might be, they were rising in their own estimation and possibly in the estimation of their womenfolk. If Edward VII., when Prince of Wales, walked up all the hills to which he was accredited, he must have been a remarkable pedestrian. These days are gone, and I hold the horse to be a noble animal in that he helped to teach man to be considerate. Of no infernal combustion engine could as much be said.

At the top of the last incline is the ruined toll of Blar a Chaoruinn, for over this hilly road there once ran the stage coach between Fort William and Glasgow, a two days' journey then. The toll-house is in ruins, but the stone pillars that once held the barricade still stand. Beyond the toll the road divides. The old Glasgow road, now a track on the hillside, continues south and then east through the valley of Mammore Forest, a deer forest in which trees are few and far between. To the south-west is the old road that once went to North Ballachulish and on this road a mile away I saw the farmhouse beside the loch. Two miles beyond the farm the road now comes to an end in a plantation of the Forestry Commission. The loch, a mile long and a furlong wide, lies NE. by SW. at the foot of the mountains Meall nan Cleireach to the north-west, and Doiree Ban to the south-east.

Half-way to the farmhouse there is a bridge over the Water of Kiachruish, and on this bridge I stopped to look downstream. Something had happened on that river forty-two years ago, something that concerned a salmon and a bullet, and I tried to remember what it was. A salmon and a bullet! Then as I watched the running water the mist over memory cleared and the past was recaptured. My uncle, Brigadier-General R. L. A. Pennington, then the youngest colonel in the British Army, and his wife, my aunt Lil, had returned from the river with a salmon. They said they had got it with a bullet, and every one had laughed when I asked if they had shot the salmon. It is best to have a story at first hand, and on returning to London I invited myself to have tea with my relatives and learnt what happened.

"Yes," said the General, "that's a really quaint story. There's not much water under the bridge where you stopped, but farther on a number of burns join the river and a mile below the bridge it becomes quite a considerable stream. That's where Lil and I were fishing trout until we came to a place where the river runs deep between large rocks into a pool ending in a waterfall. No one could possibly get a cast on to the pool. I had a salmon rod and slipped on a body-snatcher—a triangle of large hooks with a lead bullet as a sinker. You don't use gut but tie the snatcher to the end of your salmon line. Then you pop it in, let it sink to the bottom and jerk it up quickly. It's not much use if there's only one salmon in a pool, but if several are moving about you're likely to hook one. If the hooks catch in a crevice of rock, or on any other obstruction, the only thing to do is to take the line in your hands, pull until you break it and fix on another body-snatcher.

"At the first jerk I got nothing, but at the second I was

35

into him, and a salmon hooked through the body gives more play than when hooked in the mouth. I played him in the pool, and when he seemed to be exhausted I drew him towards the edge of the waterfall and told Lil to bring the gaff and gaff him. All she did was to give him a scratch that sent him back into the pool where he rushed about and finally went over the waterfall. I went down the bank below the fall, deuced awkward place to get to, and with so much loose line I expected to lose the fish. Not a bit of it. As soon as I reeled in the line he was still there. After a time I drew him towards the bank and told Lil to have another go with the gaff. Again she scratched him, and I said, 'No, no, this will never do. Give me the gaff.' I took the rod in my left hand, the gaff in my right, drew him to the bank and gaffed him myself. A clean, beautiful fish, fresh run and scaled 15 lbs. I remember the weight as I had to carry him a couple of miles back to the house. Of course, in fairness to Lil, that was the first time she had ever handled a gaff, and afterwards in British Columbia she gaffed salmon as well as any gillie I ever met.

"Illegal? Yes, the body-snatcher is illegal, and I never use it except in special circumstances. But on nearly every river, and you know it as well as I do, there are places that are quite unfishable in the ordinary way, and in those places, just now and then, you may get a lot of fun with the body-snatcher. Of course if you say that to the average fisherman he'll look down his nose and never speak to you again. Awful rot, you know! Never deceives me after what I saw on the Dovey. Years ago I was a member of their fishing association, and now and again if there was nobody in sight I sometimes used the body-snatcher. Of course I kept that to

36

myself. If the others had known they'd have rolled their eyes in holy horror. Well, one day I was casting for trout when I saw the Secretary of the Association and two workmen at a pool farther down. So I walked down the river to see what they were doing. The Secretary said that members had been complaining about some obstruction at the bottom of the pool which caused them to lose fish and casts. He was going to get it out. They located the obstruction with grappling irons, and a pair of horses was fetched to drag it out. It was the trunk of a tree, and when that log was dragged on to the bank the Secretary got the shock of his life. If there was one, there were fifty body-snatchers with bits of broken line attached to the log. 'Oh, how dreadful!' he said. 'I never thought our members would stoop to this.' 'Yes, yes,' I said, before going back to my fishing—'very sad, very sad indeed, but what a light on human nature!'

"Poaching? Yes, of course it was poaching at Lundavra. No other word for it. No use in beating about the bush and hushing things up. All the same, at that time neither your father nor I realised we were poaching. The whole thing happened so naturally, you know. One day I met the old farmer, and said: 'Look here, is there any place about here where I could have the chance of getting a salmon?' He made no bones about it, and said: 'Yes, yes, there's plenty of salmon in that river if you go farther down,' and so off I went. The same thing happened to your father about the grouse. One day your father met the old farmer, and said: 'Look here, is there any place about here where I could have the chance of shooting a grouse?' Again the old farmer made no bones about it, and said: 'Yes, yes, there's often a covey of grouse on the moor across the loch.' Afterwards your father and I discovered that the moor and the river had been let to a shooting tenant. Then, of course, we stopped, but as the man never once came near that moor or river I really don't think we did him any great wrong.

"Of course, there's poaching and poaching. You remember the shoot I had at Carlrossie up in Tain? Well, as you know it was a day's hard work for three guns and two dogs to get a decent bag off that moor. Now, I knew perfectly well that some of those local chaps were having a shot on the moor now and again. That never bothered me. Why should it? If some poor devil shoots a hare for his Sunday dinner, I can't see that he's done me any great wrong—can you? Of course, if I've spent hundreds of pounds in raising pheasants, you have no right to come along and take my birds, especially if you're going to sell them in the market. Do you agree in the difference?"

"Most emphatically, and we might define it. Poaching for the pot is a venial sin: poaching for money is a grave delinquency."

"Very sound, Hallie! Yes, I think that's a very sound definition."

At Lundavra farmhouse I knocked on the kitchen door because in all probability the front of the house had been let to summer visitors. A maid-servant opened the door, and to her I said: "I've walked from Fort William and it's forty-two years since I was last here. Could I have tea?"

"You can have it in ten minutes," and instead of asking me to come in, she closed the kitchen door.

So I wandered round the yard and was glad to find that nothing had changed. There was the same stable, the same cow-byre, and the same shed that once I had known. In that shed I had seen for the first time the killing of a sheep. How horrified was my mother when she knew that I had been allowed to see the thing done, and yet how little was the impression that it left upon me! At that time I was eight years old, for I was at Lundavra six years before General Pennington became my uncle.

It is difficult to know the psychology of a child, even if that child was once yourself. Yet I think that a child, especially a child that has lived amongst fishing rods and shot-guns, accepts the death of an animal as in the natural order of things. The gods whom a young child knows are grown-up people. The killing of a sheep was nothing to me and left no scar on my mind. Yet a year earlier, at the age of seven, I was standing with my governess, Miss Pearman, beside the sideboard in the dining-room of our house, the prison doctor's house, in Cathedral Square, Glasgow. On the previous day my father and mother had gone to Edinburgh. My Aunt Helen was very ill. She was a woman of character and ability, and an M.A. of Aberdeen. Yet she was not a favourite aunt of mine, for I thought she was too strict and she, with greater knowledge, thought that other aunts were inclined to spoil me. The bell rang, the servant handed a telegram to Miss Pearman, who opened it and said to me: "Your Aunt Helen is dead." Then for the first time did my heart, for a moment, stop beating, and I knew the Terror of Death.

"Your tea's ready," called the servant, and in I went to a sitting-room that had once been a bedroom. Here I was joined by the farmer's wife to whom I explained my visit. Not only so, but to test my memory I gave her the entire layout of the house and this, to my satisfaction, was accurate in every detail. In only three recollections was I wrong. In memory the road from Fort William was fourteen miles, whereas it was only six, and the loch which I had thought to be small was a mile long. On the loch in memory there was only one island, whereas in reality there were two. As the visitors were out, I was allowed to see the front sitting-room and it appeared to be unchanged. In that room I had the sensation of being in a waxworks, from which all the wax figures, except mine, had been removed. We went out through the porch into the small front garden overlooking the loch and the moor, and I told the farmer's wife about the grouse.

A large covey had wheeled round the shoulder of Doiree Ban and settled on the moor within a hundred yards of the loch. Five minutes later our expedition set out. My father had his own gun and my uncle borrowed the farmer's. Aunt Lil and I went as beaters. It was I who rowed them across the loch. "Muffle the oars," said my father, and the rowlocks were muffled with handkerchiefs. We landed in silence and formed a line twenty yards abreast, with Aunt Lil and myself between the guns. In a few minutes we were amongst the grouse. Only six shots were fired and we returned with two and a half brace. Good shooting.

The lady turned, looked at me, and said: "You wouldn't go and do a thing like that now?" She had a right to ask, as I had been inquiring about her terms for summer visitors, but her question so surprised me that I forgot my grammar.

"Me! Certainly not. Wouldn't dream of poaching. No, no, those happy days are over, but—is there any place about here where I could have the chance of shooting rabbits?"

Slowly and firmly she replied: "You would be allowed to shoot rabbits and nothing else."

"Quite so, ha-ha, excellent sport rabbiting—and good eating too. There's rabbit soup, boiled rabbit, stewed rabbit, roast rabbit, rabbit pie, and curried rabbit, which is the best of the lot as you don't taste the rabbit."

Then I thanked her for tea, said good-bye, and returned on my way. The lady was right, but all the same the sound of whirring wings is more exciting than the thumping of a rabbit's hind leg in a burrow. If any censorious reader should now ask why I do not have a moor of my own, I would answer that if all readers of this book made a practice of buying 365 copies every year it might be possible for me to shoot grouse without being hounded from pillar to post in this most unseemly fashion.

On the way back to Fort William I listened to the sound of rivulets under the moors and by the roadside. Their music varies from the high tinkle of water falling into a pebbly pool to the low gurgle of the stream that falls into peat; and a blind man passing that way might be able, had he good hearing, to know every incline by the music of its streams. At one place, not a yard from the road and almost completely hidden by young birches, willows, nettles, and ferns, I found a splish-splash waterfall between moss-covered rocks, and began to understand the saying of a child that these rivulets were specially made by God. The farmer's wife had told me of this saying by her son aged six, and of how, when asked his reasons for this belief, the child had quoted from the XXIII Psalm in metre:

"In pastures green: he leadeth me
the quiet waters by."

CHAPTER V

IN OBAN BAY

BACK at the hotel I asked for my bill, as I would be leaving fairly early in the morning. I also told the head waitress that I would not be taking breakfast. There would be breakfast on the *Loch Fyne* at 8 a.m., and I never breakfast in hotels when it is possible to have breakfast on a steamer. Moreover, the hotel breakfast began at 8.30 a.m.

When she returned with the bill I saw that the not-to-be-eaten breakfast was charged at three shillings.

"But this is most unfair," I said.

"It's the rule," she replied, "that bed and breakfast is eight shillings, and there's no reduction if you don't have breakfast."

"I am not blaming you," I continued quietly, "but I would like you to realise how unfair it is. You are not only getting my three shillings but you are also getting the value of the breakfast, let us say one and six, which I shall not eat."

"It's the rule," she, womanlike, persisted.

"I know it's the rule, but I would like you personally to realise that it is a most unfair rule not only to myself but to all other guests who may be sailing on the *Loch Fyne*."

"The Boots can get up at seven and give you tea and boiled eggs."

"No Boots shall rise at seven on account of me, and no

42

Boots, not even the Boots at the Savoy Hotel, shall be allowed to prepare my breakfast. That is the privilege of a *chef.*" Then I paid the bill and knew that I had a genuine grievance on which I could feast my mind in moments of depression.

This was my one and only complaint of a West Highland hotel. That is saying a great deal, because never once on my journey did I book rooms in advance either at hotels or in lodgings, and yet everywhere I found accommodation and was never overcharged. Those who idealise the "good old days" like to think of every innkeeper as a Boniface who was as little concerned about money as the guest master in a monastery. Nothing could be further from the truth, and many an old-time innkeeper could give points and a beating to the most rapacious seaside landlady of to-day. Consider what befell a shrewd London solicitor who visited the West Highlands in the 1860's. He liked to shoot grouse without the bother or responsibility of taking a moor, and had answered the following advertisement:

"*To be Let*, from August 12, two guns upon a first-rate moor in Argyllshire. Board, residence, and dogs found if required: excellent cuisine. For particulars apply to Duncan M'Doem, Doch-an-Dorris Hotel, Gaelside, Argyllshire."

Duncan M'Doem's terms were £50 for a gun on the moor from 12th August to 2nd September, and £10 a week for board and residence. This suited the solicitor, and, when he read that four guns had killed 800 brace the last season, he thought he had made a good bargain.

43

For about £100 he was going to have an excellent three weeks' holiday. At the end of the first week he asked for his bill to date, and according to a facsimile it read as follows:[1]

	£	s.	d.
To three weeks' rent for moor . . .	50	0	0
To one week's board and residence . .	10	0	0
Conveyance to and from the moor, including driver's fee	5	0	0
Hire of dogs for one week	2	2	0
Wine and spirit bill for the week . .	4	10	0
To fifty brace of grouse sent to London @ 5/6 per brace	13	15	0
Boxes for ditto, @ 2/- a box . . .	1	10	0
Postage for ditto	2	0	0
Attendance	1	10	0
Cleaning of guns	0	7	0
Paid gillie	1	5	0
Grease for shooting-boots	0	5	0
Total .	£92	4	0

Most men would have been enraged by such a bill, but solicitors know the danger of passion uncontrolled, and so the guest was content to send for the hotelkeeper, and then, holding the bill between his finger and thumb, to remark quietly: "I object to some of these items, Mr. M'Doem. Let us commence with the grouse. Am I to shoot the grouse and to pay for them too?"

M'Doem. "That is the arrangement I always make."

Solicitor. "Very well, let me pass on. I see £4, 10s. for wine. I have had but one bottle of claret daily. How is that?"

---

[1] *Glenmåhra*, by Sir Randal Roberts, Bart., London, 1870, p. 13.

M'Doem. "Claret is expensive to bring here, and I always keep the best at 12*s.* a bottle. The whisky was 6*s.*"

Solicitor. "Am I to understand that I have used 5*s.* worth of grease for my boots?"

M'Doem (getting angry and speaking broad). "Aye, surely; ye canna get grease for naething."

Solicitor. "I see you charge 25*s.* for a gillie. I have always paid 15*s.*"

M'Doem. "Ye micht, but ye see they're some dear in these pairts; the ither folks pays the same as ye, and they dinna mak a skirling aboot it."

There was no Taxing Master to whom the solicitor could appeal, but as he paid the bill he thought of a last chance of repudiating the contract. "By the way, your letter mentioned to me four guns on the moor. How is it there are six?"

"Oh, aye," said M'Doem, "there was just two vacancies at the time."

At this rate the solicitor's holiday would cost £176, 12*s.*, and if the other five guns paid the same, the total sum obtained by the hotelkeeper for three weeks' grouse shooting would be £1059, 12*s.* So much for the good old days.

On the Monday forenoon at 10.25 I landed at Oban, and for the benefit of the B.B.C. be it said that the correct pronunciation of the name is Oban, with the "a" short as in "woman" and not O-bann. Here I had to stay the night because the steamer for Iona did not sail until 9.5 a.m. on the Tuesday morning. Unfortunately, the room I might otherwise have had in the house of my friend the Bishop of Argyll and the Isles was occupied by the headmaster of

Stonyhurst, and all the hotels where I sought a room were full. Not that I called at every hotel. There was at least one that I missed, and that was the one where an enterprising young man, whom I met there, had stayed a few years previously. He had arrived by train with three very heavy suitcases containing his kit, which included everything from a golfing outfit to evening clothes and Highland dress. Despite this wealth of clothes his income was limited and so, when the hotel porter greeted him on the platform, he left the three suitcases with the porter in the belief that the man would wheel them on a barrow to the hotel, whilst he himself would walk there and thus save a taxi fare. Off he went, and then to his surprise an open taxi passed him on the esplanade. On the front seat were his three suitcases, and sitting up on the back seat was the hotel porter. He had to pay for that taxi. *Moral:* Do as I did if you are poor—carry your few belongings in a rucksack and bless the man who invented the steel frame which takes the weight from your shoulders on to your haunch bones.

As three large boarding-houses at which I called were also full I began to look for lodgings, and found that land-ladies are a sisterhood. If Mrs. McCracken has no room she refers you to Miss McDougall, and so you wander from one to another. In this way I came to hear of Miss McLucas, for the fifth landlady had said, "You might try Miss McLucas, but she's only bed and breakfast." Just what I wanted, and so I rang the bell of a small two-storied house in a terrace in sight of the sea.

The door was opened by Miss McLucas, a little old lady with white hair. Although her back was somewhat bent there was scarcely a wrinkle on her placid face, and she gave the impression of practicality and kindness. "I can only give you a room for to-night as more visitors are arriving to-morrow. It's not a proper bedroom but a little sitting-room with a bed in it, but it's a comfortable bed and the bathroom is next door. You'd better come in and see it before you decide."

I saw the room, laid my rucksack on the table, and asked if her name was West Highland. It was, and in telling me her history she spoke more freely than do most West Highland people when speaking to a total stranger. Her father was born on the Isle of Ghammin which lies west of the Ross of Mull, but went to Iona, where he married and where his children were born. The family then moved to Loch Melfort some twelve miles south of Oban, where the father worked in a cordite factory, and when this went bankrupt he set up as a boat hirer in Oban. "Oban was more select in those days. It was mostly advocates and doctors who brought their families here for the summer holidays. William Black, the novelist, was often in our house, and if you're going to the islands you'll see his memorial beyond Duart Castle on the Sound of Mull."

"Yes, Miss McLucas, and weren't there more steam yachts in those days? I was once here as a child, and seem to remember that at night in the bay and all along the Kerrera shore there was a blaze of lights from their riding-lights and portholes."

"Yes, there were hundreds of yachts then. Now there are only a few. I suppose it's become too expensive. After my father's death we three sisters moved into this little house. One of my sisters has the Sweetie Shop. Perhaps you saw it on the Promenade—a little shop next to the Bunnie Shop,

47

and she's got the only agency in Oban for Fuller's cakes. My other sister has the agency for Pullar's Dye Works. Then my brother, after serving in the War, lost his wife, and so, of course, he came to live with us."

"Have you any other visitors except myself?"

"There's three upstairs. They leave to-morrow, and four more arrive."

"That's eight people! How on earth do you manage?"

"It's just a matter of arrangement."

After this talk I went out for the rest of the day, and as I closed the gate of the tiny garden in front of the house I reflected that this kind old lady had never even asked for my name, and that for all she knew to the contrary I might be a Recidivist on the run.

The bay of Oban, surrounded by the hills of Lorne and sheltered to the west by the long island of Kerrera, provides a good anchorage for yachts; and from the south you may go there by steamer from Glasgow, or by motor coach by way of Loch Lomond and the Pass of Glencoe, or by the single railway line that begins at Stirling and over which in summer through coaches and sleeping-cars run from Euston.

A single railway line seems to bring one nearer the scenery, and had Ruskin travelled over the Callander and Oban line he might have written less unkindly about railways, for no railway in Scotland passes through more beautiful places. Here you know that you are coming from the Lowlands into the Highlands, not only by reason of the steep gradients but also by the gradual change in the colour and contour of the hills. The green hills increase in height, then heather appears by the rail side, and then mountains, crags, moors, lochs, swift rivers, the red deer in Glen Lochy and the long dark waters of Loch Awe.

In summer the railway company provides a folder with diagrams showing all stations and the places of interest on each side of the line, and if this idea was adopted on all railways it would relieve the tedium of long journeys and people would learn at least something of interest when looking out of a train. Thus, after crossing the River Forth beyond Stirling, you learn that the monument on Abbey Craig to the right is to the memory of the Scottish patriot, Sir William Wallace, who was betrayed to the English by the false Menteith, tried at Westminster and executed in 1305. By that betrayal Scotland gained her one and only lake, the Lake of Menteith, of which Scotsmen are ashamed. Do not scoff at this "potted" history, for it is well that you should know these facts lest you are put to shame, as was that English tourist who sat in the back of a charabanc last summer. He was on a conducted motor tour and when the coach stopped beyond Stirling the guide announced, "To the right and on the top of the hill you see the Wallace Monument," and then from the back of the coach came the hearty response, "Good old Edgar."

You shall have no more "potted" history for the moment, lest I begin writing a guide book, and I say this with no feeling of superiority, for I have made a careful study of these books in order to analyse and so avoid the style in which they are written. The more facts in a guide book the better it is, but as the information must be condensed and as the number of appropriate adjectives for each item is limited, the result is a piece of writing so adjectival that the reader feels that his interest is being artificially stimulated. Consequently, he begins to feel mentally tired, just as he is physically tired when rushing from the birthplace of one person to see the grave of another, for the superlative note cannot be sustained except by those who are so young and inexperienced as to think that everything is "too perfectly marvellous." Thus if I intend to go for a day's cruise in the *Loch Foam* I would be glad to read in the guide book that this steamer is either seaworthy, steady, comfortable, fast or slow, but when I read, "In the morning we all embark with keen appetites and smiling faces on the good ship," or still worse, "the brave ship *Loch Foam*, whose genial Captain is already on the shining bridge," why then, and call me Scrooge if you will, I just don't want to go. There are times when I want to rejoice and there is scenery the memory of which will abide with me it may be for ever, but these are my times and my scenery, since no two people see anything in precisely the same light, and for that reason I resent being told either that I have got to rejoice or that I must appreciate a particular scene. I'm damned if I will, and that is not profanity but good theology and part of the Faith.

On the other hand, when a writer, by the Grace of God, can enable readers to share his sensations, he has created something worth reading, and that has never yet been achieved on any page plastered with adjectives. It was my dead friend J. H. Cattanach, a minister of the Church of Scotland and a lecturer in English Literature at Edinburgh University, to whom *In My Path* is dedicated, who gave me the following advice: "Every writer should have over the foot of his bed an illuminated text so that he may see it last thing at night and first thing in the morning, and the text is, 'The Adjective is the Enemy of the Noun'."

Over the railway between Stirling and Oban I have travelled at all seasons and have always found new beauty in the mountains. Even in November when, having misread a time-table, I was stranded for seven hours at the hamlet of Crianlarich, I was glad to walk back on the road beside the line to Loch Dochart at the foot of Ben More and to seize the tints of late autumn in the Highlands. On the top of the hills the grass is olive green, on the lower slopes grey rocks streaked with quartz rise from the saffron background of withered bracken, in the woods the dying leaves of birch trees are greenish yellow, of the larch a paler yellow, all the paler when beside the copper of the beech, the dark green of pines, and darker green of spruce, and in the foreground is the blue-black water of the Loch with an island holding the grey ruins of a castle once the home of Robert the Bruce. In mid winter I have also passed this way when the mountains and frozen lochs were covered with snow and the rocks of every railway cutting festooned with cascades of glistening icicles.

The bay of Oban, as I have said, has a natural setting among the hills of Lorne, and so magnificent is that setting that the many hotels and large houses which border on the sea look even more commonplace than they are. Only one building, as yet unfinished, on the sea front has any architectural interest or value and that is the new Cathedral of St. Columba, which in the opinion of many experts will be the finest modern Gothic building in Britain. Here Sir Gilbert Scott has used granite, a material coarse and hard, but which, nevertheless, is suited to the genius of an architect who knows the value of restraint, because the shallowest splays and grooves on a block of granite serve to bring out all its weight and strength.

51

The outside walls of the cathedral are of pink granite from Peterhead and on the roofs are slates, in shades of brown and some a light yellow, which harmonise with the colour of the stonework. That in itself is an artistic achievement. Pink granite is also used for the nave columns and for the moulded four-foot dado; whereas the rest of the interior walling is of blue Inverawe granite, quarried at Kentaller twelve miles from Oban, and the eastern wall reveals the amazing beauty of blue granite masonry when the setting of the stones has been well arranged. There is no lighting in the upper part of the nave, and this, one of the discoveries of Sir Gilbert Scott, increases the effect of height because the nave seems to disappear into the gloom under the bare oak roof, a roof of Kentish oak, our Scottish oaks being too small to yield planks that would span the nave. The tower will rise 90 feet and its arch will be as high as the nave, so that from the chancel there will be a view of the ocean through three immense lancet windows in the western wall.

When pious ladies tell me that such and such a church is "so devotional," I usually suspect, by virtue of original sin, that it is a badly ventilated church and that they have mistaken the drowsiness induced by a lack of oxygen combined with an excess of carbonic acid gas for higher emotions. Yet in this small cathedral—it is only 150 feet in length—I found that the things of this world may be easily forgotten, for there has been erected in stone upon stone an environment that recalls, and *Deo volente* will recall to generations yet unborn, the story, the strength, the austere beauty, the simplicity, and the comfort of the Faith as known for centuries in Argyll and the isles.

My only regret about this cathedral is that Bishop Donald

Martin did not live to see completed the work he had to begin. I say "had to begin," because the old "cathedral," a shanty of wood and corrugated iron, had ceased to be weather-proof. So the Bishop of the poorest diocese in Scotland had to go far afield, even to the United States of America, begging for money. He died suddenly and un-expectedly in his sleep at the age of 65, and on the 9th December, 1938, three pipers playing "The Flowers of the Forest" led the cortege in a bitter wind along the mountain road that leads to the little cemetery of Pennyfuir amidst the hills of Lorne. He was a most kindly bishop, and his house was ever open to me. Every evening after supper he would go into his beloved cathedral, and I noticed that he always removed his Ring. "Some people are shy of bishops," he explained, and he was in great good humour when a tripper, mistaking him for the parish priest, gave him sixpence towards the cathedral. "Most kind of him. He looked quite a poor man, and it shows how people are affected by the cathedral. Every one who sees it wants to see it finished." He had it built literally stone by stone, for he never expended more money than he had in hand, and so at times only one mason was working on Sir Gilbert's plans. Yet one day the work will be finished.

At 9.30 p.m. I returned to my lodging, and before going to bed had a look at the books on a small shelf on the wall. They would show the old lady's taste in reading, and browsing over other people's books is always interesting. She had a varied assortment: *Old Father Antic*, by Doreen Wallace; *The Tick of the Clock*, by Herbert Asbury; *Main Street*, by Sinclair Lewis; *Works of Virgil*; *Vanity Fair*; *Wild Wales*; *Berry & Co.*, by Dornford Yates; *Betty Greig*, by

Joseph Laing Waugh; *Our Friend the Cairn*, by Rowland Johns; *The Happy Murders*, by Victor Bridges; *Lads of the Lothians*, by Escott Lynne; *John Ames, Native Commissioner*; *A Romance of the Matabele Rising*, by Bertram Milford; and then I found a book that caused me to open my door and call, "Miss McLucas, Miss McLucas!"

The old lady hurried from the kitchen. "What is it?"

"Is this book yours?" and I showed her the volume.

"No, it belongs to my sister, the one that keeps the Sweetie Shop."

"And an excellent Sweetie Shop it is! I was there this evening, and in the afternoon at the Sheriffs' house we had one of her cakes for tea. Mrs. Chambers has the greatest admiration for your sister."

"Yes, yes, but what did you want about the book?"

"I want to sign it."

"And you wrote it!"

"Every word of it."

"Won't my sister be interested to hear that! We all like the book, and in the winter my brother reads out of it aloud. It's most kind of you to sign it."

"It's you who are kind, Miss McLucas," and I signed a copy of *A Time to Keep*.

And so to bed with great content.

CHAPTER VI

FINGAL'S CAVE

FROM Oban the way to the Isles is across the Firth of
Lorne and through the Sound of Mull, which lies
north-west by south-east, and before entering the Sound
there is the Lady's Rock with its beacon almost midway
between the coast of Mull and the southern end of Lismore
(long garden), the long island in Loch Linnhe. At equi-
noctial springs the rock is submerged, and here long ago Red
Rob of the Cave planned to drown Catherine, daughter of
Archibald, that Earl of Argyll who fell in the command of
the vanguard at the battle of Flodden. At that time the
Macleans of Duart in Mull were amongst the most powerful
of the island clans, and Colin, third Earl of Argyll, gave his
sister in marriage to their chief. It is an old story and I shall
give the version that was told in my childhood.

After a time Maclean coveted the wife of Campbell of
Gometra, one of the islands in a bay on the west of Mull,
and sought to be rid of the Earl's sister. To this end he sent
for his half-brother Red Rob of the Cave, who was a pirate
and a cattle thief living in a large cave on the shore under
Ardnamurchan Point. Now Red Rob hated Campbell of
Gometra, by whose orders he had been flogged for stealing
cattle.

"Welcome, Rob of the Cave," was Maclean's greeting
next morning in the hall of Duart Castle, "thou hast not
tarried in answering my summons."

55

"Red Rob's sporran is not so full of silver or his larder so well supplied that he can afford to delay when Duart calls."

"It is well, my brother. What I have is for thine ear alone and concerns but thee and me."

"None other shall ever know."

"Then tell me, Rob, thinkest thou that the eagle can mate with the crow? Or, if perchance there was such a mating, thinkest thou that the king of birds would remain contented with his spouse?"

"Maclean can best judge of that."

"Then tell me, Rob of the Cave, what thinkest thou of Gometra's bride?"

"Gometra is a skulking fox, and the time is not far distant when the stripes he laid on Red Rob's back shall thunder on his own, repaid tenfold."

"Wouldst thou then like to repay a portion of thy debt to Campbell of Gometra and thereby earn some silver to chink in thy sporran?"

"Show me but the way, and I am ready."

Forthwith Red Rob sailed from Duart Castle to the Isle of Gometra in Loch-na-Keal, the large inlet of the sea in the west whereby Mull is nearly divided into two islands, and next day a gillie brought a message to Maclean: "Gometra was away. Meet me this evening by the shore of Loch Don."

Quick work! For Loch Don, an inlet from the Firth of Lorne, is only two and a half miles south of Duart, and Loch Tua, which is closed to the south by the Islands of Gometra and Ulva, is some forty-five miles distant by sea.

At sunset Maclean found Red Rob in a small cabin on

the shore and with him was Gometra's bride, for the vain and foolish woman had been easily persuaded to exchange her home for the splendours of Duart Castle. Only Argyll's sister now stood between Maclean and happiness. Red Rob returned alone to Duart, where he ordered the chief's skiff to be launched and demanded audience of the sister of Argyll.

"Your lord has met with a serious accident on the Island of Lismore and requests your presence. He has arranged that I take you in a boat and lead you to him."

Wrapped in a plaid the lady sat in the stern, and in the darkness of night Rob of the Cave rowed her across the Sound towards Lismore. They had started at the end of the ebb, and when half-way across a storm blew up from the west, the waves rose and spindrift was flying on the wind. The skiff touched land and Rob told the lady to go ashore. She landed in the belief that the place was Lismore, and Red Rob rowed back to Duart. In a few moments the unfortunate woman discovered that she was on a flat rock, barely 12 feet in circumference, surrounded by waves and drenched with spray. She also realised that soon the rock would be submerged and then the racing tide would carry her away into the Firth of Lorne. Above the noise of wind and waves she shrieked in despair.

Next day Maclean with his mistress returned to Duart Castle, whence he sent messengers to the Earl of Argyll. They told the Earl how his sister had died of a fever, and of Maclean's inconsolable grief on the death of his beloved wife. For a time all went well at Duart except that Maclean began to tire of his paramour. For that reason he welcomed the courteous message from the Earl inviting him to come to a hunt, and with two or three of his clan he departed for Inveraray Castle.

After a great feast the Earl condoled with Maclean on the death of his wife, and Maclean in his turn described the scene at her deathbed in most touching terms. At the end of their talk the Earl gave orders that the ladies of the castle should be admitted to the Banqueting Hall. Then Maclean to his horror saw that the first woman to enter the hall was his intended victim. Argyll, smiling grimly, led his sister to Maclean. "Do you recognise this lady? In her name I bid you welcome to Inveraray." An Inveraray fisherman had heard her shrieks as his boat was passing the rock that night.

Maclean stood silent.

"And now," said the Earl, in a louder voice, "I must know if you are satisfied with the banquet to which I have entertained you, or if there be aught else for which your soul craves, for if there be naught else, your head shall roll on the cobble stones in the castle yard ere many more moments have passed."

Maclean remained silent; in silence they led him below to the yard where the block and executioner were awaiting him, and there in the presence of his wife he was beheaded.

At the western end of the Sound of Mull through which I was now passing on my way to Iona in the *King George V.*, is the Bay of Tobermory (Well of Mary)—a natural harbour sheltered to the east by Calve Island—and the small town which consists of a single row of shops, hotels, and houses around the bay, and of scattered residences on the wooded hillside. The trees make the place beautiful, for trees are so scarce in Mull that Dr. Johnson remarked on the island having gained some timber when he left his walking-stick there. Of all West Highland towns that I knew as a child Tobermory is the least changed. Even the new hotel on the hill above the pier seemed familiar, and I was told that an old hotel, long since burnt down, had once stood there. The Spanish galleon *Florida*, that was blown up and sunk in 1588, together with her treasure of which so much has been written and so little seen, is still buried in the sand at the bottom of the bay. As a child I watched divers descending from their barge, and probably in the near future the tenth, or would it be the twentieth, syndicate of co-optimists will undertake the work of salvage. Yet what interested me most was on the face of a small precipice, twenty to thirty feet high and about fifty yards north of the pier, namely the text, painted in large white letters, "God is Love."

Concerning this I made enquiry of a ship's officer: "Who painted that text on the cliff? Is it some religious organisation?"

"No, no, it's painted every year by the boys on the mail steamer."

This astonished me, for although sailors are far from being godless men the painting of texts seemed to be a work of supererogation, and I asked why they did it.

"When they're painting the mail boat there's always a little white paint left over, and so they get a ladder and re-paint the text every year. Before they did it, people in the town used to do it."

"I was wondering if I'd seen it years ago."

"If you were here as a boy you'd certainly have seen it."

"It must have a story?"

"Aye, there's a story right enough, and it happened generations ago—long before you or I were born. There was a man in Tobermory who was a bit careless, you understand, about drink and women and suchlike, but he had a wee boy to whom he was devoted. One day the child was playing on the top of that cliff and fell over. Now the queer thing was that he wasn't hurt. That changed the man's whole life and he painted on the cliff 'God is Love'. He repainted it every year until he died."

"And there it remains."

"Aye, there it remains. I've heard there was once some Jack-in-Office who thought it should be rubbed out. He soon learnt sense, and there it stays."

Outside the harbour a strong southern wind was blowing up the Sound, and when the *King George* rounded the Thu Na Gael lighthouse on the westerly shore a heavy sea was running in which, to the north, a small yacht was flying obvious signals of distress in that her mainsail, ripped in two places from leech to luff, was flapping like two large ragged flags, and under a jib and mizzen she was being held into the wind. The *King George* altered course, and the captain, when within hailing distance, shouted: "Do you want help?" On the foredeck of the plunging yacht stood a hatless man in oilskins, barefooted and with his trousers rolled up to the knees. With one hand he grasped the forestay to keep his balance, and through the other, cupped to his mouth, he shouted back: "Tow us to Tobermory." In the cockpit another man was at the tiller and brought the yacht astern of the steamer. In such a sea it was too hazardous to bring her so close that a line could be thrown, and so on the steamer a towing rope was fixed to a lifebuoy which was thrown overboard and drifted down wind to the yacht. A line was also tied to the lifebuoy in order that it could be recovered after the towing rope had been taken on board the yacht. It was a most seamanlike manœuvre and occupied only a few minutes, after which the *King George* at slow speed headed for Tobermory.

The yacht was the *Eriska*, eleven tons with auxiliary motor. She had left Tobermory on the previous evening and sailed north-east to the Loch Drimbuie entrance to Loch Sunart, where she anchored for the night. That morning they had left with the intention of going north, but after clearing the entrance of Loch Sunart they met with terrific squalls and the mainsail was torn. Heavy seas breaking on board had already put the motor out of action, and only with the help of jib and mizzen did they clear the dangerous Ardnamurchan coast of rocks, cliffs and caves, to reach the partly sheltered coast of Mull. They must have had a bad time, and the scene reminded me of when I stood on the foredeck of the plunging *Marion*[1] in mid-channel after the jib had been blown away and saw the Channel steamer from Boulogne passing astern. These men had a much worse time, because the *Marion's* sails, with the exception of the jib, were intact and there was no lee shore.

Once the natural excitement amongst the passengers on the *King George* had subsided, a middle-aged lady accosted me on deck, and asked: "Why is the steamer going slow?"

"Well," said I, always glad to air what little nautical knowledge I possess, "if we went any faster the tow might part or the yacht might ship more water than was good for her."

[1] *A Time to Keep*, p. 188.

"Then are we going to take this yacht all the way with us to Staffa and Iona and back to Oban?"

"No, we're taking her back to Tobermory now."

"That will make us late!"

"Yes, I daresay it will."

"Well, I consider it's perfectly disgraceful."

It is not often that I am totally flabbergasted and utterly dumbfounded, but her last remark left me so astonished and speechless that without a word I turned away, went to the smoke-room and pressed the bell.

Beyond the Sound of Mull the steamer turns south round Caliach Point at the north-west of Mull, and eleven miles to the south, almost in the centre of the wide entrance to Loch-na-Keal and six miles from Iona, is the volcanic Isle of Staffa, flat-topped, with perpendicular sides, and one and a half miles in circumference. The isle was produced by a volcanic eruption that extended in a line from Skye through Rum, Eigg, Mull, Staffa, Jura, Islay to Rathlain and the Giant's Causeway in Ireland, and Staffa is a perfect example of the columnar structure that results when a mass of lava cools from the surface.

As it cools, each particle on the surface tends to shrink and to draw towards its neighbouring particles. The result is an evenly distributed tension which splits the surface into closely packed hexagons, and as the cooling process extends downwards so also do the hexagonal cracks, and thus the entire mass of lava is broken up into symmetrical columns. In this case the uniform circular tension caused by shrinking has been exerted from within, but a simple experiment will prove that the same result occurs when a uniform circular tension is exerted from without. Take a large handful of cigarettes and hold them upright in your hand. Every cigarette in the centre will be touching six other circular cigarettes until you squeeze the handful, when every cigarette in the centre will become a hexagon.

The name Staffa is derived from the Norse meaning Island of Pillars, and the longest pillars, rising 140 feet, are on the south-west side around the entrance to Fingal's Cave. This cave is 227 feet long and 66 feet in height above the surface of the water at mean tide, when the water is 66 feet deep and yet so clear that the bottom is visible. The ground, sides, and roof, on which sunshine is reflected from the waves, are of black hexagonal or pentagonal pillars joined every 2 feet. In moderately calm weather the cave may be entered by boats or by a pathway protected by a handrail, but to-day the sea was too rough for the boats that come four miles from Gometra to land passengers, and this must have been a disappointment to the Manchester excursionists on board. Yet the steamer went near enough for a view of the pillars at the entrance of a cavern whose floor is the ever-moving sea. I was a child when first I saw this cave, sat in giant Fingal's Chair outside, and wished my wish—for strawberries and cream.

Fingal's Cave is one of the wonders of the world and a challenge to man's descriptive power in all the arts. In music Mendelssohn comes so near reality as to make me wish that Sibelius had seen this cavern of the sea. As to the poets I wish that Swinburne had been there instead of Wordsworth, who wrote:

> " We saw, but surely, in the motley crowd,
> Not one of us had felt the far-famed sight ;
> How *could* we feel it? each the other's blight,
> Hurried and hurrying, volatile and loud."

That is not William at his best, and indeed I think it is William at his very worst. If the use of italics in prose is a sign of weakness, how much greater is that weakness in a poet. The poem merely expresses regret that the poet had gone with his fellow creatures on an excursion. Nevertheless it pleases me because as a boy the poem I most disliked was the *Excursion* by William Wordsworth. How fares Sir Walter Scott? Very much better, and this is what he wrote:

> " Nor of a theme less solemn tells
> That mighty surge that ebbs and swells,
> And still, between each awful pause,
> From the high vault an answer draws,
> In varied tone, prolonged and high,
> That mocks the organ's melody."

When we come to prose I think Sir Robert Peel must have had Sir Walter's verse in mind when he wrote that he "had seen the temple not made with hands, had felt the majestic swell of the ocean—the pulsation of the great Atlantic—beating in its inmost sanctuary, and swelling a note of praise nobler far than any that ever pealed from human organ."

The cave must have been known for centuries to those who lived on neighbouring islands, but to the outside world it was unknown until visited by Sir Joseph Banks on his voyage to Iceland in 1772. St. Adamnan, who wrote from Iona in the seventh century his Life of Columba, never refers to Staffa, and it may be that to the monks in their coracles the booming of the Atlantic in Fingal's Cave was the noise of demons.

CHAPTER VII

COLUMBA ON IONA

ON Iona, long before Columba landed, there dwelt a witch so famous that Natholocus, King of the Picts, sent a trusted messenger to consult her about the outcome of the war he was waging against his subjects. The witch, having consulted her familiar spirits, declared that Natholocus would be murdered, not by his open enemies but by a friend in whom he had such faith as to entrust him with a secret mission.

"By whose hand shall the King die?" demanded the messenger.

"Even by thine," was the answer, "as shall be well known within these few days."

Then did the King's messenger curse the witch and swear that he would see her killed ere he would commit so villainous a deed; and yet already he was bewitched. In *Marius the Epicurean* I have read that the witches of Thessaly, where Medea left the black art intact, extract from moonlight a white fluid—sometimes also found on high moorlands— the lunar virus, which is poison and "a touch of which will drive men mad." Deadlier was the virus used by the witch of Iona, for it was one of the invisible mental poisons which rot the mind, and on leaving Iona the messenger brooded on what he had heard. If he told his friend the King what the witch had said, the King in fear might put him to death. If he concealed the prophesy and said that the witch had failed to read the future, his life would be in no less danger, as the King might hear the news from others. So the messenger determined on the surest way to save himself, and when the King took him aside so that no others might learn what the witch had said, the messenger told the truth, and then "falling forthwith upon Natholocus with a dagger, he slew him outright."

Nearly two centuries before Columba came to Iona, Scotland was so infested with witches that St. Patrick had to flee the country. In the year 388 the good life led by Patrick so incensed the Devil that he incited the covens of witches to attack the saint *en masse*. To escape their wiles Patrick fled to the River Clyde, where he found a coracle in which he made his escape to Ireland, then a pagan country. Witches are unable to cross running water, and so they hurled an enormous rock after the coracle, but their aim was so inaccurate that the rock fell on the river's bank where it may be seen to this day as the Rock of Dumbarton.

Even in Columba's time there were demons in Iona, as witness the one found in a milk pail which the boy milker had omitted to bless with the Sign of the Cross before pouring in the milk; and in Scotland the Devil's disciples became so active that King Kenneth, a century after Columba's death, ordained death at the stake for all jugglers, wizards, necromancers, and such as call up spirits. A fearful penalty, but at this time, according to the Scottish Chronicles, there were parts of the country where it rained blood. Still worse, during service in the church at Camelon the bishop's crozier went on fire and burnt as fiercely as if it had been made of Thermite, because "by no means could it be quenched till it was burnt even to ashes." Moreover, at noon on a clear day there was heard all over Scotland the clash of steel upon steel, the clatter of armour, the neighing of horses, and so much noise as to make folk think there was a war on between Picts and Scots, whereby many people "were put in great feare." Such were the times in which Columba and his successors lived on Iona.

On Iona to-day there are no relics of Columba save the soil, the small hills, the place-names and the sea. Most beautiful are those place-names—The Field of the Tillage; Hill of the Bones; A Place of Shells; Hill of the Well; the Graveyard of the Craftsmen, and many others.

On the eve of Pentecost 563, Columba, then aged forty-four, landed on Iona, where he died thirty-four years later in 597. He thus lived during a period of obscurity in Scottish and English history, and over a century before his birth the links between the Continent and south-eastern Britain snapped when the Roman Legions were recalled in 410, and it was not until the year of Columba's death that St. Augustine landed. This makes it all the more remarkable that by reason of Adamnan's *Life*[1] and the *Irish Life*, we know more about St. Columba than about any other historical character of that time in our country. Adamnan in youth may have met men who knew Columba, must have had access to manuscripts written by him, wrote the life within a century after his death, and has left a vivid picture of a man of great stature and athletic build, whose voice was "so loud and melodious it could be heard a mile off."

At baptism he was named Colum (Dove), to which in childhood by reason of his early inclinations the word Cille

[1] Routledge's Universal Series, 4th impression, 1939.

("of the church") was added, and among his teachers was Finbar the Irishman who had been trained at Candida Casa. At Moville, on the southern border of Ulster, Colum-Cille became a pupil of St. Finian by whom he was ordained. At the age of twenty-four he founded his first monastery at Derry, and during the next fifteen years established many other foundations in Ireland. His former master Finian was now Abbot of Clonard, and there Colum-Cille went on a visit which led to momentous happenings. Finian possessed a copy of St. Jerome's psalter which he had brought from Rome, the only copy in Ireland, and this Colum-Cille borrowed. Then, sitting up for many nights, he surreptitiously copied on waxed goatskin the entire manuscript of the psalms. Finian discovered that the psalter had been copied and demanded the transcript, but Colum-Cille refused to give it up and appealed to the High King Dairmait, who decided this case of copyright in the following judgment: "To every cow her calf, and to every book its son-book. Therefore the copy you have made, O Colum-Cille, belongs to Finian."

Columba (to use his later name) resented this decision and was imprisoned by the King at Tara, from where he escaped to join his clansmen in Tirconnel. Soon he had another grievance against the King, whose men had killed his kinsman Prince Curnan of Connaught, who had sought sanctuary with Columba after fatally injuring an opponent in a hurling match on the Feast of Tara. Columba now instigated his clansmen to rise against the King, and at the battle of Cooldrevny in 561, 3000 of the King's army were slain.

The past can never be read in terms of the present, and these things happened at a time when monks and women took their place in the battle line, and when public opinion thought as lightly of battles, which after all were fought with a purpose, as do we about the senseless weekly slaughter on the roads of Britain. Indeed, it was Columba who later on secured the exemption of women from military service, but priests were not exempted until a century after his death. Nevertheless, for his part in the battle of Cooldrevny, he was excommunicated by the Irish bishops in synod at Teltown, Meath, although the sentence was revoked by the intercession of St. Brendan. There is no evidence that Columba was exiled from Ireland for life, and in point of fact he returned publicly on several occasions.

Thus the *Irish Life of St. Colum-Cille*[1], of which the oldest text, transcribed about 1397, is in the Irish Academy Library, gives a remarkable account of his appearance at the Convention of Drumceatt in County Meath on 575. The King wished to abolish the bards, of whom there were so many that they had become an intolerable nuisance, but Columba, being a bard, defended the poets and the enduring value of poetry. Moreover, he demanded the release of Scannlan, who appears in the narrative as one of the thirstiest of all poets; and in every other line the dominating personality of Columba is apparent.

"The clerics came subsequently into the assembly. The King rose and bade them welcome.

"'Our demand must be granted,' said Colum-Cille.

"'You shall get it truly,' said the King.

"'The poets must be retained,' said Colum-Cille.

"'It shall not be done,' said the King, 'for their evils against us are great.'

[1] Skene, *Celtic Scotland*, vol. ii, 2nd edition, p. 499.

"'Say not so,' observed the cleric, 'for the praises they shall sing for thee shall be enduring, as the praises the poets sung for him are enduring for Cormac, grandson of Conn. And the treasures that were given for them were transitory, while the praises live long after them. . . .'

"'Release Scannlan,' said Colum-Cille.

"'I shall not do so,' answered the King, 'until he die in the hut where he is.'

"'We will not pursue the subject further,' said Colum-Cille, 'but if it be pleasing to God, may it be he that shall take off my shoes to-night, at matins, in whatsoever place I may be.'"

Columba proceeded to Derry and meanwhile, according to tradition, after a thunderbolt had fallen on the Convention an angel released Scannlan from his chains and prison. That night, as Columba came through the chancel-screen to matins it was Scannlan who assisted him to remove his shoes.

"And what Colum-Cille said is, 'Who is this?'

"'Scannlan,' answered he.

"'Hast any news?' asked Colum-Cille.

"'A drink,' said Scannlan.

"'Hast brought us a blessing?' asked Colum-Cille.

"'A drink,' said Scannlan.

"'Delay in answering attend thy successors,' said Colum-Cille.

"'Speak not so,' said Scannlan. 'Thou shalt always have their rents, and their tributes and customs.'

"'May bishops and kings be of thy race for ever,' said Colum-Cille. 'Here is one drink for thee,' said he, 'to wit, a vessel of ale containing enough for three.'"

70

"Scannlan then lifted the vessel between his two hands and drank the contents in one drink. And he afterwards ate his meal, to wit, seven joints of old bacon and ten wheaten cakes; after which he lay down and was three days and three nights in one sleep." That is a very human story, well told, and be it noted that in those days a common form of torture was to feed prisoners with small quantities of salted meat and deprive them of water.

Tradition is probably right in ascribing Columba's missionary journey to Scotland as the result of his remorse for the deaths he had caused, and of a penance imposed upon him by St. Laisren that he should leave Ireland and win as many souls for Christ as there had been men and women killed in the battle. Yet in Murray's Guide Book of 1884 you would have read: "In the darkest of the dark ages (A.D. 563) St. Columba, an Irish monk, of royal descent, disgusted with the sanguinary feuds of his countrymen, left Ireland, and sought refuge in Iona, out of sight of his native land." Most comforting history, and it reminds me of what I once read about Waterloo in one of my school books: "Wellington gave the order, 'Up, Guards, and at them'. The Old Guard of France wavered, broke, and fled. Waterloo was won."

Apart from their meaning some words are beautiful in themselves, and Iona is one of the most beautiful. I have read somewhere that it means "the Isle of the Waves," but a more probable meaning and derivation would be "The Island of Columba." Thus Adamnan, whose knowledge of Hebrew, Greek, Latin, in addition to his native Celtic, raises a doubt as to whether "the dark ages" were so very dark, refers to Columba as "having the same name as Jonas,

71

the prophet, for, though differing in sound of the three different languages, it means one and the same thing: what in Hebrew (Yonah) is pronounced Iona, in Greek is uttered Peristera, and in the Latin tongue is called Columba." All these words mean Dove, and if the Celtic word Hy or Hi, meaning island, were placed before the Hebrew we would have Hy Yonah, from which, although I know nothing of philology, it seems an easy step to Iona meaning, since there are no doves on the island, the Island of Columba. Thus the *Irish Life* records that "he reached the place the name of which to-day is Hii-Coluim-Cille." [1]

The greatest mystery concerns the first death on the island, and, according to the *Irish Life*: "Colum-Cille then said to his people, 'It is good for us that our roots should go under the ground here.' And he said to them, 'It is permitted to you, that some one of you may go under the clay of this island, to consecrate it.'

"Odran rose up obediently, and what he said was, 'If you would accept me,' said he, 'I am ready for that.'

"'O Odran,' said Colum-Cille, 'thou shalt have the reward therefore, viz. his prayer shall not be granted to any one at my grave, unless it is from thee he asks it first.' Odran went then to heaven. He (Colum) founded the Church of Hy (Iona) there." [2]

This story may be a distorted version of some conversation between Columba and Odran, but, according to Adamnan, a certain Brito "was seized with bodily illness and brought to the last extremity," and Columba then refers to "the soul of this exile, the first who has died among us in this island." Now Adamnan may have been referring to Odran by his

1 Skene, *loc. cit.*, p. 491.   2 Skene, *loc. cit.*, p. 492.

nationality, Brito the Briton, to show that he was British and not a Gael. Although Adamnan never mentions Odran, nevertheless the most famous place on the island is called Reilig Odrhain, the traditional site of Columba's wooden church and afterwards the burial-place of kings where forty-eight Scottish, four Irish, and eight Norwegian kings were buried, the latter after the conversion of Norway in the eleventh century. Popular tradition is wont to pile horror upon horror, and so the story, for which there is not a shred of documentary evidence, goes that after three days Columba wished to see the face of his friend Odran once more, and had the grave reopened. Odran was still alive and announced that there was no hell, whereupon Columba called, "More earth on Odran," and that phrase in Gaelic is used to this day in the Western Isles as a rebuke to anyone who talks foolishly.

Columba's bravery is outstanding, and during his second year on Iona he risked his life when with two Pictish-speaking companions he visited the King of the Picts at Inverness, overcame the opposition of the Druids and won the confidence of King Brude. He travelled by the chain of lochs now united by the Caledonian Canal, and was the first to describe the Loch Ness Monster which he saw in the River Ness. Some of the local inhabitants were burying a man who, when swimming in the river, had been savagely bitten by some aquatic monster. Columba ordered one of his companions to swim across the river and fetch a cobble beached on the other side. His companion obeyed and swam towards the other side. "But the monster, which was lying in the river bed, and whose appetite was rather whetted for more prey than sated with what it already had, perceiving the surface of the water disturbed by the swimmer, suddenly comes up and moves towards the man as he swam in mid stream, and with a great roar rushes on him with open mouth, while all who were there, barbarians as well as brethren, were greatly terror-struck." Columba made the Sign of the Cross, and in the Name of God commanded the monster: "Go thou no further, nor touch the man; go back at once."[1] The monster obeyed.

By some modern critics Columba has been accused of being the political agent of the Irish Kings of Dalriada (Argyll and the Isles), and he certainly persuaded the northern Picts to abandon their suzerainty over Dalriada. His greatest diplomatic achievement was in 574 when he secured the election of Aidan as King of Dalriada and later the consent of the northern Picts to his election.

Aidan was solemnly consecrated King by Columba on Iona, and during the service Aidan sat on the Stone of Fate above which King George VI was consecrated and crowned at Westminster in 1937. Once Aidan was consecrated, Columba took him to Ireland, and at the Convention of Drumceatt secured the political, financial, and military independence of Scottish Dalriada from its former subjection to the Kings of Ireland. These were great political achievements, but only an ignorant critic would suggest that statecraft is incompatible with genuine piety. Both are to be found side by side in the Hebrew prophets, in W. E. Gladstone, and in the late General Booth, to name but a few.

Of modern appraisements of Columba the best I know is that of the late Father Tom Burke, the Irish Dominican and famous wit: "At the beginning of his life, Columba was vindictive, passionate, bold—a man of strife, born a soldier

---

[1] *St. Columba.* Routledge's Universal Series, 1939, p. 137.

rather than a monk. Often in his lifetime he was involved in fighting, and, when the Irish were fighting their battles, they would cry out, 'Columba, pray for us,' and his soul went out from his cell into the thick of the fight with them. He was, at the same time, full of contradictions and contrasts. He was tender and irritable, rude and courageous, ironical and compassionate, caressing, imperious, grateful, revengeful, led by pity as well as by wrong; ever moved by generous passions, and, among all passions, fired to the last by the love of poetry and the love of Ireland; little inclined to melancholy, when he had once surmounted the great sorrow of his life—his well-won exile. Thus, full of contradictions, though harmonised by Divine Grace, he lived and died a Saint."[1]

When the Norse pirates were raiding the coast of Scotland in the eighth century, Columba's bones were removed for safe custody, some to Kells and others to Dunkeld. Then in the *Irish Annals* comes the laconic entry: "Devastation of all the islands by the heathen," and in 801 Columba's monastery was burnt to the ground. Of all buildings now on the island the most ancient was built nearly five centuries after Columba and is, therefore, out of place and time in this narrative. Yet the place-names have survived, and by staying a night in the island, on which are two hotels, you may follow in the footsteps of the Saint.

Iona, three miles long, one and a half miles wide, is treeless and looks barren and rocky, but the soil grows good turf with thyme and clover, which at one time supported 200 cows, 600 sheep, and 25 horses. Oats and barley may be grown there but not corn. At the southern end is the

---

[1] From a sermon preached in St. Columba's Chapel, New York. Quoted by J. F. S. Gordon in *Iona*, Glasgow, 1885, p. xi.

Port of the Coracle, where Columba landed, a little bay between red gneiss rocks with a beach of coloured pebbles, green serpentine, green quartz, and pink felspar. The sea is transparent green and on the white sandy bottom are beds of purple Algæ. Near by is the "Cairn with the back turned upon Erin," the hill from which the Saint could not see his native land. You may walk by the Cliff of the Rowan, the Hill of the Window, and the Hill of the Mass to the place where, on the day of his death at the age of seventy-seven, he blessed the granary and thanked the monks for having worked so well that there would be enough grain to last for a year after his death. They begged him not to speak of dying, but he replied: "This day is called the Sabbath, which is, interpreted, Rest. And this day is truly a Sabbath day for me, because it is for me the last day of this present laborious life, on which I rest after the fatigues of my labours; and this night, at midnight, when begins the solemn day of the Lord, according to the saying of the Scriptures, I shall go the way of my fathers."

As he was returning to the monastery he stopped to rest and "behold the white horse, a faithful servant, runs up to him, the one which used to carry the milk pails to and fro between the byre and the monastery. He, coming up to the Saint, wonderful to tell, lays his head against his breast— began to whinny and to shed copious tears into the lap of the Saint as though he had been a man, and weeping, and foaming at the mouth. And the attendant, seeing this, began to drive away the weeping mourner, but the Saint forbade him, saying: 'Let him alone, let him alone, for he loves me . . .' And so saying, he blessed his servant the horse, as it sadly turned to go away from him."

76

At the top of the hill above the monastery he stopped again, raised both hands in blessing the monastery, and then uttered the amazing prophecy that has been and is being fulfilled to this day: "Upon this place, small though it be, and mean, not only the Kings of the Scotic people, with their people, but also the rulers of barbarous and foreign races, with the people subject to them, shall confer great and no common honour: by the Saints also even of other churches shall no common reverence be accorded to it."

On the way back to Oban by the southern route the steamer, before rounding the Isle of Earraid, close in to the south-western corner of the Ross of Mull, makes her way through channels in the Torran reefs and, so clear is the water, the submerged ledges are visible. The Torran reefs extend from the Ross for fifteen miles to the south-west, and the last reef is the Dhu Heartach from which one black oval rock rises above the sea, the Rock of St. John, on which is the lighthouse that warns shipping from the south of the dangers that lie so far from shore. This lighthouse took five years to build and the builder was Thomas Stevenson. All the stones were quarried and dressed on the Isle of Earraid whence, when the sea ran low on the reef, they were towed in barges to the rock over fifteen sea miles out into the open Atlantic.

At the age of seventeen, R. L. S., the first of a trinity, for the only other writers known by their initials are G. K. C. and G. B. S., lived for a time among the rocky and heathery hummocks of Earraid, and so came to know "The earthy savour of the bog plants, the rude disorder of the boulders, the inimitable seaside brightness of the air, the brine and the iodine, the lap of the billows among the weedy reefs, the

77

sudden springing up of a great run of dashing surf along the sea-front of the isle. . . ." This was the island on which he landed David Balfour after the wreck of the *Covenant* in *Kidnapped*.

Some modern writers, especially those who believe that books, like legal documents, are improved by lack of punctuation, belittle Stevenson for what they call his complacent philosophy and midnight oil prose, but no man who suffered so much ill-health could have made life tolerable without a contented, heroic, and charitable outlook. In the essays it may well be that sentences are sometimes too well balanced, and assuredly the prose of his imitators is stamped with preciosity, but be it noted that he himself used the words midnight oil when telling of how he played the "sedulous ape" to the great writers of the past and of the difficulties of his apprenticeship. Writing may come very easily to those who are inspired either by God or the Devil, but for most writers it is a hard task, and in all probability the more readable a book the more difficult it was to write. R. L. S. is read to-day by boys and girls who might be his great-grandchildren, and it is posterity that either awards or withholds the palm. "The trouble about *Treasure Island* and *Kidnapped*," said a public librarian, the other day, "is the difficulty we have in getting them back on the shelves." To have written the unfinished *Weir of Hermiston*, or to be able to complete it, I for one would give ten years of life, and now Alfred Noyes has declared that the poem "To My Wife" is not only the greatest love poem in the English language but also is in a metre never previously used by any British poet. Good prose is not unpunctuated and great poetry is not obscure.

CHAPTER VIII

LOOKING FOR LODGINGS

DUE west and eight miles from the Sound of Mull is the Island of Coll, and to the south-west, two miles distant, the adjacent Island of Tiree. Coll is twelve and a half miles long, for the most part about three miles wide and lies north-east by south-west. At all seasons and in all weathers I have crossed to the Hebrides, but the most memorable crossing was in December, 1933. The *Lochearn* leaves Oban at 6 a.m., and I had slept on board. At 7 a.m. I dressed and went on deck into the night, for the sun had not yet risen. The night was calm, cold with five degrees of frost, and the sky so ablaze with stars as to remind me that constellations in the north are more numerous and brilliant than those of the southern hemisphere. Behind the mountains of Scotland a long faint streak of light appeared and slowly rose until all the stars were extinguished save Venus, whose flashes of crimson, blue, and yellow continued almost to the rising of the sun:

> " Thou lingering star with lessening ray,
> That lovest to greet the early morn."

The snow-clad mountains were now visible, some of the peaks lit with golden light, and then the first blinding rays of sunlight reached the ship. The sun rose in a cloudless sky, over a calm sea as blue as the Mediterranean on a clear day, and astern was a panorama of white summits, the Coolins, the heights of Rum and Eigg, the mountains

79

of Ross, the hills of Lorne, Ben More in Mull, and the Paps of Jura. To the south among the Treshnich Isles the Dutchman's Cap, covered with snow, looked like an iceberg. On that day visibility was eighty miles, and the first officer said, "This weather is sensational." He was right, and for once an overworked adjective was not abused.

At Coll the *Lochearn* stops at the entrance of Loch Ithiuirne, one and a half miles long, three-quarters of a mile wide at the mouth, two-thirds dry at low water, and so shallow that a motor-boat from the stone jetty at Arinagour ferries passengers and goods, cattle and sheep, from and to the shore. Last summer I landed in heavy rain, and amongst those who came on board was a boy scout escorted by two companions, and from the vacant look on his face I wondered if he was suffering from the second stage of sunstroke, in which there is drowsiness and even coma.

Arinagour is on the south-western shore of the loch which lies between low rocky hills with patches of grass. On the north-eastern shore are a few acres of meadow land with a derelict farmhouse whose roof is falling in and whose windows are broken. At low tide it may be reached by a cart track, at other times by boat, and it looked a desirable abode for a modern anchorite. The village, two hundred yards in length, consists of a row of a dozen well-built white-washed cottages roofed with galvanised iron painted terra-cotta, facing the road and the loch, and extending from the post office to two semi-detached two-storied villas, one of which is the shop where one can buy almost anything from a newspaper to a pair of boots. On the roadside opposite one of the cottages were seven small lime trees, which were planted from cuttings taken from the manse garden by a visitor forty years ago. Beyond the villas is the smithy, and beyond that a small hill where the loch becomes very narrow. At the foot of the hill is the Coll Hotel, half-way up is the Church of Scotland, and on the top is a small cairn of stones to commemorate the men of Coll who fell in the Great War, a simple memorial which one day might be impressive if every one who climbed the hill carried up a stone in accordance with the old Highland custom.

As I have said, rain was falling fast, but so contrary is my nature that I feel exhilarated when walking in the rain. Yet I do not enjoy looking for lodgings, although such a quest is good for the soul, inasmuch as it teaches humility and hope, and would make an excellent penance for all to whom Life is a personally conducted tour with accommodation booked in advance. Looking for lodgings also teaches self-reliance, and the values of dress and address, because you are knocking at doors where your features are unknown.

As to dress, it is a mistake to be too well dressed lest the people whose shelter you seek should imagine that you are better than they are, and so feel ashamed to have you in their home. Nor should you keep the limousine purring outside the cottage door lest they think you are mean. Above all, if you call at a farm late in the evening, do not ask the farmer if you may sleep on the hay in his barn, as did a couple of "hikers" in the West Highlands last summer. The farmer answered that even if they had no money he would give them a couple of beds for the night. "Oh, no, we've plenty of money, but want the experience of sleeping on hay in a barn." Whereupon he cursed them and drove them away, and rightly. In the last war I have slept on a straw palliasse sodden with rain on the floor of a leaky hut at Lake Down on Salisbury Plain. I have also slept of necessity on heather, but none except pampered fools in search of a new sensation would choose such couches in preference to a mattress and a bed. Moreover, hay is valuable because it sustains cattle, and cattle are clean feeders who might not eat the hay on which humans had slept.

For myself I wore brown shoes with studs, flannel trousers, flannel shirt, riding coat, a raincoat and a panama hat. Do not jeer at the panama hat, for I hold with Mr. Hilaire Belloc that of all headgears it is the best. It may be carried in the pocket, on the head it is light and lets the rain through as easily as any other hat save the sou'wester, which on shore is apt to overheat the brain. The only place where the panama hat should not be worn is in great cities, as I discovered in Edinburgh, where it attracted the attention of undesirable touts who mistook me, an Edinburgh graduate, for a tourist and an immoral tourist to boot. We cannot all carry a bishop's crozier on our travels, but next to that a fishing-rod carried in the hand and displayed on the doorstep is usually accepted as a token of inoffensive respectability, and as a sign that you are not selling silk stockings.

Beyond the smithy I went up a steep rough road, now running with water like a shallow burn, and knocked at the door of a dairy farm, where doubtless there would be plenty of cream, which I like although it does not like me. The door was only half-opened by a woman, who looked tired and anxious. "I was told you take lodgers, and I'd like to stay for a week." She shook her head decisively. "No, I cannot take anyone. My daughter is very ill and I'm nursing her. If the minister was at home he'd give you a room in the manse. There's a divinity student there now, and

he only comes here for meals. Have you tried in the village?
No, well you might try Miss MacLean, Mrs. MacKinnon,
Mrs. MacFadger, or Miss Kennedy."

Having thanked her I returned down the watery road to
the village, only to find Miss MacLean, and Mistresses
MacKinnon and MacFadger had each two visitors and
could not take a third.

Miss Kennedy seemed the last chance. She was of medium
height, stout, in age between fifty and sixty, with grey hair
and large eyes, and gave the impression of being a hard
worker with a kindly disposition, and yet: "No, no, I can't
manage it. I'm very busy. There's visitors coming on
Monday and I've got to get their house ready. I'd have no
time to look after you."

"But, Miss Kennedy, I don't need any looking after."

At this point her brother, a tall, lean man of seventy with
a white moustache, came from the kitchen looked at me and
spoke to her in Gaelic.

"Would you not try some other place first and then——?"

"Ah," said I, with a smile, "now you're thawing, Miss
Kennedy. I've tried four already—and surely it's an awful
thing for a Highlander to be looking for lodgings in the
rain?"

"Well, you'd better come in and get your wet things
dried." The door was opened wide, and my cottage was
opposite the lime trees. Of those who plant trees Dr.
Johnson has written sonorously and redundantly. "Plantation is naturally the employment of a mind unburdened with
care, and vacant to futurity, saturated with present good,
and at leisure to derive gratification from the prospect of
posterity. He that pines with hunger, is in little care how

others shall be fed. The poor man is seldom studious to make his grandson rich."

And what would I have done if Miss Kennedy had not let me in? I would have played my trump card, as I did at 2 a.m. at Tarbert, Harris, but what that card is I shall not tell you until we get there in the dark.

My bed-sitting-room was to the left of the front door, a fairly large room with a double bed, a circular table, two chairs, one an easychair, a wash-stand, above it a small shaving mirror on the wall, a sideboard on which stood a large paraffin lamp and an old gramophone, a china cupboard, a clothes cupboard, a chest of drawers, and on the floor waxcloth and rugs. In the window were two geraniums, and in a corner of the room a palm that had known better days. On the mantelshelf were china ornaments, also wax roses under glass, and on the wall above, a plaster bas-relief of Glasgow University in a frame of clam shells. On the other walls was a picture text of, "I will praise Thee with my whole heart," with the coloured picture of a woodland scene and a waterwheel. Another picture was of a sunset behind a windmill, and the whole room was dominated by a composite engraving of "Queen Victoria and the Royal Family of Great Britain in 1897," in which I counted no less than thirty royal personages ("We made a wonderful row of royalties," as the Queen wrote in her diary after attending a gala performance of *Macbeth* in January 1858)—Grandmother Sutherland would have known all their names and birthdays.

Assuredly the room was not under-furnished, and the advantage of a bed-sitting-room is that you may read and write in peace and more comfortably than in the bedrooms

84

of small hotels. Nevertheless, I told Miss Kennedy that if she had no objection I would prefer to have my meals in the kitchen with her brother and herself, and to this she agreed.

At supper I learnt that her brother's name in Gaelic was Malcolm, son of Charles, son of John, which did not surprise me, because in Lochaber there was an old man who could remember the names of his father's fathers for twenty generations. I told them my name and that I was a doctor.

"Oh, you're a doctor," said Miss Kennedy, "and that's strange because our last visitor was a professor from London with ten letters after his name! He collected flies on the island and sent them away in bottles—a nice gentleman, and I had a kind letter from his mother thanking me for looking after him. Many visitors? Most of them are travellers selling meal, flour, clothes, butter, and baking soda."

"Aye," said Malcolm, son of Charles, son of John, "and the one I'd like to see again is the travelling watch-maker who repaired that grandfather clock. It's one hundred years old, and the man who repaired it said it would go for five years. It did and then it stopped. I'm thinking that if I was to tighten it up it would go for another twenty years."

"No, no, Malcolm, leave the clock till the man comes this way again. Is your tea to your liking, doctor? If it looks black it's only the peat. Where we had our farm there was a spring of clear water, but here it's peaty. I spoke to the old doctor, the one before Dr. Somerville, about the water, and he said, 'It is good water. I sent a bottle to a professor in Edinburgh, and had word that it was very good wood water. The colour does not matter.'"

My hosts had good manners, self-possession, and treated me as their equal.

CHAPTER IX

THE FAIRIES

AFTER supper we sat around the kitchen peat-burning range, she knitting, he smoking a pipe and I cigarettes. After a pause in our talk, I asked: "Are there many fairies on the island?"

She looked at me sharply. "You don't believe in fairies?"

"I do believe in fairies," said I, and told them of the Phantasmagoria I had seen in a Lapland forest.[1]

"Well, well," she said, patting me on the shoulder, "you're as bad as my brother."

"Of course there are fairies," said the old man, "plenty of fairies in the north end of the island."

I rejoiced that the ice was broken, and asked if he'd ever seen them.

"No, I've never seen them myself, but I had a friend who often saw them. He was a piper, and there is a steep rock beyond the Windy Gap—you'll see it if you go there—that used to open, inside the fairies were dancing, and he'd go inside and play the pipes to them. Mind you, I believe what my friend said, but I cannot understand how a solid rock can open."

"Anything may happen in fairyland."

"That's right, and you may have heard tell of that man in Lochaber—it was long before my time—who went with a friend of his, a piper, to a dance. On the way to the dance

[1] *Lapland Journey*, p. 145.

they were passing a rock and the rock opened. Inside the fairies were dancing and the piper went in to play to them. The rock closed, and his friend went back alone to tell what had happened. No one would believe him. They thought he had murdered his friend, and for a time he was kept in prison at Fort William. I daresay they tortured him. But he stuck to his story, and as the body of his friend was never found they had to let him out. Now the queer thing was that five years later this man and four others were on their way to a cattle fair when they passed a rock that was open and inside was his friend the piper playing to the fairies. They called to him to come out, and when he came out all he said was: 'I've only been here for five minutes.' Yes, yes, it is well known that the fairies take people away."

"And for a long time," said I, "because their time is not our time. There was the piper who promised to play to them for a year and a day. Then he escaped and returned to his father's house, but the house was a ruin and no one in the neighbourhood recognised him, until a very old man remembered hearing as a child a grandfather's story of a piper who had been taken by the fairies."

"That's right; their time is not our time."

Then I told them about Mr. Robert Kirk, who graduated M.A. at Edinburgh, studied Divinity at St. Mary's College, St. Andrews, became minister at Balquhidder, then at Aberfoyle, and was "taken" to Fairyland *circa* 1692 after he had written the *Secret Commonwealth* of *Elves, Fauns, and Fairies*.[1]

---

[1] With comment by Andrew Lang. Introduction by R. C. Cunninghame Graham. Aneas Mackay, Stirling, 1933.

The story of Robert Kirk's fate was first published in *Sketches of Perthshire*[1] by the Rev. Patrick Graham, D.D., Minister of Aberfoyle from 1787 to 1835: "The Reverend Robert Kirk, the first translator of the Psalms into Gaelic verse, had formerly been minister at Balquhidder; and died minister of Aberfoyle in 1688 at the early age of fifty-two. His grave-stone, which may be seen near the east end of the church of Aberfoyle, bears this inscription:

Robertus Kirk, A.M. Linguae Hibernii, (c) oe bumen, obiit, etc.

He was walking, it is said, one evening in his nightgown, upon the little eminence to the west of the present manse, which is still reckoned a *Dun shi'*.[2] He fell down dead, as was believed; but this was not his fate:

> " It was between the night and day,
>   When the fairy king has power,
> That he sunk down (but not) in sinful fray,
> And, 'twixt life and death, was snatched away,
>   To the joyless Elfin bower."

"Mr. Kirk was the near relation of Graham of Duchray, the ancestor of the present General Graham Stirling. Shortly after his funeral, he appeared in the dress in which he had sunk down, to a mutual relation of his own and of Duchray. 'Go,' said he to him, 'to my cousin Duchray, and tell him I am not dead; I fell down in a swoon and was carried into Fairyland, where I now am. Tell him, that when he and my friends are assembled at the baptism of my child (for he had left his wife pregnant), I will appear in the room, and that if he throws the knife which he holds in his hand over my head, I will be released and restored to human society.' The man,

[1] Edinburgh, 1812, p. 253 (British Museum copy).
[2] Fairy Hill.

88

it seems, neglected, for some time, to deliver the message. Mr. Kirk appeared to him a second time threatening to haunt him night and day till he executed his commission, which, at length, he did. The time of the baptism arrived. They were seated at the table; Mr. Kirk entered, but the laird of Duchray, by some unaccountable fatality, neglected to perform the prescribed ceremony. Mr. Kirk retired by another door and was seen no more. It is firmly believed that he is, at this day, in Fairyland."

The fairies have not yet released Mr. Robert Kirk, and play tricks on those who are over-interested in this affair. Thus Sir Walter Scott, in his *Demonology and Witchcraft* (1830, p. 163), says that the *Secret Commonwealth* "was printed with the author's name in 1691, and reprinted in 1815 for Longman and Co." Yet Scott had never seen a copy of the 1691 edition, nor is there a copy in any of the great libraries. Moreover, the supposed "reprint" of 1815, of which there were a hundred copies, was published by Ballantyne and was made, as it states, from "a manuscript copy preserved in the Advocates Library," now the National Library of Scotland. On this manuscript there was a "Note by the Transcriber," the person who wrote the manuscript, "See the rest in a little manuscript belonging to Coline Kirk." Now Colin Kirk, Writer to the Signet, was the son of Robert Kirk by his first wife Isobel (daughter of Sir Colin Campbell of Mochester) who died in 1680.

There is also a practical reason why the *Secret Commonwealth* was not published in the author's lifetime. Mr. Kirk must have been aware of the penalty for witchcraft, because he knew of the "damnable Practice" of evil angels who suck the "Blood and Spirits" out of a witch's body, "leaving what we call the Witches Mark behind; a Spot, that I have seen, as a small Mole, horny, and brown-coloured; throw which Mark, when a large Brass Pin was thrust (both in Buttock, Nose, and Rooff of the Mouth) till it bowed and became crooked, the Witches, both Men and Women, nather felt a Pain, nor did bleed, nor knew the precise Time when this was adoing to them, (there Eyes only being covered)."[1]

The penalty of death at the stake for witchcraft was not repealed until 1735, and had the contents of the *Secret Commonwealth* been known to the Covenanters, the minister of Aberfoyle, albeit north of the Highland Line,[2] might have come to an even more untimely end.

Sir Walter also refers to Patrick Graham's book as *Sketches of Picturesque Scenery*, the title of the first edition published in 1810 in which there is no reference to Kirk, who appears in the second edition of 1812, which is called *Sketches of Perthshire*. Andrew Lang copied this mistake, and that is a good example of a literary changeling which led me a fine old dance round the Reading Room of the British Museum, even into one of the inner chambers, where under the eye of a custodian you are allowed to read rare books, only to discover that Sir Walter in his *Demonology and Witchcraft* had both quoted and misquoted Graham on Kirk. For myself, I ought to be now writing under a rowan tree, because Lang also says, again following Sir Walter, that Kirk's "tomb, in Scott's time, was to be seen

[1] *Loc. cit.*, p. 115.
[2] An imaginary line drawn from Helensburgh on the Clyde to Stonehaven in Kincardineshire.

in the east end of the churchyard of Aberfoyle; but the ashes of Mr. Kirk *are not there*." Well, neither is the stone which with its inscription was found last summer by Miss Isabel Macdonald, S.R.N.,[1] to be close to the wall of the now roofless church. "Near the east end of the church," wrote Patrick Graham in 1812, and he was right.

The kindness of Dr. L. W. Sharp, Keeper of Manuscripts at Edinburgh University, where there are eight volumes of Kirk manuscripts, enabled me to glean some further particulars of this elusive author. He was probably born at Aberfoyle where his father James Kirk was minister from 1634 to his death in 1658. Robert was the youngest and seventh son, and in the *Secret Commonwealth* he explains how the inborn gifts, including the second sight, of a seventh son may come from "some secret virtue in the womb of the parent, which increaseth untill the seventh son be borne, and decreaseth by the same degree afterwards." Alas, in our time there are few if any seventh sons, which may explain why tuberculous glands (scrofula) are now treated with tuberculin, and are no longer healed by touch as in the days of yore.

He was probably born in the year 1645 or 1646, because in an original manuscript of *Occasional Thoughts and Meditations*, begun on 5th August 1669, there is written at the beginning "aetat 23." Now if Kirk was accurate about his age it means that when he matriculated at Edinburgh, in the class of John Wishart, on 22nd October 1657, he was a boy of twelve or thirteen, a not unusual age at which to go to a university in those days. He took the usual four years'

---

[1] *The Fairy Tradition in the Highlands,* published in aid of charity by the Royal British Nurses' Association, London, 1938, p. 28.

course in Arts, and there is the original manuscript of his notes, in Latin, on Wishart's lectures, on prelections, "begun on January 12, 1660." He graduated M.A. on 19th July 1661, at the age of sixteen or seventeen. Then there is the manuscript of his notes on lectures at St. Andrews which end, "Finished June 21, 1664." Other manuscripts are *Meditations* and *Excerpts* from books he had read, pieces on Scottish charms and spells, and some poems, chiefly elegies, occasionally written both in Gaelic and English.

Those of my readers who read complicated detective stories may remember that, according to Dr. Patrick Graham, Kirk died "in 1688 at the early age of 52." Yet if Kirk knew his age and died in 1688, he was only forty-two or forty-three when he died. In point of fact, he did not die in 1688, because one manuscript in Kirk's handwriting is *A description of London in* 1689, and it was probably in 1692 when he was aged forty-six or forty-seven that "he went to his own Herd."

Only last summer when Miss Isabel Macdonald asked an old man at Aberfoyle if he knew anything about Robert Kirk, she got this answer: "All I know is that he knew more than was good for him." Assuredly he knew more about the metaphysics of Fairyland than anyone else has ever known, and he has even described the nature of fairies, who are an order of beings between men and angels, intelligent and studious, with light changeable bodies, like those called Astral, "somewhat of the Nature of a condensed Cloud, and best seen in Twilight. . . . They are Distributed in Tribes and Orders, and have Children, Nurses, Mariages, Deaths, and Burialls, in appearance even as we (unless they so do for a Mock-show, or to prognosticate some such Things among

92

us)." When human beings, "Superterraneans," as Mr. Kirk
calls them, find themselves in the Fairy Halls, they should
behave discreetly and neither seek to discover any of the
mysteries nor make use of the magic ointment which
confers invisibility, lest the fairies "smite them without
Paine, as with a Puff of Wind, and bereave them of both
the naturall and acquired Sights in the twinkling of ane
Eye (both these Sights, where once they come, being in the
same Organ and inseparable), or they strick them Dumb."

In proof of what he writes Mr. Kirk quotes cases of
"undoubted Verity," where he interviewed the people concerned and the eye-witnesses of what happened. There was
"the Woman taken out of her Child-bed," and in her place
the fairies left a lingering image who decayed, died, and was
buried. Two years later the woman returned to her husband,
who recognised her, and took her back. "Among other
Reports she gave her husband," was that in the Fairy Hill
"She found the Place full of Light, without any Fountain or
Lamp from where it did spring." In this case Mr. Kirk's
only anxiety is what would have happened if the husband
had married again during her sojourn in Fairyland, and he
fears that it would be a matter of dispute amongst casuists
whether the man would be obliged to divorce his second
spouse. I can foresee an even greater dispute in the event
of the fairies releasing Mr. Robert Kirk and of his return to
the manse at Aberfoyle in his nightgown.

He must have been happy as he wandered around his
parish, an oasis of peace in a time of wars and rumours of
wars, and happier still when at twilight he rested on some
rock on the Fairy Hill with the Good People, decked in green,
all around. As he has explained it is wise to call them the

Good People, because it is wise to speak well of those who may do you harm.

Yet in his study there were, I think, times when he smelt the faggots and knew fear, because at the end of the *Secret Commonwealth* are five short questions and five long answers on the lines of the Westminster, or as we call it in Scotland the Longer, Catechism, to justify his beliefs. "Question 1. How do you salve [save] the Second Sight from Compact [with the Devil] and Witchcraft?" Mr. Kirk "salved" all his questions, and thus answered "Objections against the Reality and Lawfulness of this Speculation."

The universality of a belief in fairies who live underground and are of a different order of being from ourselves is one of the mysteries of folklore, of history, and of psychology. Some have thought it may be the survival of a belief in an early race of dwarfs who peopled the earth. "Thus, as it seems to me," wrote Andrew Lang, "the Scots and Celts possessed a theory of a legendary people, as did the Greeks. Whether any actual traditions of an earlier, perhaps a Finnish race, was at the bottom of the legend is an obscure question. But, having such a belief, the Scotch easily discovered homes for the fancied people in the sepulchral howes: 'they combined their information.'" So far as the Finns are concerned the question is not obscure, for they are not and never were a dwarf race. Even if the Lapps were the first race on earth, the explanation would imply that a dwarfish race was distributed over the whole earth, because even Tibetans believe in fairies.

Another explanation is that mankind once possessed a sixth sense—the second sight, in which I for one believe, and could see beings of a different order than ourselves.

Those who have studied spiritualism will, I think, agree that there is evidence for the existence of discarnate intelligences who control the medium. Whilst there is a vast amount of fraud in spiritualism there are undoubtedly honest mediums who see forms which other persons do not see and who receive information which cannot be explained by telepathy. Now the most honest mediums have admitted that they can never be certain about the identity of these "controls," who often play tricks as spiteful as those of the fairies. It is the uncertainty, the anonymity, and the contradictions in the messages received which preclude spiritualism being ranked as a religion, but nevertheless, it tends to establish the existence of intelligences other than human. Moreover, if you believe that mediums do see these discarnate forms, there seems to be no reason why those with the second sight should not see and converse with fairies.

For myself, only once did I see "Subterranean Inhabitants," and then in a Lapland forest. Cunninghame Graham, when writing of Mr. Robert Kirk and the fairies, says: "He saw them, for what we are convinced we see exists for us, as certainly as if we had touched it, so that a man who is convinced that he has seen a ghost has seen it actually— with the interior vision, that vision a thousand times more vivid than the exterior eye,"—and that was the opinion of one of the greatest writers and sceptics of the last generation.

Of this writer I also like to remember the story of how he closed a conversation at his club. Some seasoned travellers were discussing the merits and demerits of women of different nationalities, when Cunninghame Graham interrupted, "You're all wrong. There's nothing to beat a red-haired Scotch Presbyterian."

CHAPTER X

TALE OF A HAGGIS

NEXT day I called on Dr. J. A. Somerville, and found him in a new house, or rather in the garden around a new house half a mile from the village. He and his brother, a skin specialist from Glasgow on holiday, were planting a rock garden on ground which the builders had littered. In three days the brothers had constructed a large rock garden, bringing the rocks in a car from a quarry a mile off, and when I saw the size of the rocks I wondered whether the floor of the car was stronger than the strength of the brothers. Both are keen gardeners and first-class botanists. They were planting the rockery with wild flowers—thyme, a pale heliotrope; blue geraniums; purple orchis; and the yellow mignonette. As I say, they were first-class botanists, but neither could tell me what is the difference between a wild flower and a weed. I have often and in vain asked that question, and assume that it concerns æsthetics rather than botany, a subject in which I nearly failed in the First Professional Examination at Edinburgh by reason of the complicated life cycle of ferns, whose sexual and asexual activities almost reduced me to tears. So I assume that a weed is an unwanted wild flower.

"At the moment," said Dr. J. A. Somerville, "there's not much sickness on the island, but two days ago I had a sad case —a boy scout in the camp from Glasgow—dementia præcox —a poor ending for a holiday, and rotten for his parents."

"I saw him taken on board the *Lochearn* and thought of sunstroke."

"Yes, I had that in mind, but there's been no sun for a week."

Dementia præcox is one of the least painful forms of insanity, and is described by modern writers as a variety of schizophrenia or splitting of the personality, although it would be more accurate to say that the personality disintegrates. It is a "psychosis of psychogenetic origin," which in plain English means a mental disease without structural changes in the brain and without a definite tangible cause, albeit that in a few cases dementia præcox has followed a great moral or physical shock. The disease is characterised by lethargy followed by stupor, and has never been better described than by Henry Maudsley in his masterpiece *The Pathology of Mind*: "The most characteristic symptoms are—vacant and expressionless countenance, oft-times dilated and sluggish pupils; confused and aimless excitement, alternating sometimes with periods of stupor; dullness of sensibility so that pain seems not felt or, if felt, only felt and responded to in a vague and confused way; seeing without perceiving, and hearing without understanding; no sense to take food, nor the sense to make definite resistance to it, but aimless and random oppositions; speechlessness or incoherent muttering, or senseless sentences or half-sentences muttered or ejaculated; inattention to the calls of nature. There is practically a mental void, and there is no memory, therefore, after recovery, of anything having passed in the mind. With these symptoms go lowered reflex action, small and perhaps scarcely perceptible, but frequent pulse and bad nutrition, for the nervous collapse

97

tells inertly on all the functions of the body." That is an example of how clinical medicine should be written, and I make no apology for introducing it here, because *The Pathology of Mind* might be read by every educated adolescent with advantage to themselves. It is the sanest book ever written on insanity, and one of my regrets is that I was born too late to have had the chance of meeting the author.

Henry Maudsley was one of the few doctors who have made a fortune in the practice of medicine, and he left his wealth to found the Maudsley Hospital for the Prevention of Mental Disease. Although an agnostic, Maudsley had partly solved the eternal problem of suffering because he concluded that imbeciles, idiots, and the incurably insane have their place in the scheme of things, if for no other reason than that their plight should arouse feelings of pity and thankfulness in the minds of those who have mental health. In this he was ahead of the materialism of the last century and of the moral defectives of our own time who advocate euthanasia as a measure of social reform.

In the afternoon we motored to Arnabost on the western side of the island, and turned north-east through the grazing lands of Gallanach, a large farm which carries 100 cattle, 1000 sheep, and once produced fifteen tons of cheese a year. Beyond the farm a steep hill, whose gradient is one in ten, rises to a narrow pass at the top of the hills, the Windy Gap through which, against strong north-easterly or south-westerly winds, pedestrians have difficulty in making their way, for the wind is deflected into the Gap from the sides of the hills and from the rising ground below. In a gale it might be impassable, because on an open road on the Island of Barra I have walked in the path of a wind so strong that I had to lean back against it lest I was thrown on my face.

From the Windy Gap I saw a strange country the like of which I had never seen, because it was Highland scenery in miniature. The road looked long, the heather-clad hills were high, the lochans lochs, the rocks huge, and to the north-east was a range of great mountains. Yet on coming near the mountains I found them to be hills not more than 200 feet high, and once the illusion was dispelled, I felt like Gulliver in Lilliput. You may have seen those miniature gardens or villages so constructed to scale that in a photograph they cannot be distinguished from a real garden or a real village unless a child is seen towering above a house or a tree. Such was my impression of this scenery in broad daylight, but to the Little People who at twilight come out of their mounds, of which there are many, the small hills would be real mountains.

A mile and a half north of the Windy Gap the road approaches the western shore near the site of a Norwegian fort, the Dun a' Bhuirbd, and near by is the entrance to a cave which is supposed to be one entrance to a subterranean passage that runs under the island for two and a half miles to the eastern shore at Dun Lórachain. Once upon a time a piper, accompanied by his dog, entered the cave at Lórachain with the intention of playing his way under the island from sea to sea, but at the Dun a' Bhuirbd only the dog emerged. There are similar pipers' caves on many of the islands, and although I bear no illwill towards pipers I cannot understand why any piper, unless extremely deaf, should wish to play the bagpipes in a subterranean passage. There is music in the pipes when played in a Highland glen at a

99

reasonable distance from the listener, but every year all over the world, on Burns's Nicht and on St. Andrew's Day, thousands of my fellow-countrymen and their guests suffer from temporary deafness when the haggis, on a silver dish, carried by the chef with uplifted arms, followed by a waiter holding aloft a bottle of whisky in each hand, and preceded by bagpipes in full blast, is marched round the room.

In thus honouring the haggis Scotsmen also do penance for their general neglect of our national dish, which many of us eat only twice a year, and then only after pouring neat whisky over a most tasty and nutritious food—a custom which arouses in strangers the suspicion that the contents of a haggis require to be disinfected. Yet I know one Lord of Appeal who dines once a week on haggis and without the relish of whisky. It is the national dish of a people once so poor and short of meat that when a sheep was killed they could not afford to throw away any part that was edible. Hence the haggis, about which there is no mystery. It consists of sheep's liver, heart and lungs boiled, then chopped fine, and well mixed with half a pint of oatmeal, one pound finely chopped beef suet, two finely chopped Spanish onions, two tablespoonfuls of salt, one teaspoonful of pepper, half a grated nutmeg, the juice of a lemon and one and a half pints of stock. The sheep's paunch, cleansed and turned inside out, is filled with the mixture and the opening is sewn up. Then the haggis, "Great Chieftain o' the puddin' race," is placed in boiling water and boiled gently for three hours. A large haggis will serve nine people, and a smaller one may be prepared from the same parts of a lamb.

Not always have I been entirely orthodox on the question of haggis, and I came to grief in July, 1916, when attached to the Royal Marine Depot at Deal. A Highland regiment was under canvas in the vicinity, and I suggested to our mess president, Major Scott, that if he would invite the Highland officers to a guest night I would provide the haggis. To this he readily agreed, and I ordered a large haggis to be sent from Edinburgh. Then by reason of what were euphemistically called "the exigencies of the Service," I was moved for temporary duty to Wales. This was a disappointment, but the Major said he would postpone the guest night until my return, provided the haggis, which had not yet arrived, would keep.

"Keep!" said I. "Of course it will keep. As a matter of fact these things are rather like Christmas puddings, the longer you keep them the better they are."

At the end of three weeks I returned, and to the Mess Sergeant my first question was: "Well, sergeant, did my haggis arrive all right?"

"Yes, sir, your 'aggis arrived all right."

"Splendid."

"No, sir, if I may say so, it's not splendid."

"What's the matter with it?"

"Well, sir, it's buried in the flower-bed outside the porch."

"Ah, I see, the hot weather; it didn't keep."

"No, sir, it did not keep, and Major nearly had the drains up before the cause of the—unpleasantness—was discovered."

Yet in the letter rack was the bill for my buried haggis, and so I wrote a letter of protest to the makers, who replied that there seemed to have been a complete misunderstanding, since had they known that I proposed to keep the haggis for three weeks they would have packed it in a hermetically sealed tin, such as they used when sending haggis out East, to India or to the tropics. Under the circumstances they would remit the bill, and for that reason I name the old-established firm of Messrs. Gibson of Princes Street.

From the Piper's Cave, and he might be the Pied Piper by reason of the distance he has led me astray, the road continues north-east and then crosses the top of the island to end at Sorasdal Bay on the eastern side—a white sandy bay guarded by red gneiss rocks not too precipitous. On the turf above the shore wild flowers were in bloom, sea pinks, snowcrop (summer-snow), deep blue speedwell, and pale forget-me-nots. Around the Bay were about a dozen crofters' houses, all of which save two were in ruins, and the children who once lived there must have kept rabbits for, in addition to wild rabbits, the place was overrun with black, white, and speckled rabbits, all now reduced to the size of the wild rabbit. In one of the houses an old woman still cards and spins wool dyed from seaweeds, and sends it to Helmsdale for weaving. I saw no young people, and outside I spoke to her husband, aged seventy-two: "No, there's no young people left. They're not content to work on the land. It gives you a living but little money. There's no money in the 'lazy fields.' " In that he was right because a "lazy field" is a small plot where furrows to grow corn are ploughed between strips of turf. Of the fishing, he said: "There's no fishing and no ling. It's the trawlers. In a westerly gale I've seen them within half a mile of this shore."

"Might they not be taking shelter?"

"No, no, they're taking the fish."

The truth of the matter as I see it is that anyone could get plenty of fish around these islands, where the seals flourish; and from the rocks of Barra I have caught fish in the Atlantic. There are flounders in the bays, ling, whiting, and mackerel farther out, but the people of the islands will not eat mackerel, as it feeds, so they say, on drowned bodies. A man could supply his own household with fish, but he has no means of bringing fish to the markets where money is made. Are men lazy, wise, or foolish who refuse to fish except for money? If there were more people on the island there might be a local market, but the population is now under 300, with only thirty children of school age in the four schools. To-day only three MacLeans and two MacKinnons, names native to Coll, hold land on the island, whereas prior to the evictions of 1856, twenty-six MacLeans and fourteen Mac-Kinnons were paying rent for land. In the south-western corner of the island, in the township of Feall, there were 200 people, until they were cleared out by Captain Donald Campbell in the middle of the last century. The place is now uninhabited. Of the evictions the old man had heard when a boy: "When the first Stewart laird bought the main part of the islands from the MacLeans, he raised the rents. The tenants could not pay, so he had them evicted. In one place ten holders and six sub-tenants were evicted. Many went to America. Now you can go from Glasgow to America in ten days. At that time, the time of sailing-ships, it took one year. Yes, one year to get to America."

To the north of Sorasdal is a small hill, called in Gaelic the *Cnoc Mor* or Great Hill, since everything here is relative, and from the top of this hill there is a view to the north-east of a cluster of small skerries and islands, of which *Eilean Mor*, the Great Island, is almost circular and less than a quarter of a mile in diameter. These skerries and islands are inhabited by colonies of seals, each colony being a harem of one male to ten females and their cubs. The males fight any other male who seeks to encroach on their territory, but on the Island of Treshnich, off Tiree, there is an old seal who lands with impunity on any of the islands.

On the coast of Coll, north of the *Cnoc Mor*, is a small bay almost enclosed by rocks, through which there is a narrow entrance, called the Sound of Breaking Oars. Long ago, when Iain Garbh of Coll was held prisoner by his stepfather MacNeill on the Island of Barra, he escaped in a six-oared galley. His galley was pursued by an eight-oared MacNeill galley and was almost overtaken at the narrow entrance to the bay. Iain's men knew the place and banked their oars, so that their galley shot through the narrow channel to safety. MacNeill's men continued rowing and their oars were smashed against the sides of the rocks. Thus the channel was called the Sound of Breaking Oars. There are hundreds of place names around the coasts of Coll and all the other islands, and on the maps in the local guidebooks they are printed in Gaelic. Let it be so, but I would suggest to the authors of these books that a glossary in English might also be included, because even in English these place names are beautiful and almost all of them have a story.

In the southern part of Coll undulating moors, whose heather is not in bloom until August, lead to a sandy plain— the Field of Flowers, and to the sand dunes in the south-western corner of the island. The few rocks rising above the moorland are of white gneiss, a hard white stone rough as a file, and on the day I passed that way the surface of the peaty lochs was a deep blue under a clear sky, in which a hawk hovered, on the alert for birds on the moor. At Acha is the roofless derelict mill whose waterwheel once ground the barley and the corn. To-day barley and corn are raised for cattle fodder, whilst flour, bleached white by electric shocks and adulterated with "improvers," is imported from the mainland. In all the islands are derelict mills, tokens of a devastation greater, because it is more enduring, than that which followed the fire and sword of the Vikings.

To the south of the Field of Flowers and on the western shore of Loch Bhreacachaidh are the ruins of an old castle above whose entrance was once a stone that bore in Gaelic the words that follow: "If any of the Clan MacElonich shall appear before this place, although at midnight, with a man's head in his hand, he will find admittance and protection against all but the King." The castle was that of the MacLeans, and when John, one of their early chieftains, was at war in Lochaber he was accompanied by his young wife who was pregnant. In the hour of her husband's defeat she was delivered of a son and heir, and both mother and child might have perished had not one of the Clan Mac-Elonich given them protection and brought them back to the safety of the castle in Coll. Hence the inscription on the stone, and for many generations the chiefs of the MacLeans provided for the education of the eldest son of the reigning chief of the MacElonichs.

On rising ground south of the old castle is the mansion house, a square bleak building with sham baronial turrets, where Dr. Johnson and Boswell were entertained by Mac-Lean of Coll in 1773. In his Journal the doctor wrote that they lived "very commodiously" in "a neat new house, erected near the old castle"; and according to Boswell it was "a neat new-built gentleman's house, better than any they had seen since they were at Lord Errol's." Yet the doctor in conversation with Boswell, remarked, "there was nothing becoming a chief about it: it was a mere tradesman's box." With Dr. Johnson's second thoughts I agree.

The Field of Flowers and the sides of the great sand dunes to the west were a blaze of purple, for it was late in July and the wild geraniums were in bloom. Never before had I seen wild flowers in such profusion. I climbed to the top of the sand dunes made by the wind and held in place not by the scanty soil or the wild flowers but by the sharp bent grass whose roots go deeper into the sand. On the top of the dunes was a circular crater about a hundred feet deep, and on its white walls layer upon layer of sand told of successive tempests in which the dunes were built. Then came the whirlwind that scooped out the crater and undid the work of other storms.

This white sand, found also at the southern end of Tiree, is not the sand of the sea but the pulverised shells of two or three species of small land snails that live and die in myriads on clover pastures near the shore. When they die their tiny shells crumble into fine white sand, which in the course of time may raise the surface of the soil by many feet, because the grass and clover continues to grow on the top of the sand. The danger is that in a great wind the thin top soil may be broken so that the wind gets under the surface of the soil and blows it away as there is no resistance in the white sand beneath. For that reason bent grass is grown on these pastures. In the south of Tiree is a deserted church which marks the time when, in a great gale, the fields of neighbouring farms were literally blown away.

On the day that I left Coll, Miss Kennedy gave me a root of bog myrtle and of southern wood, a fragrant herb, to send home—"In London they will remind you of Coll," but alas, those fragrant plants do not thrive in the soil of cities.

CHAPTER XI

A RINGING STONE

THE strange story told to me by Agnes Porter, M.D., the bacteriologist, led me to the Island of Tiree. On her way to the island in 1919 she made acquaintance on the steamer with a young newly-married couple, apparently well-to-do, whose name was Maclaren. They were first cousins, and each was a Maclaren descended from a Doctor Maclaren who once lived in the Island House on Tiree, where they hoped to learn something about their ancestor. On the island they announced their descent and made their enquiries, to which the islanders replied gravely, politely, and laconically: "Doctor Maclaren—in Island House— yes, he was factor and doctor—I've heard of him—he was before my time." Behind the backs of the descendants the islanders seethed with suppressed excitement. That anyone would claim such an ancestor, who had never married, was strange enough, but that two would make this claim, and marry each other, was almost unbelievable. Thus Agnes Porter came to hear of the wicked Doctor Maclaren.

An old woman aged eighty-five, mother of Mrs. Campbell the washerwoman who lived near the pier, said (in 1919) that Doctor Maclaren had died a few years before she was born. He was a properly trained doctor from the south, but in Tiree practised black magic. As the years went on he became more and more wicked and terrible, for he could kill people from a distance. If anyone asked him to visit a patient, then, according to the amount of the fee and the previous behaviour of the applicant, he would say either: "It's no use going to your father, seeing he will die at three in the morning," or "I don't need to see your mother. She will take a turn for the better at two in the morning." Invariably the patient either died or recovered at the predicted hour.

Doctor Maclaren had a Familiar who was a Sea Maid, and after their quarrels this Sea Maid, who was also a sort of Poltergeist, used to slip out of the sea at night, enter the Island House by one of the windows, turn the furniture upside down and smash the crockery. At last things got so bad that "the Medical Faculty of the University of Edinburgh" decided that Doctor Maclaren's wickedness and black magic could not be tolerated any longer, and they held meetings to decide how he could be controlled. Eventually all agreed that the only thing to do was to poison Doctor Maclaren. To this end a great dinner was held in Edinburgh to which every doctor was invited. At each doctor's place was a piece of paper with his name on it, and a glass of wine. In Doctor Maclaren's wine was poison, and he came in last when all the other doctors were already seated. Knowing by his magic that the wine was poisoned, and wishing to show the others that his magic was greater than their science, he drank the wine and walked out of the place. Once outside he placed an onion under each armpit and chewed some raw cabbage. An hour later he removed the onions and the cabbage, all of which had turned black, and he was free of the poison.

When Dr. Agnes Porter heard the story she immediately remembered having heard it in her childhood in Edinburgh, and when she mentioned it to Colonel Beaton of the Board of Health, he told her that the story, which until that moment he had entirely forgotten, was very frequently told throughout the Highlands when he was a child, but of what doctor it was told he could not remember.

For my part I never heard of Doctor Maclaren until 1935, and immediately wrote to my friend Mr. T. F. Harley, Secretary of Edinburgh University, to ask if they knew anything about him. Dr. L. W. Sharp found no records in the Library, and Dr. John D. Comrie, Lecturer on the History of Medicine, sent the following comment: "The story is a very good one, and if it is not true, it ought to be, and with a few touches might be made into a very good tale.

"The first Dr. Maclaren who graduated at Edinburgh did so in 1824, which is too late for the period given in the letter, as Dr. Maclaren of Tiree must have died round about that time.

"Island House is the name of the factor's house at present, so that if Maclaren was factor as well as doctor, the story has that amount of substantial basis. It is quite likely that a doctor who was somewhat lazy or addicted say to laudanum, might be loth to go and see patients at three o'clock in the morning, and as it would be easy for him to know every one in Tiree with their probable ailments, he might make the predictions mentioned with reasonable certitude and without any recourse to black magic. With regard to the story of the medical faculty dinner, obviously the only source of information that the islanders could have would be Dr. Maclaren himself, and he might have wished to give a highly coloured version of what transpired, with a view to increasing his sinister reputation.

"I fear, however, that Edinburgh University must, for the reason I have stated, reluctantly abandon the idea of being the Alma Mater of this Dr. Maclaren. St. Andrews appears to me to be more likely!"

From Coll the *Lochearn* took me to Tiree, an hour's cruise to the south-west, and the first officer said I was fortunate in that on the previous day they had evacuated two hundred Glasgow summer visitors from the island where otherwise I might have been unable to find lodgings. On the way we passed close to the Cormorant's Rock, from which hundreds of these long black birds with yellow beaks rose laboriously one after the other in the air and with rapid beats from powerful wings, feet and neck outstretched, flew off in a single line only a few feet above the sea, from which by short dives they catch and kill fish near the surface. It was a good day for the sea birds, and the solan goose, with yellowish head, bluish beak, and white, black-tipped wings, was also fishing, flying in circles at a great height and then, on seeing a fish deep in the sea, the goose rose higher before diving obliquely and head first to the depths, where its prey was killed and swallowed. A passenger throws a herring into the air where it is caught by one of the gulls following the ship. The herring sticks in the gull's throat and he makes off for the shore, followed by his companions, screaming in the hope that the fish will be disgorged in flight.

Tiree, to the south-west of Coll, lies almost due east and west, is about ten and a half miles long, and in the centre is two miles wide. Here the island is divided into two parts, east and west, by the reef, a level plain from shore to shore and about one and a quarter miles in width. This plain, whose soil is almost pure shell sand, growing excellent pasture, was once the bottom of the sea when Tiree consisted of two islands. Indeed, the central and eastern parts of the island are so little above sea-level that from a few miles to seaward the land can scarcely be distinguished, and houses rise against the skyline like a line of battleships at anchor abreast in a sound. The absence of high hills also accounts for the low rainfall, one of the lowest in Western Scotland, because rain-bearing clouds from the Atlantic pass over this low-lying island to break on the mountains of Mull and Argyll. Humidity is as high as 27 degrees, and the ocean winds carry the tang of salt tempered with the scent of wild flowers and thyme.

The pier is at the western extremity of Gott Bay in the south of the eastern half of the island, and here a large number of inhabitants, most of them potential landladies, await the coming and going of the *Lochearn*, for the staple of Tiree appears to be the importation of summer visitors. I got a lodging at Scarnish, about a mile south-west of the pier in the guest-house of a farm. The guest-house was a small, two-storied modern building on the roadside about a hundred yards from the farm, and during the summer holidays was run by two of the farmer's daughters who were school teachers in the island. They were pleasant, conscientious people and I was made comfortable, but, and it may be they suspected me of being a writer in spite of the fishing rod well displayed, they were not so communicative as my friends on Coll. Moreover, they knew nothing about Doctor Maclaren and were not over-anxious to discuss the second sight, although on Coll I had been told: "Every other one of them on Tiree has the second sight, and if you

were going to die to-morrow they would know it to-day."
Such are the repressions of modern education, and yet
millions of people, presumably educated, profess an interest
in astrology and seek to guide their conduct by the stars,
to which they refer such questions, for example, as whether a
particular day is good or bad for beginning or discontinuing
litigation.

To the west of the reef and about a mile from the shore
is the factor's residence, the Island House, a plain substantial house built on what once was the island in Loch an
Eilein (Loch of the one Island). On this island stood the
ancient castle of the MacLeans of Tiree until their estates
were seized, on claims for debt, by the Earl of Argyll in
1674. The old castle had a drawbridge between the front
entrance and the shore, and at the back there was a sunken
causeway in the Loch, across which those who knew the
way might escape in time of peril. The present Island
House was built in 1748 by the new proprietor, the Earl
of Argyll, and the narrow channel once spanned by the
drawbridge was filled in by forced crofter labour. The
story as told by one of the oldest inhabitants is recorded in
the local guide-book.[1]

The factor's name was Maclaren, and one day he ordered
the crofters of a particular township to attend to the work
of filling in the channel. At evening a crofter, who was so
poor that he had to borrow a neighbour's horse and cart to
bring the stones and rocks, had discharged his last load and
was preparing to go home when Maclaren ordered him to
bring another load. The crofter protested, and was told to
obey the order or await the consequences of disobedience.

[1] Handbook to Coll and Tiree. Macdougall & Cameron, Glasgow, p. 117

So he obeyed, but stung by the injustice of the order he turned on Maclaren and said: "I'll do what you bid me, then, but let me tell you that you will never pass a night of your life under that roof." In due course the Island House was built, but before it was ready for occupation Maclaren was taken seriously ill. His one anxiety in his illness was to belie the crofter's prophesy, and so he ordered four retainers to carry him in a blanket to the Island House. This they did, and just as he was being carried over the threshold he died. This happened *circa* 1748, and such a man seems capable of having sired the sinister Doctor Maclaren who may have succeeded him. No more of this matter could I discover on the island, and perhaps the old custom, of stories being handed down from one generation to another in the long winter evenings round the hearth, is dying, and if so more's the pity. Yet it may be that more will be known of Doctor Maclaren, although possibly not in our time, when the archives at Inveraray Castle are allowed to be inspected for the purpose of historical research.

Some of the people on the island asked me if I liked Tiree better than Coll, and as this was a delicate question I answered by telling them the story of the Wise Man of Bonar Bridge. At one time there was so much jealousy between the Royal Burgh of Tain and the town of Dornoch that at last the citizens of both towns agreed to ask the Wise Man of Bonar to decide which was the better town. Accordingly a deputation of citizens from Tain and Dornoch visited Bonar Bridge and asked the Wise Man to give judgment. The Wise Man lived on a small croft and sustained himself with frugal fare—porridge, milk, and potatoes. He received the citizens and said: "It is a momentous question you are asking me to decide, and until I have seen both towns it is not possible to make a decision." Thereupon the citizens of Tain invited the Wise Man to enjoy their hospitality. They wined and dined him for a week, and thereafter he enjoyed similar hospitality at Dornoch. After the festivities the Wise Man returned to Bonar Bridge to consider the problem. A month passed, and again the deputation went to Bonar Bridge where the Wise Man said: "I have not yet seen enough of your towns to enable me to decide." Another fortnight of hospitality followed, and the Wise Man promised to give judgment a month later. In due course the deputation went to Bonar Bridge and the Wise Man spoke the words that follow: "To this momentous question I have given the greatest consideration, contemplation, and meditation, and I have now come to the opinion that Tain is neither worse nor better than Dornoch, nor Dornoch nor Tain."[1]

Gott Bay, about three and a half miles round, is half empty at low tide, and on the white sand a hundred yards from the shore is a small flat black rock called Mallachdaig (Cursed One), to which Columba once made fast his coracle by fixing the anchor on a bunch of seaweed growing there. When he returned the tide had risen, the seaweed had broken from the rock and his coracle was adrift. Whereupon Columba cursed the rock in order that nothing should ever grow on it again. For that reason I inspected the rock and found only a few baby barnacles which could never reach maturity for the simple reason that during two-thirds of each tide they are exposed to the air. Moreover, Columba with his great experience of boats would never have made

---

[1] The final "nor" is used in the old sense of "than."

fast to a bunch of seaweed in a hard sandy bay where he could have easily dragged his coracle above high-water mark. To anyone who knows the Hebridean seas it is clear that Columba and his monks must also have been skilled in forecasting and choosing their weather before setting out in their boats of wattle covered with skins.

In Columba's time, as indicated by place-names, there were seven monastic settlements on Tiree (Land of Corn), and this island was the granary of Iona. A few hundred yards north of the middle shore of Gott Bay are the ancient chapels of Kirkapol (North Church Town) and Oran's Graveyard, in which is the foundation wall of a Columban chapel. A few yards distant is the Little Graveyard with the ruins of an eleventh- or twelfth-century chapel. Both these burial-grounds are still used, but on a rock a hundred and fifty yards to the north is a more ancient and interesting chapel, which is probably the one that was dedicated to St. Columba and to which in 1375 the Pope appointed Ayg Mac Petris as Vicar.

To reach the rock and the chapel I crossed a meadow where wild yellow mustard and blue vetch were knee high, and so thick was the growth that my feet were entangled at every step. It reminded me of the thick and tangled undergrowth around enchanted castles, and thus musing I fell headlong into an open field drain which, fortunately, was dry, and where I was completely hidden by the vetch and mustard whereby it was concealed, an excellent sanctuary for anyone who wished to elude the police.

In the main I am not over-interested in ancient ruins, but this roofless chapel shows the strength of mortar used by masons long ago. The small doorway with a round

Saxon arch is intact, as also is a small round window in the northern wall, but a similar window in the south wall has been enlarged to a width of six feet by local vandals who removed stones for building. At last they desisted, because no doubt they found it easier to quarry stones than to remove them from those well-mortared walls. The top of the widened window is a horizontal six-foot bridge of large stones, a foot in depth, held in position by nothing except mortar.

Within living memory such mortar has been made in the Western Isles. A solid circular layer of peats is built on the ground to the size of a cart wheel, with a space in the centre for a kindling fire to which air is led through four equidistant channels in the layer of peat. On the top of the first layer a second layer of peats is arranged without air channel, and this is covered with cockle shells to a depth of six inches. Then come more alternate layers of peats and shells until a structure shaped like a bee skep six feet high has been erected. This is covered all over with turf except at the entrance to the air channels next the ground. In the centre the kindling fire is lit, and the peat kiln burns itself out and collapses in the course of a week. Under the burnt turf there is nothing save a white powder of peat ashes and quicklime. This mixture, when slaked and with the addition of dry sand, not seashore sand, forms the mortar whereby to this day in old ruins enormous stones are suspended against the law of gravity.

From the chapel I intended to walk across the moors to the northern shore of the island, here only a mile and a quarter wide, to see the Ringing Stone on the Sands of Saltaig (Salt Bay). Yet before setting off I decided to speak to two men who were working in an outhouse of a farm half a mile east of the chapel. On my way to the farm I was glad of my unwonted prudence, because to get to the men I had not only to walk round swamps but also had to take running jumps over two ditches full of water.

The men were carpenters and their first question, a tribute to the Panama hat, was: "Are you from the Big House?" In the United States of America the "Big House" is the film name for a convict prison, but thanks to the guide-book I knew that on this island the Big House was "The Lodge, for many years the residence of Lady Victoria Campbell, and afterwards of her sister, Lady Francis Balfour." The men advised me to take the road to Balephetrish Bay, and then walk east along the coast. There were many swamps on the moor, and no houses where I could ask the way. I took their advice because, although it is possible to cross an unknown moor dryshod if you keep to the heather and bog myrtle, avoiding what looks like dry grass, but proves to be swamp grass, there are also moors where hillocks of heather rise from a swamp and where jumping from hillock to hillock makes progress slow. These moors were cleared of peat by the beginning of the nineteenth century, and then workers and horses had to be ferried in open boats to the shores of Mull and Coll, where peat was and is to be found in abundance. Later the Tiree sailing smacks brought coal from Ardrossan, Ayr, and Irving, and peat was no longer used. Neither of the carpenters had ever seen the Ringing Stone, and this aroused my suspicions because it is well to distrust anything of interest to visitors only. Next day my suspicions were confirmed.

On my way across the island I made the ascent of Ben Gott, which rises to the west of the roadside. That sentence has an Alpine flavour and it is right to add that I was climbing for at least five minutes, since Gott is the smallest ben I have ever climbed. Yet the climb was worth the effort, because from the top were views with violent contrasts. The sky was clouded, but Gott Bay lay in a semi-circle of bright white sand, against which the colours of the sea passed from translucent green inshore to paler and darker blues beyond, so that even on a dull day there was life and movement there. To the north was a desolate rocky moor from which almost all the peat had been taken away long ago. Thus I sensed the difference between those extremes of experience, hope and despair, for such is the magic of scenery well seen.

At Balephetrish Bay sheep were being dipped in a fank near a farmhouse on the hillside, and above the bleating of sheep rose the voice of the shepherd shouting orders in Gaelic to a collie rounding up an escaped sheep in the distance. Racing in a wide circle, the collie headed the sheep, who stopped and looked at the dog now sitting on his haunches eyeing his charge. As seen by the sheep the collie must represent law and order, or else the sheep would charge and butt the dog who, if sheep only knew, is not allowed to bite, and elsewhere I have seen a Cairn terrier, tail down, chased off a moorland grazing by charging sheep. In a few minutes the sheep that objected to dipping was back in the pen.

From the pen the sheep are driven into a narrow, fenced passage holding them in single file, and leading to the entrance of the fank, where an inclined board, with trans-

verse slats for a foothold, descends into the narrow wooden
tank four feet deep in the centre and filled with disinfectant
solution. The dipper, who needs the strength of a black-
smith, seizes the sheep by the wool on its back and drags
it down the incline into the fank, where it begins swimming
and is submerged up to the neck. The head is then submerged for a moment, after which the sheep is released and
swims for the inclined plane at the exit. As their heads
emerged from the ducking their faces expressed such mild
indignation as to make me remark, "That must be a surprise," at which the man laughed and answered: "Aye, to
them it must be another world." The sheep-dipper told
me to walk a mile to the east, keeping well up on the hillside, to avoid soft marsh ground above the shore, until I
saw a flat boulder above the high-water mark in a small
bay. Thus did I find the Ringing Stone, a rock about five
feet long, three wide wide and two feet deep, resting on a
tripod of three rocks projecting about ten inches above the
sand. When struck with another stone the Ringing Stone
emits a high ringing note painful to the ear, and best heard
when the ear is applied to the Stone. The note is due to
vibrations in the crystals of the Stone and in pitch is just
below the upper threshold of human hearing, twenty
thousand vibrations a second. Hence the pain.

So far so good, but according to the guide-book "This
glacial relic is deeply pitted with cup markings." Now
whatever else it may be the Stone is not a "glacial relic,"
because it shows no ice marks and consists of red gneiss
granite of which there is a large outcrop at this place. On
the Stone I saw two shallow, smooth, circular hollows—the
"cup markings"—and on the rocks of the neighbouring

outcrop I found similar "cup markings." So far as I know these hollows are formed in the course of centuries when a hard rounded stone, resting in the crevice of a rock, is given a circular movement either by the waves or by eddies in the tide.

To my mind that is a rational explanation, but the guide-book will have none of it. "That they are real cup markings and connected with some form of worship is undeniable." Yet I for one deny it. "It is puerile to suggest as some have, that the deep pits on the surface of this boulder could have been caused by the ringing propensities of the visitors to the spot." Puerile is too mild a word, because only mental defectives could have made the suggestion. "The visitors are comparatively few; and there are many hundreds living in Tiree that never saw it. Besides, it would take an army of such casual ringers incalculable years to form one cup, even if it were pre-arranged that each should strike in one marked spot. No; the natural curiosity of visitors makes them strike all over the boulder's face and listen to the variety of its notes. The marks of their handiwork are only too evident." This last seems a trifle hard on visitors who, like myself, have been incited to visit the boulder and to hit it with a stone, but no matter because "Mr. Ludovic MacLellan Mann, is satisfied that these markings are according to a system that is to be traced all round the world, and pertained to a religion that was older than that of the Druids, who were the precursors of Christian teachers in the west."

Since we know next to nothing about the religion of the Druids, I should have thought that we knew absolutely nothing about an older religion. Yet the gentleman may be right, and in that case I think that these cup marks are associated with the religion of the mermen and mermaids, because in the tidal rocks at Bermeray I found a much deeper cup and within it the hard round stone that was doing the grinding. Indeed, to facilitate the grinding I removed sand from the bottom of the cup and replaced the stone. This cup lies about two feet west of the jetty below the lighthouse, and perhaps in a couple of thousand years one of my readers will be so kind as to remove any further accumulation of sand in order that the good work may continue.

From the shore I walked inland for a hundred yards across sward on which there were yellow goat's-beard, butter-cups, the scentless mayweed, ox-eye daisies, and also white cockle shells, the latter thrown and blown ashore by Atlantic gales. There was also a large whelk shell and a polished beach pebble weighing about half a pound near the place where I rested. These had been thrown ashore by the sea, and the shell puzzled me because the whelk is a deep-sea shellfish found on rocks below tide levels from the Mediterranean to Greenland. It is an edible shellfish obtained by dredging, and you may eat it, amongst other places, at Margate. How came this deep-sea shell to be blown ashore in a gale. The shell itself gave the answer. When the whelk died its shell was occupied by the sponge *Cliona*, whose burrowings from within had pitted the white walls from apex to mouth. In time the sponge died and a hermit crab lived in the shell and moved it towards the beach, whence it was blown inland during a storm. At the Natural History Museum at South Kensington the Curators of Shells and of Sponges told me the story of this shell, and that is an example of genuine science in which everything is proved.

The place where I rested was a peaceful spot with not a house in sight, albeit there was much activity in the air. Sand-pipers busy about nothing flew from one sandy bay to another. Overhead were plovers and wild duck, and from a marsh near by rose a wisp of snipe. Removing my shoes and socks I gave my feet an air bath in the cool breeze blowing from the sea, and wondered why, on an island so rich in genuine relics of antiquity, anyone should go out of his way to get beyond the Druids.

CHAPTER XII

THE SECOND SIGHT

ON my way back I stopped near the farmhouse to watch two men digging a drain, and was startled when one of them looked up and shouted at the top of his voice: "Well, and did you find the stone?"

Thinking the man was deaf, I shouted: "Yes, is there any buttermilk?"

"Any what?" and his companion translated my question into Gaelic.

"Yes, yes, come this way," said the shouter, in an ordinary voice. He was not deaf, but his knowledge of English was limited, and it may be that he gained self-confidence by shouting in what to him was a foreign language. When next abroad I shall give this method a trial. Speaking softly in Gaelic he led me to the house, where in the same language he explained my words to his wife, who, having good English, showed me into the parlour and asked me "to excuse the house, because we have visitors with children, and you know what children are." I assured her that I knew what children were, and indeed there was nothing to excuse save a few stains on the white tablecloth. She offered me fresh milk, but I told her that I thirsted for buttermilk, than which no drink is more cooling. Having drunk three glasses I asked what I owed, but she refused to accept any payment, and remarked, with a smile, "We feed it to cows." I was glad she mentioned cows because in some places they "feed it to pigs."

Refreshed by the buttermilk, I took the road back to Scarinish, but was glad when overtaken by a dogcart drawn by a Highland pony and driven by an old man of seventy who offered me a lift. In the back of the cart was a killed sheep for the butcher, and I sat in front with the driver, who was most communicative. He pointed to a squatter's house, a well-built cottage by the roadside, and explained how it was that the occupier paid no rates. If in Scotland, with the consent of your neighbours, you build a house on common land and occupy it for seven years, you have a presumptive title of ownership unless someone has a better title to own the land. In England I understand that a presumptive title is gained after twenty years of occupation.

The cottage by the roadside had been built by a squatter whose children migrated to Glasgow. On the death of their parents the children regarded the cottage as an ideal summer residence, but some years elapsed before any of them could afford a holiday, and when they did return to Tiree there were strangers in possession. The strangers refused to vacate the cottage, and the family were advised by Glasgow lawyers that it would be a waste of money to go to law. Let no reader make any mistake about the Law of Squatting, for a Lord of Appeal has kindly advised me that I have no right to take up residence in any unoccupied house. You may only squat on land or in houses to which no one has a title, and such places are so few and far between that I do not think it would be worth while to go in search of them. Even in the case cited, the Duke of Argyll, had he thought the rent of the cottage worth the cost of a lawsuit, probably could have proved his prescriptive rights, because if a squatter leaves his house the house becomes the property of the landlord on whose land it is built.

The driver also told me of the Tiree crofter who died fifteen years ago leaving £60,000. "Aye, sixty thousand pounds! And how did he make it? I'll tell you how he made it—by going round the crofts buying cattle cheap from those who did not know their value, and then selling them at a big profit in the Oban market." *Moral:* A man who can scent money will make it wherever he happens to be.

Yet there is a limit beyond which people will rebel against exploitation, by which I mean taking advantage of their ignorance or weakness, and I was glad to hear the story of the "rising" of 1886. The crofters then rebelled, not against the exactions of landlord or factor but against the treachery of their own leader. The McNeils were a crofter family, and one son was the ex-captain of a coastal vessel. This McNeil was also a politician, and when a farm of fifty acres in the west of Tiree fell vacant, he toured the island to advocate that the farm should be broken up into crofts. Provided no crofter made a bid for the farm it would assuredly be broken up into crofts, and if anyone of them made a bid he deserved to be hanged from the farmhouse chimney. To this eloquence the people responded nobly and at the sale not a single bid was made for the farm. "Aye, not a bid was made. Then one fine day the news spreads that the farm had been bought behind the backs of the people by McNeil himself. It's a wonder they did not hang him. All they did was to surround the farm and prevent the traitor from taking possession. McNeil appealed to the Government, and so H.M.S. *Ajax* and *Assistance* steamed into Scarinish Bay. Aye, and when they dropped their anchors the rattle of the cables shook the very ground. You'd have thought it was an earthquake. Disturbance? There was no disturbance. Tiree was as quiet as it is this afternoon. Marines were landed, and sailors too, and they held their summer sports on the reef."

The Highland pony or "sholtag" was taking things easy, and there was no reason why he should do otherwise because although there was a layer of tar on each side of the road, for the benefit of motor-car wheels, the centre over which the horse went was stony. Nor did I wish the animal to hurry for now was the time to mention the second sight to the friendly driver. "No, I haven't got it myself, but lots of them on the island have it. You wouldn't find me going out at night if I had it, for who wants to see these Things. A friend of mine had it, aye, and when I was a boy he told me how at night he saw great black masses coming along the road so fast that he jumped out of their way. You'll know what they would be?"

"No, I don't."

"The motor-cars that were to come. What else could they have been?"

"Nothing else."

Yet I was disappointed not to have met anyone who confessed to having the second sight, and, therefore, I was glad when some weeks later I met a man who is a seer. I had met him off and on in the Hebrides during the past five years, and I shall write nothing that might reveal his identity lest his life be made a burden by others as curious as myself. One night I spoke to him about the second sight, and he, knowing my interest to be sincere, answered:

"Yes, my father had it. One night he and my mother

were in bed. They were old folk then, but being Christians they still shared the same bed. You know what I mean. Well, this night my mother was awake and listened to hear their clock strike twelve. She counted, and the clock struck thirteen. So she woke my father and told him, but all he said was, 'Yes, Dugald is drowned in the loch.' Now Dugald was a friend of his who drank too much, and that night he had mistaken the way and walked over a small cliff into the loch.

"It was after my father's death that my mother told me the story, but I had known all along that my father had the second sight. As a laddie of twelve I used to help him to sail his ketch which brought cargoes, including cattle and sheep, to and from the islands and the mainland. One night we were lying empty alongside the quay on the mainland, and my father and I were asleep in the fo'castle. Suddenly I was wakened by the noise of an awful clattering as if some-one was throwing iron things into the empty hold. I was feared and called out: 'Father, did you hear yon?' 'Aye, I heard it, and now you will rise and make sure that nothing's been thrown into the hold.' So I rose, went on deck, down the ladder, struck a light, and sure enough there was nothing in the hold.

"When I got back to the fo'castle, I said to my father: 'There's nothing in the hold.'

"'Aye, and what did you think the noise sounded like?'

"'Like spades being thrown into the hold.'

"'You're right, lad, and to-morrow they will put in the hold a coffin for burial on the island, and the grave-diggers will throw their spades down after it.'

"And so it happened next day."

As he was telling me this story I was not looking at him but was trying to memorise every word. When I looked up he was looking at me in a way in which he had never looked at me before. His eyes were wide open, his face was expressionless and he seemed to be looking beyond me.

In a flash of memory I was back in Lapland, because there only had I seen that look before, and then on the face of a Lapp. Twelve months previously I was approaching the entrance to the hotel at Inari when I saw a Lapp whom I thought I knew, but as we approached I saw that he was a stranger. He stopped me by holding up his left hand, and said nothing. Then I noticed that he had what I can best describe as mesmeric eyes, and this annoyed me. A fortune-teller, no doubt, but he could get nothing from me because I did not know his language. I held his gaze, and after a few seconds he said something in Lappish, bowed, moved to one side and passed on.

In the hotel I sought out the hostess, she who, in *Lapland Journey*,[1] I have called "a Brave Girl," and asked: "Who is that Lapp?"

"What Lapp?"

"The one who stopped me outside. Look, you can see him through the window."

"That's a Lapp wizard, and he can make little devils dance on a table."

"Have you ever seen him do it?"

"No, but some of the servants have seen it, and I went to see one of his seances."

Some weeks later I mentioned this encounter to Wolter Stenbäck, who knows the Lapps as no other man in Finland

---

[1] *Lapland Journey*, p. 186.

knows them. "No, he's not a wizard, and I don't believe he can make the little devils dance on a table, but he's what the Lapps call the One Who Knows. You've got the same thing in Scotland, but there, I think, you call it the Second Sight."

Now it has taken me some minutes to write about that Lapland experience, but when I saw the fixed gaze of the Hebridean seer the whole scene came back to memory in an instant, and a thrill ran down my spine. For a moment I was prepared to defy God or the Devil, and said, in a level voice: "Your father had the second sight and I know that you've got it. What are you seeing beyond me now?"

His eyes blinked and he shook himself. "Doctor, if I've got it and if I saw anything beyond you I would not tell you. Who wants to have the second sight?"

"You're right," said I, "because if we knew the future how many of us could face it?"

"That's the truest word you've ever said."

Many seers in the Western Highlands have had prevision of events that were to happen in later years, and "a highly educated percipient" told Andrew Lang of a remarkable example of collective second hearing when four or five people on the Ballachulish-Oban road in 1881 were alarmed by the thunder of an invisible train on the road, although there was then no railway in the district. Lang suggests that conceivably at that moment an engineer was planning the railway track which in 1903 was laid on the old road. Again, at Ballachulish early in the last century a seer was troubled by visions of armed men in uniform drilling in a field by the sea. He did not know who the men were

and their uniforms were not "England's cruel red." Therefore he foretold an invasion, and said: "It must be of
Americans, for the soldiers do not look like foreigners."
In 1859 the Volunteers came into being, and companies
were drilled on that field.

Most of the visions seen by percipients are of shrouds,
corpse candles, fore-goes, and spectral lights, although the
latter have also been seen by many who lack the second
sight. Thus the Rev. Dr. Stewart, of Nether Lochaber,
told Andrew Lang that a woman, one of his parishioners,
called him to his door and pointed out to him that on the
shore there was a rock which "shone in a kind of phosphor-
escent brilliance." The minister attributed the phosphor-
escent light to decaying seaweed, but the woman said:
"No, a corpse will be landed there to-morrow." Next day a
dead body was brought in a boat, and prior to burial was
laid at the foot of the rock, on which Dr. Stewart found no
decaying seaweed.

Be it said that I myself have not the second sight, nor,
so far as I know, had any of my forebears, who all came from
Caithness where the Gael never settled and where the people
were originally of Pictish and Viking stock. Moreover,
even amongst the Gaels the second sight has always been
more prevalent in the Western Isles than in Ireland. According to Dr. Johnson: "The Second Sight is an impression
made either by the mind upon the eye, or by the eye upon the
mind, by which things distant or future are perceived, and
seen as if they were present." To that I would add that those
who have the second sight may perceive things happening
at a distance at the moment of their occurrence.

Thus Mr. Taylor of Bankton, a farmer, stolid and sober-minded, and an elder of the Free Church at Prestonpans, where my uncle the Rev. Patrick R. Mackay, D.D., became minister on 6th February 1879, was driving with a friend in a gig along the shore road to Cockenzie in pouring rain on a dark winter's night. The wind was blowing a gale, and at times the farmer feared that the gig would be blown over, when suddenly his friend shouted above the noise of the storm: "My God!" The elder was shocked by this exclamation which to him was a breach of the Commandment: "Thou shalt not take the name of the Lord thy God in vain," and, turning to his companion, he asked: "Are you ill?"

"No, no, I'm not ill, but the Tay Bridge is down. I saw it."

"Nonsense," said Mr. Taylor, "the storm is getting on your nerves."

Yet it was not nonsense, for at that moment on the night of 28th December 1879 the Tay Bridge, thirty miles to the north and beyond the hills of Fife, went down and with it a train in which eighty lost their lives.

The mystery of the second sight cannot be explained by asserting that the percipient was suffering from hallucination, the apparent perception of an object not present, because, as Andrew Lang has said: "This experience has occurred to the sane, the unimaginative, the healthy, the free from superstition, and in circumstances by no means mystic, when the person supposed to be seen was not dying, nor distressed, nor in any but the most normal condition. Indeed, the cases in which there was nothing abnormal in the state of the person seen are far more numerous in my personal experience, than those in which the person was seen dying, or dead, or excited." In that case, the apparent perception of a person not present would not warrant the assumption that visual impressions may be conveyed from mind to mind without the aid of the senses and from a distance of thousands of miles; but Lang's experience was not endorsed by the Society for Psychical Research, who investigated nearly 17,000 instances of this phenomenon. As a result of these enquiries Professor Sidgwick[1] concluded that "The actual proportion of coincidental to non-coincidental cases, after all deduction for possible sources of error, was, in fact, such that the probability against the supposition of chance coincidence became enormous, on the assumption of ordinary accuracy on the part of the informants."

The second sight is not inherited and, according to Martin Martin, an M.A. of Edinburgh who visited the islands *circa* 1695,[2] cannot be communicated to others. When a seer has a vision his eyes are wide open and he is seen to be staring at what others cannot see, and when two seers are together both do not always see the vision, unless one of them touches the other. The time when a vision is seen is an index of when the event foretold is going to happen. Thus a vision seen in the early morning will materialise in a few hours; if seen at noon, the event foreseen will occur that day; if seen in the evening, it may happen that night, but visions seen at night will come to pass weeks, months, or even years afterwards, according to the lateness of the hour. Such was Martin's belief, although the instances I have already quoted do not bear this out.

When shrouds are seen, the length of the shroud indicates

---

[1] Proc. S.P.R., vol. viii, p. 607.
[2] *A Description of the Western Islands of Scotland*, 1703. Reprinted 1706 and 1884.

the time of death. Thus if the shroud does not reach above the waist, the person seen will not die until a year has elapsed, but in cases when the shroud reaches towards the head, death is to be expected within a few days or hours. Another omen of death is by means of the second hearing, when the seers hear a loud cry called the taisk, which exactly resembles the voice of the person whose death it foretells. Five women sitting together in a room in the village of Rigg in Skye all heard a loud cry, which passed by the window and so resembled the voice of one of those who heard it that she blushed although she had uttered no cry. She contracted a fever next day and died that week.

Amongst happier prognostications, if a woman be seen standing to the left of a man she will become his wife, or if two or three women are seen to the left each in turn will become his wife, and this irrespective of whether they are unmarried or married to others at the time of the apparition. Horses and cows have the second sight, and when horses have stampeded without any apparent cause, seers who were near at hand have seen the vision at which the horse took fright; and when a woman with the second sight is milking a cow and sees a vision, the cow runs away and remains restive for some time. Children may also see these visions as clearly as do men and women of advanced years. "I was present," writes Martin, "in a house where a child cried of a sudden, and being asked the reason of it, he answered that he had seen a great white thing lying on the board which was in the corner: but he was not believed, until a seer who was present told them that the child was in the right, for, said he, 'I saw a corpse and the shroud about it, and the board will be used as part of a coffin, or some way employed about a corpse'; and, accordingly, it was made into a coffin for one who was in perfect health at the time of the vision."

Dr. Johnson's father gave him a copy of Martin's book, of which the doctor had a poor opinion albeit he took it with him on his journey to the Hebrides. "No man," said he to Boswell, "now writes so ill as Martin's account of the Hebrides is written." Although somewhat quaint, Martin's style is interesting, and were it not for his descriptions we would have no knowledge of many Highland customs now extinct. Martin Martin graduated M.A. at Edinburgh in 1681, when his age may have been anything from fifteen to twenty, and died in 1719. The Dictionary of National Biography says he entered Leyden University on 6th March 1710, where he later graduated M.D., but in view of the dates this may refer to a son.

The west of Tiree is a plain of fertile sandy soil with two hills, Ben Hough in the north and Ben Hynish in the south. In Columba's time Tiree was the granary of Iona, and even in the days of rack-rents before the Crofters Act gave security of tenure there was a saying that "Tiree could yield two crops in one year were it not for fear of two rents," and on the slopes of Ben Gott I was shown a place now uncultivated where once two crops of corn were sown and reaped in a year. At the south-western corner of Tiree the land rises to Kenavara Headland, an overhanging cliff with ledges that are beds of bluebells, geraniums, sea-thrift, vetch, ferns, and grasses where wild geese, swans, falcons, goosanders, and the great northern diver rest in safety. The lower ledges are white with cormorants, overlooking a colony of seals, and at sea level are two caves. One is the inevitable "Piper's Cave," and in the other a pair of ravens make their nest and rear their young until old enough to be banished. This last cave is inaccessible without the aid of ropes, but within living memory the raven's nest was harried by a barefooted boy who made an unaided descent and ascent. Twelve miles to the south-west of this headland is the Skerryvore Lighthouse, built by Alan Stevenson in 1844 on a reef only uncovered at low tide and inhabited by sea rats.

In the Kenavara district are the ruins of a kelp factory built by an Irishman at the beginning of the nineteenth century. Kelp is the ash produced by burning at a low temperature the seaweeds that grow on the western coasts of Scotland and Ireland. These seaweeds—the knobbed, sugar, black and bladder wracks—are cut from the rocks at low tide, dried in the sun and burnt in a hollow on the ground until the ashes fuse. The fused ash is sprinkled with cold water which causes it to crack into smaller pieces. Kelp was once the source of carbonate soda for making soap and glass, and of iodine obtained by distilling a solution of the ash.

It was a tedious process because 20 tons of wet seaweed produced 1 ton of kelp, and that in turn produced only 3 or 4 lb. of iodine, although from a ton of drift weed kelp made from deep-sea tangle blown ashore in storms as much as 15 lb. of iodine could be obtained. Iodine is now made by a much simpler process from the sodium iodate in Chile saltpetre, and the rise and decline of the kelp industry in Tiree was accompanied by a rise and decline in population. Thus in the fifty-four years between 1792 and 1846, the year of the potato famine, the population was more than doubled, rising from 2416 to 5000. By 1881 there were only 2730 people on Tiree, and in 1931 the population had fallen to 1446. Every statesman should be made to live for at least one month every year on a small island in order to study economic problems in their simplest dimensions, and Tiree is a good example of how population is influenced by commerce.

Nowhere, not even on the South Downs, have I seen so many larks as on the western plain of Tiree. There were also green, ringed, and golden plover, snipe in abundance, and in one of the lochs a pair of heron who come over from Mull to fish. I saw pheasants and hares, but there are no rabbits. At Balevulin Bay in the north-western corner of Tiree, I rested on the slope of a small hill, once the site of an ancient fort called Dun Bornaige Moire (Fort of the Larger Fortification), whose outlines remain. The Duns, of which there are hundreds in the Hebrides, consisted of at least two concentric circular walls or mounds separated by a trench, the inner circle being occupied by the defenders. The external diameter of this dun was 65 feet, and the inner circle was 40 feet wide, and these simple defences embodied the two essential principles of all fortification—to protect the defenders and to obstruct the enemy. These forts were probably built against the Vikings, were near likely landing-places, and were generally within sight of each other, whereby signalling was possible. They doubtless served their purpose, and Dr. Johnson was no strategist when he suggested that forts and castles would be better placed in the centre of an island.

Balevulin means the town of the Mill, and in the centre of the bay the White River, a tiny stream which once turned the old mill wheel, runs into the sea. In the bad old days a miller's son had been ordered to do some work for the

137

Chieftain MacLean, and failed to appear. He was arrested
and brought to the island castle, where his excuses were
ignored and he was sentenced to be hanged on the Hanging
Knoll, a sandy hillock, in the neighbourhood. His sister on
hearing of the sentence hastened to the Chief and begged
for her brother's life. She was too late, and was told by
MacLean that had she arrived earlier her brother would
have been spared. The crime was commemorated in a poem
of which only three lines survive:

> " Son of him from Balevulin
> That possessed the kiln, the grain, the mill,
> At the Bay you were dishonoured."

There is no town at Balevulin, although a row of small
houses is called the Red Street, and in the neighbourhood
are seventeen large crofts. Never have I seen pasture so rich
with brighteye, red and white clover, daisies, ox-eye daisies,
ragged robin, heliotrope orchis, yellow bedstraw, scentless
mayweed, and wild thyme. The day was calm and sunny,
the tide was out, and in the bay a lagoon of pale green water
stretched from the shore to a strand of silver sand on which
cows had taken refuge from the warble fly, which lays eggs
in their nostrils. Beyond the silver strand the colour of the
sea changed to purple over a patch of deep sea wrack, and
then from purple to blue.

CHAPTER XIII

THE WICKED PRINCESS

BERNERAY, the most southern island of the Outer Hebrides, is two miles long by less than a mile wide, and from the eastern end the land rises fairly gently to a cliff of 622 feet in the west. The most southerly point of the island is Barra Head. Near the western cliff is the lighthouse, sixty feet high, from which a light is shown at an elevation of 683 feet above the sea and a radio beam is transmitted. Yet high as it is, the courtyard of the lighthouse is often knee deep with salt water from the spray thrown up in westerly and south-westerly gales. On looking over the parapet on the brink of the cliff I saw what to me was an awful view. The Atlantic surge was rising and falling at the foot of the cliff, pouring into and out of caverns, and yet no sound of the sea reached the parapet. Hundreds of small creatures that seemed like white moths were flitting in and out of caves, but these were sea birds whose cries I could not hear. Terror seized my mind and I shrank from the parapet lest I threw myself into the abyss, a sign no doubt of age, because as a boy I could have stood on the brink without knowing even fear. Now of reasonable fear no one need be ashamed, because it is a natural instinct of self-protection, whereas insensate terror may lead to self-destruction, and I believe that many who leap to death from a great height are not to be held accountable. Anyone can walk twenty yards along a plank two feet wide if the latter be laid on the ground, but how few could walk the same plank if it bridged a chasm of fifty feet.

Yet a past secretary of the Alpine Club tells me that by training it is possible to become accustomed to great heights. "Goethe was sensitive to heights, but he overcame this by walking round the parapet of a cathedral every day. Of course you've got to be in first-class condition. After the War, when I went back to Switzerland, I went for an easy climb—no ropes, no chimneys, no hanging on by your eyelashes to a narrow ridge with a drop of 2000 feet— just an easy climb, and I didn't like it. I was out of practice, but after a day or two everything was all right, although I've never really enjoyed walking along the unguarded parapet of a high building."

North of the lighthouse grassy slopes fall away to the narrow Sound of Berneray across which is the Island of Mingulay. So transparent was the water in this Sound that all the rocks and seaweeds on the bottom were visible, and so clear was the day that I saw in the north and fifteen miles away what reminded me of fairyland, the mountains of Barra seen through a blue haze. I had come to the lighthouse in the relief motor-boat from Castlebay, and on the way we had called at Mingulay with stores for a sheep farmer. At only one place is it possible to land passengers or stores, and at that place the eastern cliff is ten feet above the sea, so that in rough weather landings are impossible.

Mingulay is a grazing island two and a half miles long by a mile wide, and its western coast is a sheer precipice rising to a greatest height of 747 feet. The sheep farmer had once farmed in Australia and now lived in the solitary house on the island. During the winter he was alone, but in spring and summer shepherds came from Barra to help in the lambing, dipping, and clipping, and he showed hospitality to the few strangers who ever visited his retreat. Months later, in London, I heard that when he wished to sell the island one of the prospective purchasers proved to be the man who had been his partner on an Australian sheep run twenty years ago.

There are other grazing islands between Mingulay and Barra, these being Pabbay, Sandray, and Vatersay, but it is curious that the names of some of the smaller islands in the Outer Hebrides should be duplicated and even triplicated. There is a Pabbay in the Sound of Harris between North Uist and South Harris, and there is likewise a Berneray not only in this Sound but also to the north-east of St. Kilda.

The Outer Hebrides were known and described by Pliny the elder and by Ptolemy, and extend in a north-north-easterly direction from Berneray in the south for about 113 miles to the Butt of Lewis, but excepting for the channels between the smaller grazing islands south of Barra, the only navigable channels between the larger islands are the Sound of Barra and the Sound of Harris. In the latter Sound are strange tides, of which the Admiralty Pilot says: "The tidal streams in the Sound of Harris are very remarkable, and do not appear to be much influenced by the wind. Generally in summer, during neaps, the south-east-going stream from the Atlantic runs during the whole of the day, and the north-west-going stream from the Minch during the whole of the night. In winter this operation is nearly reversed, the north-west-going stream running during the day, and the south-east-going stream during part of the night."

The Outer are divided from the Inner Hebrides and from the north-western coast of Scotland by the Hebridean Sea, by the Little Minch, and by the Great Minch. The Hebridean Sea, twenty-six miles wide between Berneray and Tiree, extends eighty-five miles north-north-east to a line drawn between Usinish promontory in North Uist and Ness Point at the extreme west of Skye. From that line the Little Minch extends for about forty miles north-north-east to a line that runs from Rudha na h Aiseig at the northern end of Skye through the Shiant Islands to the coast of Lewis, and thus separates North Uist, Harris, and part of Lewis from the north-western coast of Skye. The average width of the Little Minch is twelve miles. Beyond the Little is the Great Minch, which ends in a line between Cape Wrath and the Butt of Lewis.

At Castlebay in the south of Barra is a good albeit a small natural harbour protected from the north, east, and west by its own hills and to the south by the Island of Vatersay. So well sheltered is this harbour that both it and the small town of Castlebay on its northern shore are invisible until the steamer has turned the Islet of Orosay.

In harbour were four Norwegian ships with sail and auxiliary power, on their decks hundreds of barrels of cured mackerel, and that night in the hotel bar one of the Norwegian skippers declared, "It is a poor boat that will not get £5000 for a cargo." He may have been boasting, but here was an industry that we have presented to Norway. Not so long ago the Norwegians netted mackerel in the Minch, until our fishermen said, "Why trouble to fish?

If you stay in port we will sell you all the mackerel caught in our herring nets." The Norwegians followed this advice and now buy from British boats all the mackerel they need at two shillings a basket and cure them on board. Our fishermen do not like mackerel, as they may tear or eat through the herring nets. Neither will they eat mackerel, believing that this fish lives on dead bodies, nor did they know how to cure mackerel, because unlike the herring all blood must be washed from mackerel before they will cure, whereas no washed herring could ever be cured. So the Norwegians sail from one fishing port to another buying mackerel and curing them on board, and from Norway these cured mackerel are shipped to the United States, where they fetch a good price as delicatessen. All this was news to me, although I knew that we sent herring to Germany, where they are treated with salt, cloves, and brown sugar, before being returned to Britain as Bismark Herrings.

A few hundred yards from the pier at Castlebay is a small isle or rather rock, Kisamul, on which are the ruins of MacNeil's Castle. Four square walls about two stories high rise from the sea, and within the walls are the ruins of a tower, a hall, and a few dwellings. When Martin visited the place, *circa* 1695, MacNeil and his lady were away from home, but the Constable of the Castle was standing on the walls and Martin was not permitted to enter, because in the tower was a small powder magazine and a knowledge of its whereabouts might have been of service to some foreign power. When a MacNeil was in residence and had dined, it was customary for the Constable to stand on the walls, whence he shouted to the four points of the compass: "The MacNeil of Barra has dined, and the kings and princes of the world may now sit down to eat." Of an earlier MacNeil it is told that when offered a place in Noah's Ark he refused, and said, "The MacNeil has a boat of his own." Yet this was and is a small castle, and Dr. Johnson was right when he said that from the stones of one great medieval castle in England or Wales all the castles he ever saw in Scotland could have been built.

Nevertheless, every Highland chieftain had his retinue, which included two stewards or *marischal taeh*. One was a master of ceremonies well versed in the pedigree of the clans, and it was his duty to indicate with a white wand where each guest, according to his quality, should sit at table. The other marshal had outdoor duties corresponding to those of a factor; there was also a cupbearer who drank the first draught before passing the cup round the company; and a purse-bearer who kept the chief's money. All these officers had an hereditary right to the appointments, and each was paid in kind and land for his services.

At one time the chiefs exercised summary jurisdiction, which included death by hanging or by being burnt between two fires, and to the right of the road up the west coast of Barra is a small plateau on the hillside called the Place of Justice, where MacNeil sat in judgment, and near by is a small knoll where malefactors were hanged. Yet even in those days and up to the end of the seventeenth century there was a patriarchal relation between chief and clan. Thus, in addition to a fixed rent in kind, a tenant, if one of his cows had two calves or a sheep two ewes, gave one of the twins to his master. Nor was this a unilateral arrangement, because if the tenant's wife gave birth to twins the master was obliged to rear one of them with his own family, and Martin states: "I have known a gentleman who had sixteen of these twins in his family at a time."

Moreover, when a tenant's wife died he would advise the chief of his loss and request that another be recommended, as without a wife he could neither manage his affairs nor beget followers for MacNeil. The chief would then find a suitable partner, advise the tenant of the woman's name, and their marriage would follow. Widows likewise were enabled to find new husbands without the uncertainties of courtship.

Along the shore at Castlebay are curing yards. The town is on the lower slopes of Ben Heava (1260), and I took the western road for North Bay which, being five miles distant and almost in the centre of the eastern side of the island, is misnamed to the confusion of strangers, who see the sun rising in what appears to be the north and setting in the south. A mile from Castlebay I passed Loch More, where only a few years ago many people witnessed a curious event in the lives of swans. A flock of swans rested on the loch one evening, and in the morning continued their flight in wedge formation, all save one pair who stayed on the loch. Now these birds mate for life and the cob had apparently stayed behind to look after his pen, whom observers thought to be injured or sick, as he gave her the best feeding-places by the side of the loch. After a few hours the cob decided to desert his mate and took to the air, but by evening the whole flock returned from the direction in which they had flown. Next morning they went off, leaving the pair on the loch, and this time the cob waited a day and a night before he once more deserted. Two days later every one near the loch heard the sonorous "klung klung" overhead, where one swan was being savagely attacked by the others in the air, and was forced to alight on the loch. This time the cob was so injured that he stayed with his mate until both had recovered.

At Gariemore, one and a half miles further on, I stopped to call on Father John Macmillan, who knows every foot of this island, on which he was born, and the names and stories of its creeks, rocks, and bays. In his old age he is entitled to leisure, but unless these names and stories are recorded they are likely to be lost. There is the Creek of the Frenchman's Gold, the Rock of the Viking Witch who, when told of rocks ahead of her galley, shouted: "Rocks, that's only little Barra! My galley will pass over it," and many other names which should at least be placed on a local map. Yet it was not to ask him for stories that I had called, but for a bath. Father John is a tall man, built on Columban lines, and when I mentioned "bath" he shouted: "A bath! There's not a bath in the house. What do you want with a bath when the Atlantic is at the door? Take a towel and go into the ocean. If you swim far enough the first land you'll touch will be Labrador."

So I walked down the firm sandy bay, the tide being out, to a ledge of rocks beside a clear fresh-water stream running over the sand. I would have a swim followed by a fresh-water bath. The sea was neither too rough nor too cold, but after swimming a few yards out of my depth my legs became partially entangled in a mass of deep-sea wrack coming in on the tide, and I returned to the peaceful security of the fresh-water stream.

On returning to the house Father John gave me a good lunch of fresh herrings and potatoes, and from him I heard

146

the story of the Wicked Princess. In the telling he was obviously thinking in Gaelic and speaking in English, but from notes I made at the time this is the story:

In olden time on the Isle of Barra there lived a band of heroes called the Feinn, and their chief was called Fionn. Each of the heroes was very brave, and every one of them had taken a mighty oath before he became a member of the band. He had sworn that if he was killed in battle none of his friends was expected to avenge his death; that he would never do harm to a woman; that he would never refuse to marry a girl because she was poor; that he would be kind to the weak; and that he would never refuse to fight single-handed against nine men of any other nation if they attacked him.

Before a man could join the Feinn he had to prove himself a perfect swordsman, and so strong that he could take his broad-sword by the tip between thumb and forefinger and hold it out at arm's length without a tremor. His long hair was tied with a ribbon at the nape of the neck, and even when he was chasing animals with his spear over the moors or through the woods, his hair had to remain tidy. If at the end of the chase the ribbon was untied and his hair was towsled, he was not worthy to belong to the Feinn. Each of the Feinns had to prove that he was able to jump over a tree as high as his forehead, to creep under a tree no higher than his knee without shaking the leaves, to stand so lightly on a rotten branch that it did not break, and, most difficult of all, to pull a thorn out of his foot when running at full speed. In addition to these accomplishments each of the Feinns had to compose a war song.

All the Feinns, fourteen in number, were equally brave, and Fionn their chief was no braver than his companions. In one way only did he excel them. When something had to be decided, Fionn placed his thumb under his wisdom tooth, and at once he knew what should be done. The Feinns had golden hair and blue eyes, because they were descended from the Vikings who had sailed and settled all over the known world. Over shirt and kilt they wore a plaid or sleeveless cloak. Each was armed with a two-handled sword buckled round his waist, a shield carried on the left forearm, and a dirk or dagger placed between the top of the stocking and the skin of his right leg. For foot-wear they had moccasins. When hunting animals they discarded swords and shields and carried spears.

One day the Feinns were sitting in their castle, and Fionn, having put his thumb under his wisdom tooth, said: "Let us put out our boat, prow to sea and stern to shore, hoist the speckled flapping sails, and visit Dubhan, the King of Ireland across the sea."

After two days they reached the shore of Ireland late in the afternoon, and King Dubhan came down to the beach to bid them welcome. As the boat was approaching the shore, the King saw that Fionn had fourteen companions, and so he chose fourteen of his dark-haired warriors as a bodyguard equal in number to that of Fionn.

When the prow touched the sand, Fionn and his companions jumped overboard, dragged their boat beyond high-water mark and approached the King.

"I am Fionn, the son of the daughter of a sea-king."

"Welcome," said King Dubhan, "and come to the palace where a banquet is prepared for you, for your coming was known to our Druids, who are great magicians. He led them to the banqueting hall, a large room with a stone floor and a vaulted roof. There were no windows, and the room was lit by torches in brackets on the walls. At one end of the hall a huge fire of blazing logs roared up an open chimney. Then Fionn and his companions, having piled their swords and shields in a corner of the hall, sat on benches at the long table, laden with food. The King sat at the head of the table, and on his right was Fionn. To the left of the King sat his only daughter, the black-haired, dark-eyed Princess, whose lips were the colour of pink coral, and whose skin was as white and smooth as ivory. At the sides of the table were Fionn's fourteen companions, and each had sitting beside him a dark-haired warrior.

The feast included oysters, hare soup, roast quail, venison, boar's head with seakale and wheaten cakes. They had no spoons or forks, and each man cut up the meat with his dirk and ate with his fingers. There was ale and for dessert they had sweets made of honey, butter, and cream.

Then did Fionn say: "O King, hear my request for your daughter in marriage."

"It shall not be granted," said the King, "for never would I give my daughter to the son of a sea-wolf."

"Say not so," said Fionn, "but await the morning."

In the morning the Princess said, "O my father, let the royal galley be launched for the sea is calm, and let us show the noble Fionn and his companions the wild wave-swept cliffs, where the sea-fowl nest."

"Say not so," said the King, "for our royal galley holds but sixteen, you, myself, and our fourteen trusted followers.

Would you have me risk the lives of the noble Fionn and his companions?"

"Nay, my father, the sea is calm, and there is room for us all."

"Your request shall be granted," said the King.

The sea was smooth, and a gentle breeze carried the royal galley beyond the high headland to the great cliffs where the sea-fowl nested on ridges and in which are caverns where the sea booms. At noon the sky became overcast and the breeze increased. Soon the sea rose and the over-loaded galley was in peril in the trough of the waves.

"We must lighten the ship, O King," said the navigator, a dark-haired warrior nicknamed the Horse, by reason of his countenance, "and some must be thrown overboard."

King Dubhan was sore at heart that anyone should be thrown overboard. Yet the galley was overloaded and waves were breaking over the side. Unless some of the men were thrown into the sea all would be drowned. The King did not wish to lose any of his black-haired warriors, nor did he wish to see any of his guests, Fionn and his fair-haired followers, thrown overboard, and he bowed his head in thought, but all his men murmured: "Some must go."

Then the King spoke: "Let my daughter, the Princess, choose who are to be thrown into the sea," and all his men answered: "Let the Princess choose. We will obey."

So the King turned to his daughter and said: "Choose the victims, for fifteen men must die if our ship is to reach the land."

"O my father," said the Princess, "let the choice be by lot, and first I shall give to each his place in the galley." She sat on the middle thwart, facing the stern, and spoke as follows: "On my right in the stern let there stand four followers of Fionn, most glorious and beautiful.

"Next to them I place five dark-haired warriors from the palace of my father, the King of Ireland," and as she spoke the men took their places.

"Now, two followers of Fionn, the son of Cumhail.

"And one dark-haired warrior—he that is called the Horse.

"In the bow three followers of Fionn, the stalwart and lovely one."

By this arrangement nine of Fionn's and six of her father's men were in line along the port side of the galley, and the Princess continued:

"In the starboard bow I place one of my father's men.

"Next to him comes Fionn.

"The brave Fionn would not stand there unless I placed two dark-haired warriors beside him on his left.

"Then let two fair stalwarts from the palace of Fionn take their places.

"You, my father, King of Ireland, shall stand amidships, with a trusted dark-haired warrior on either side of you.

"Now I place a follower of Fionn.

"Let two dark-haired giants stand beside him.

"Then two of Fionn's men.

"Next to them let the last of the King's warriors take his place.

"And now, O my father, you shall count, beginning where I began, and every ninth man will be thrown overboard."

Then did King Dubhan begin to count from the first of the men in the stern on the port side, and every ninth man was one of his trusted followers. Fifteen times did he make the count and then he himself was thrown into the sea. In order that readers may understand how this crime of parricide and treachery was achieved, I shall draw a plan of the galley, showing how the Princess arranged the men. The large white circle is Fionn, and the small white circles are his men. The large black circle shows where the King of Ireland stood, and the small black circles are his dark-haired warriors.

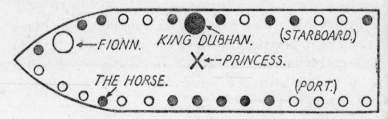

The story is commemorated in a Gaelic poem, which translated by Father John Macmillan is as follows:

"Four from the Fionns of glorious beautiful appearance,
Let them stand aside
With five black men after them, from the dwelling of Dubhan.
Two from Macumhal anew
And one from Dubhan, the Horse,
Three from the Fionn, of glorious beautiful appearance,
And one from Dubhan, put him out,
Fionn will not sit in the white stream,
Without two black fellows on his left,
Without two others after them, of the habitation of Fionn,
Three blacks one on each side of the Dubhan,
One fair of Fionn watching these,
Two black giants after that,
Two from Fionn and one from Dubhan."

After this cold-blooded massacre the royal galley sailed to Barra, where Fionn married the Princess, and that perhaps was the bravest thing he ever did. Yet even in our own time, whenever a woman has been acquitted of murder, there are brave men who offer to marry her.

For centuries and centuries up to this day the children of Barra play this game on the long level sands, using cockle shells for Fionn and his followers, and mussel shells for the King of Ireland and his dark-haired warriors, and apart from a moral lesson it teaches them to count.

CHAPTER XIV

THE LOCH OF THE RED-HAIRED GIRL

A MILE north of Gariemore the road goes east to the miscalled North Bay, and then south to complete a twelve-and-a-half-mile circuit of the island. At North Bay is a small hamlet, with church, presbytery, post office, and scattered crofts. The road descends at the eastern side of the island to a small natural harbour, dry at low water, opening out of Hirivagh Bay, and at the entrance to this bay a long narrow arm of the sea, Hulavagh Bay, runs northwards for a mile. Both these bays are sheltered from North Bay by the Black Island, which leaves two channels through which small craft may enter the inner bays. There are other islets in North Bay and the entrance to the inner bays may be easily missed by a stranger, as it was by me in broad daylight. Yet even on dark nights local fishermen made the entrance because when the Black Isle opened on the inner bays they saw on the shore a guiding light. They did not know what the light was, but it always appeared, and this I was told not by one but by many fishermen. These guiding lights have been seen in other parts of the Western Isles, and assuredly they are not will o' the wisps, these latter being wandering lights seen on marsh land and possibly caused by some electric disturbance on the ground. The guiding light is no longer seen at North Bay; nor is it needed, because when a house was being built on the road above the harbour where it used to appear, Father

John paid for the building of an extra window on condition that a lamp would be shown there whenever boats were out at night.

On the south side of the inner bay is the church, presbytery, post office, which is part of a general shop, and a wooden boarding-house which in the summer is packed with visitors. In the dry dyke around the church a geologist noticed a stone foreign to the Hebrides but common enough in Cornwall, and discovered that it had come as ballast in the days when sailing-boats came from Cornwall to Barra to buy kelp. On my first visit I stayed at the boarding-house which is run by the postmaster, who runs many other things including a motor boat, and represents Barra on the Inverness County Council. This short, burly man with white hair, moustache, and grey eyes is called the Coddie. His real name I do not know, and on this island very few people are known by their real names, but a letter or telegram to Coddie, Barra, would be delivered. I specified for a single room, and the Coddie was able to give me a room to myself until a visitor who had booked it in advance arrived.

The room was small and square with wooden walls and roof, and held two twin beds, side by side with space for a chair between. On the chair I placed the lamp, on the spare bed my clothes and belongings, and got into the other bed. There are times when one is fortunate in getting a bed and not a sofa, and, as Dr. Johnson said, "He that shall complain of his fare in the Hebrides has improved his delicacy more than his manhood." Moreover, the room was mine until the man, who had booked it in advance, arrived. He came three hours later, at 1 a.m., and I awoke to hear him fumbling about in the dark. "Who's there?" I asked.

155

"It's me," said he. "I booked this room in advance, and the steamer arrived at midnight."

"You weren't expected," said I, lighting the lamp, "but you may move my things off the other bed, and I'll clear out in the morning."

"I'm sorry to have disturbed you," said the man.

"Not at all," said I, and went to sleep. Some time later I was awakened by the man talking in his sleep, which was disconcerting, although all that I heard were the words: "God is very good. Be grateful to God," which bespoke a tranquil mind in the speaker asleep.

Next day I climbed Ben Erival which is near North Bay and to the north of the road crossing the island. The lower slopes are mainly swamp, but there is a dry patch a hundred yards beyond a large boulder on the roadside, and this boulder is unmistakable because it shows a perfect profile of the late Queen Victoria. The Ben can be climbed in half an hour's easy going and is worth climbing because on the flattened summit is a small loch into which no streams run. A girl tending sheep on the Ben once saw a stranger, a young man of great beauty and with golden hair, sitting on the bank of the loch. He beckoned her, and when she approached he grasped the hem of her skirt. To escape she loosened her skirt, leaving it in his hands, and fled, but already his hands had changed into hoofs, and on looking back from the edge of the Ben she saw a horse savaging the skirt and lashing out at the rocks with his hind feet until at last he leapt into the loch and disappeared. To this day there are hoof marks on the hard rocks around the Loch of the Water Horse. One of the visitors at the Coddie's boarding house was an English professional photographer to whom I told the story, which so interested him that he took a photograph of the place. Some weeks later he sent me a print, and in his covering letter wrote that until the plate was developed he did not realise that the loch in its shape resembled a horse lashing out, as indeed it does in the print.

That night I got a room in a large croft north of the inner bay and known as the Crookles, this being the nickname of the crofter and fisherman who owns it. Here I shared a sitting-room with a singer and his accompanist, and next morning after breakfast we stayed indoors on account of the rain, but the entertainment they provided more than compensated for the rain. The singer had a magnificent tenor voice, and he sang arias, Highland and Irish songs, unaccompanied because the piano was out of tune. Indeed, it was so out of tune that it reminded the accompanist of the piano on which he had once played in a small cinema to provide atmosphere for the silent films. Of this "atmo-sphere" he gave an imitation on the piano which made me shed tears of laughter, and as he played I almost saw once more the old silent films—galloping horses, mother's farewell, the storm that became a cyclone, a maiden's prayer, death of the big bad man, at which for no apparent reason someone always pointed to the sky, the dawn of love, in the teeth of the gale, shot and shell, and the wedding march.

This was not the singer's first holiday in Barra, and when first he came he was not a singer but a Glasgow school teacher, who disliked teaching as much as he liked singing in amateur choirs. At a ceilidh[1] in the North Bay church hall

---

[1] Originally a gathering at a neighbour's house where songs were sung and stories told round the fire, but now applied to small Gaelic concerts in the Islands.

he sang solo, and was afterwards advised by Mr. Compton Mackenzie to give up teaching and to have his voice trained. The advice was taken, and in London his voice was trained by Plunket Greene. Then Count John McCormack gave him an audition, praised his voice and promised an American tour. The singer was now awaiting the details of this tour, and to all his friends he seemed to be on the high road to fame. Moreover, great singers amass money, and some say that McCormack's royalties on American gramophone records amounted to £20,000 a year. When next I met the singer he was singing at Londonderry House in Park Lane, and then came a successful tour of the United States and of Australia. Last year he sent me a Christmas card from Rome. He was not singing there in the Opera House but was studying at the Scots College for the priesthood—and I was not astonished.

On another day I went to fish the Loch of the Red-haired Girl, which is reached by a track that leaves the main road beyond Queen Victoria's boulder and goes south-east for about a mile. Leaving the track one continues for another half-mile through the heather. It is a small loch encircled by hillocks that form the horizon, and has one small islet on which are the ruins of a stone hut. There is an under-water causeway to the islet, and at one place on the causeway is a knocking stone, namely a balanced stone which knocks when stepped upon, the knock being heard by anyone on the shore or on the islet. On this islet a MacNeil chieftain imprisoned the red-haired daughter of a Viking who had his stronghold on Fuday, a small island north of Barra. MacNeil's son fell in love with the girl, visited her on the islet, and by him she had a son who grew up and joined MacNeil's forces, although MacNeil refused to acknowledge either the boy or his red-haired mother. In time MacNeil's own son was killed in battle, and then the boy went to his mother and asked her how he could avenge his father's death. She told him the date of a pagan festival, after which all the Vikings on Fuday would be drunk. The boy brought the news to MacNeil, who acted upon it, surprised the Vikings and slew every one of them. Thereafter MacNeil recognised the red-haired girl and adopted her child as his son and heir.

I caught no fish that day, but I stayed by the loch until sunset. Next day the postman took me with him to deliver letters in the northern end of Barra, which is reached by a rough road running north from Castlebay. This postman had a car which he said was ten years old, by which he probably meant that he had bought it second-hand ten years previously, because never before or since have I seen a car whose engine was partly fixed to the chassis by wires and ropes. Yet the engine worked when once it was started, usually after five minutes' cranking. The car was the least part of the postman's troubles, because to reach some of the crofts entailed a walk of a mile or even more, and to-day he had a heavy mail, as this was the day on which the dole arrived. At one distant croft he who was to receive the dole was sitting at the end of his house, and made no effort to rise and meet the postman. That was the last straw. "Can you not get up to receive your wages?"

"Ye get well paid yoursel'," shouted the crofter.

"I'm not well paid, but I work for it," shouted the postman, as we turned back towards the road.

The crofters had made a fine art of getting the dole.

A would employ B to make a road in front of A's croft, and as wages A would stamp B's employment card until B was qualified to draw the dole. Then B would employ A on the same terms. The authorities have now stopped that procedure, but they have not solved the problem of unemployment. Indeed, some newspapers suggest that there must always be unemployment. Why? There is no unemployment in the Isle of Man, where every able-bodied unemployed man is given well-paid work on the roads. How is it that all children in London between the age of fourteen and sixteen can find work? Because child labour is cheap, and they in turn will be sacked when they ask for better wages. If the family be large the children may be the sole support of a father who has been unemployed for years, and thus children may be tempted to despise him. To save their self-respect many of these unfortunate men do all the housework while the wives and children are employed outside the home. Why is there little or no unemployment in countries so different as Finland and Germany? And above all, how is it that chronic unemployment should be the perquisite of the "great free democracies" of America, Britain, and France. Many people who are neither revolutionaries nor socialists are beginning to wonder whether the root cause is not our monetary system. They are also wondering whether this monetary system, whereby money has ceased to be a token of exchange and has become a commodity to be bought or sold, is maintained for the benefit of a comparatively small number of very rich men in the "free democracies."

On this motor-walking tour with the postman there was time to see something of the northern end of Barra. At low water we motored across the Traigh Mhor, a large sandy bay, once the richest ground in Europe for blue cockles. On the sands we stopped to talk to a lad who was digging for cockles, and he was also getting "razor fish," a mollusc so-called because its shell in shape resembles an old-fashioned razor. The only other place where I had ever seen "razor fish" was on the sands of Sea View in the Isle of Wight, where we used to coax them out of their burrows by putting salt over the holes. The salt made a saturated solution which sank into the burrow and so irritated the mollusc that it would leap out of the sand. In the Isle of Wight we never ate these fish, but here in Barra I followed the example of the lad who was digging and ate one raw. It was edible, but a long way behind Whitstable oysters. Let not the most squeamish reader shudder because, believe it or not, raw fish is slightly more digestible than cooked fish, and raw meat is much more digestible than cooked meat.

At Eoligary are the ruins of an ancient chapel and an old burial ground, but near by was Eoligary House, a bleak, square building whose owner was the last of his race and the house the last of his possessions. His collection of stuffed birds had caused me to knock on the door, and the knocking echoed as it might have echoed from an empty house. The day was warm and sunny, but as I stood on the doorstep I remembered the phantom listeners in Walter de la Mare's poem:

> "Hearkening in an air stilled and shaken
> By the lonely traveller's call."

Soft shuffling steps answered my knocking, and an old bent woman let me in to a carpetless hall walled with cases of stuffed birds, and then into what once had been a dining-room. There was a mahogany table, chairs, a bare side-board, and stuffed birds in glass cases on the walls were the only decorations. There was no carpet in the room, and it must have been years since a fire had been lit in the empty grate, or windows had been opened, because the room smelt of mildew, damp, and dust. At last the owner of the house appeared, a tall, pallid, gaunt old man, who gave me a chair and drew one from the table for himself. I mentioned the stuffed birds, but in them he was no longer interested, because after his brother's death the best specimens had been given to the museum at Inverness. He talked incessantly of people and of times I had never known, and was petulant when I revealed my ignorance. His grievance was that no one ever came to see him, but from what I heard from the postman neither he nor his forebears had ever sought friendship in the days of their manhood. For one thing only was I grateful, namely that he neither offered me food nor drink in that house, and at the end of half an hour I rose and declared that I must leave him lest the postman returned without me. The old man asked me to call again, but as I left his decaying abode I knew that I would never return.

When the time came to leave Barra I crossed to Pol-lachar by motor-boat on the day of the South Uist Games. There were two boats of the same make, each had a full complement of passengers, and there was rivalry as to which would win on the eight-mile crossing, with a stiff south breeze, a following sea in the Sound of Barra between the islands of Fuday and Eriskay (where Prince Charles Stuart first landed in Scotland on 23rd July 1745), and more sea as we approached Pollachar. The two boats, within hailing distance, were almost abreast when our propeller was fouled by drifting seaweed and the Coddie's boat took the lead. Our skipper, a little old man in oilskins, removed his sou'-wester and leant far over the side in the stern. With each wave his head was under water, but within a couple of minutes he had cleared the propeller and apparently regarded this manœuvre as an everyday occurrence. Our boat was the first to reach the jetty.

CHAPTER XV

THE SINGING SANDS

AT Pollachar near the jetty is an inn which is said to date from the reign of Charles I., who authorised a ferry between South Uist and Eriskay on condition that an inn was built at this desolate south-western corner of the island. No inn, no ferry, was his maxim, and such a monarch must have had an irksome time when sojourning with the ranting Covenanters. The walls of this inn are of masonry two feet thick, the windows are small and the door of the sitting-room is of oak blackened by age. From an inn such as this David Balfour might have set forth on his adventures, had he not stayed at the Hawes Inn, South Queensferry.

Outside the inn I met a man who had lost an arm by being mauled by a tiger when shooting in India. Having written an excellent book about tigers, he was trout fishing at Pollachar before returning to India in order to make a film about tigers. I asked him if he had felt pain when the tiger was mauling his arm.

"Not the slightest pain," said he.

"That's very interesting, because Livingstone had the same experience when being mauled by a lion."

"The only pain I felt was when my friend in trying to shoot the tiger missed, and like a damn fool put the bullet through my foot. That stung a bit."

From Pollachar we went in motor lorries to Askernish

where the games were being held, of which I have little to say because Highland Games do not interest me. They are usually held on a cold, windy and rainy day, and nobody knows from the programme what is happening, because either nothing is happening or too many events are happening at the same time. Nevertheless, these games give Englishmen who have married Scottish wives an opportunity of wearing the kilt of their wives' tartan, but I have also known Englishmen to appear in a tartan which only a few Scotsmen of Royal descent have the right to wear. Apart from competitors, the only people who really seem to enjoy Highland Games are the officials, who wear large rosettes which give them the privilege of going into a tent in the middle of the field, and the more they go into that tent the more do they seem to enjoy the games. *Moral:* Wear a rosette. It keeps out the cold.

At Loch Boisdale, the port of South Uist, I went on board the *Lochmor* at midnight on my way to the Island of Eigg. There were no vacant berths, but I found a cushioned seat in a small lounge on the deck. A woman was lying at one end of the seat, and using my rucksack as a pillow at a safe distance from her feet, I also lay down. Presently a nun and three schoolgirls entered the lounge, where they sat on chairs until the nun, looking at me and the woman, remarked to the girls: "These two might be closer together." Whereupon I moved my rucksack and myself nearer the woman's feet, which made room for one of the girls to lie on the seat. Only the nun and two girls would have to sit up all night, but, nevertheless, my conscience pricked me. Did not good manners demand that I give up my place to the nun? They did, but on the other hand the nun was more accustomed than I was to long vigils and early rising. This would be no new experience for her, and although she looked past middle-age there was not a wrinkle on her face. Nevertheless, I ought at least to offer her my place, and there was always a chance that she might refuse. At that moment the stewardess entered and said there were berths for the four of them.

After a few hours' sleep I chanced to wake and saw through the port a crimson light in the sky which brought me on deck, and then on to the upper deck near the bridge where the Second Officer was on duty. The time was just past 4 a.m., the sun was rising north-east by east behind the Coolins of Skye, and against a great half-circle of crimson I counted thirty-five peaks, including those of mountains on the mainland. Overhead the clouds were tinted crimson; through gaps in the Coolins this light also fell on a calm lead-grey sea, and between crimson streaks on the water were long black shadows of pinnacled peaks, some smooth, some ragged. Slowly the colour changed to pale orange, and then to green, until at last the sun had risen in a blue sky. To the east a carpet of sea fog was drifting out of the Sound of Sleat, and on those low billowy clouds the mountains of western Inverness seemed to be resting. During the transformation scene I had made rough notes of the colours and now asked the second officer for his impressions, but he shook his head: "I'm not colour-blind. I'm colour-ignorant, and there's been a score of colours in as many minutes." He was right, and of the score I have only captured a few.

The *Lochmor* stopped half a mile from the jetty at the south-eastern end of Eigg, and I was the only passenger

who went ashore with the mails in the motor ferry boat.
The ferry fare is one shilling per journey to or from
the island, and on the jetty I asked the ferryman about
the nearest hotel, for it was now 6.30 a.m. and I was
hungry.

"There's no hotel on this island."

"Then where can I have breakfast?"

"If you wait till you see smoke going up from the
houses, you might get breakfast at one of them."

"And what time does the smoke go up?"

"About seven o'clock, but it's early yet."

"Then where is the priest's house?"

"He's on the other side of the island at the Bay of
Laig. It's a three-mile walk, and if you wait a minute
or two you can follow the post cart. It's going in that
direction."

After fifteen minutes the ferryman and his brother the
postman harnessed their horse to the cart that carried the
mails. The postman drove and I walked alongside, for
he had explained that it was against regulations to give me
a lift, but he kindly put my rucksack in the cart. From
north to south the island is five miles long, its greatest
width being three and a half miles, and from the jetty to
Laig Bay the road runs almost due north. For the first
mile the road went through wooded country not only of
pines and silver birches but also of palm trees, with ferns,
hydrangeas, and azaleas by the roadside. Beyond the
woods the road skirted the foot of moors rising to mountains in the west, and to the east was pasture land on the
slopes of Kinloch Glen, while half a mile from the road an
Ionic cross marks the place where St. Donnan and his

167

followers were massacred in A.D. 617, after celebrating the sacrament of the Last Supper.[1]

Accounts differ as to whether they were massacred by robbers or by Frisian Vikings, but it appears that "They settled where the chief-lady of the district was wont to keep her sheep. This was told to the lady. 'Let them all be killed.' 'That would be impious,' replied every one. But, at length, men came to slay them. The cleric was now at the *Oifrend* (the celebration of the Eucharist). 'Let us have respite till the *Oifrend* is ended,' asked Donnan. 'It will be granted,' replied they. Afterwards, the whole company was massacred together."

From the same source there is an account of St. Donnan's visit to Columba on Iona: "It is this Donnan who went to Columcille to get him to be a soul-friend ("amncharait"). Columcille replied to him, 'I shall not be soul-friend to folk *destined* to red-martyrdom,'[2] says he, 'thou shalt go to red-martyrdom, thou and thy muinntir (community) with thee;' and so it *afterwards* happened."

At the head of the glen was a green hill invaded by whins, but when the postman was a young boy that hill was cultivated land. "There were more people on the island then, and at the school there were over two score children and two teachers. Now there are only a hundred people and only ten children at the school." The cart stopped at the post office on top of the hill above Laig Bay, and I made my way down to the priest's house. Both house and church were open but there was nobody about,

---

[1] According to the *Feilire of Aengus*, quoted by A. B. Scott in *The Pictish Nation : its People and its Church*, 1918; p. 271.

[2] Massacre.

and so I wandered round to the back where I met a tall, lanky lad who touched his cap and in answer to my enquiry for the priest, replied: "He should be about." That was not helpful, and when I saw a woman returning with a pail from the milking, I gave her my card. "If you go to the front door I'll tell Father Campbell." A minute later Father Joseph Campbell, whom I had never met previously, came down from his study and gave me a Highland welcome: "You must be tired and hungry. Would you like to go to bed, or would you like to hear Mass now and have a good breakfast afterwards? And how long can you stay?"

So I heard Mass, which was served by the lanky lad, and for the first time I was a congregation in myself. Moreover, in my pew I found a bank note which I put in my pocket. Father Campbell, who was lithe, dark-haired and of middle age, provided an excellent breakfast of porridge and cream, bacon and eggs, coffee, scones, oatcakes, butter, marmalade, and heather honey. As we took our seats, he said: "Eat your breakfast. We can talk afterwards."

"No, Father," said I. "In the first place, a mystery has got to be cleared up."

"What mystery? What are you talking about?"

"Have you noticed any foreigners recently in the island?"

"No. But why do you want to know?"

"Because I have reason to believe that a foreigner has been on the island, and not so long ago."

"Now that you remind me, an Englishman and his wife were staying on the island. She was a Portuguese, but they left last week."

"Had they recently been to Portugal?"

"Yes, but what on earth is all this about?"

"It explains the mystery."

"What mystery? Are you writing a detective story?"

"No, but something has been found in your church."

"What's been found in my church?"

"This." And I handed him a five-escudo note on the Bank of Portugal.

"Where did you find it?"

"On the ledge at the aisle end of the pew where I was sitting."

"Not dropped or hidden in any way?"

"No, lying there where anyone could see it."

"How like a woman to leave it there! I'll tell you what happened. One morning when coming in to Mass she broke the Holy Water Stoup. She was very upset and wanted to pay for the damage. I refused to take anything, and told her that I could get another at Woolworth's. So she goes and leaves that note on the ledge of the pew."

"You must have a very small congregation?"

"Not at all. Although there are only forty Catholics on the island, there's always a good attendance on Sundays, but they're much too honest to touch a note lying on the ledge of a pew."

I looked at Father Campbell, but his face seemed free from guile, and we changed the conversation.

Around the Bay of Eigg are crofts of seven to eight acres running down to the shore, with well-built iron-roofed houses which would be better if they were thatched to avoid the noise of rain falling on corrugated iron. The rents are £2 a year, and the crofters keep sheep, a horse, four cows, and their stirks. Sheep feed on the common grazing land, stirks on the crofts, and so famous are these stirks that when the cattle buyers come to the island they charter a special steamer to take the animals to the mainland. In May a good stirk may fetch £15, and in September £10. Wool is another source of income, and the only necessities of life that a crofter needs to buy are tea, sugar, salt, meal, clothes, and boots.

In a good year a crofter may make £70 clear, which seems very little to city-minded folk who fail to realise that an income of £100 on an island such as this is worth £500 in a city like Glasgow where, in addition to high rents and rates, every one of the necessities of life must be bought. Moreover, on the island a man is his own master, and it is a commonplace of human nature that a man tends to work better for himself than for another. Yet the younger generation are leaving their island security for the cities, where most of them will answer the whistle of a factory which for all they know may close down to-morrow. Conditions on the island would be better if transport were improved, because during the winter there is only one steamer a week to Mallaig, thirteen miles distant on the mainland. Thus eggs on the island are destroyed at a time when the people of Mallaig are obtaining eggs and other farm produce from Glasgow. The owner of the island is that millionaire English shipowner Lord Runciman, who worked so hard in the interests of the people of Czechoslovakia.

During the visit I saw one of the wonders of the world— the Singing Sands, which are found, so far as I know, in only one other place, namely at Manchester on Massachusetts Bay, U.S.A. The Singing Sands are in a small bay to the north of the Bay of Laig and are reached by descending a rather steep ravine with grassy sides. Down the side of this double incline both Father Campbell and Growler, his West Highland terrier, were at their ease, but I preferred to descend on the bed of a dried-up stream which served as a crude staircase at the bottom of the ravine. Fortunately the tide was half out because the sands only sing when dry. When you walk, or better when you slide your feet, over this sand it emits a long musical note— ooh, ooh—and this note is also obtained by stroking the surface of the sand with the palm of the hand. This is a fine grained quartz sand, the grains being circular in outline, and the sound is due to friction between the grains and to the minute air-pockets around them.

On this beach I also saw the Cathedral Cave, which could be more accurately called the Cathedral Arch, since only the entrance to the cave now remains. In an enormous and roughly rectangular mass of limestone rising from the sand the sea has fashioned a great arch resembling the entrance to a Gothic cathedral. Beyond the arch is an open space between the cliff and other masses of limestone rising from the sand. Here I found a small smooth stone bored with holes as if by some large worm, and this was a pebble of calcareous grit bored by molluscs. The geology of Eigg includes the Scuir or Squrr, a vertical cliff of basaltic columnar rock near the southern coast and rising to a height of 1282 feet, which may be climbed from its north-western side. This rock is all that remains of the lava that once flowed from a great volcano on the neighbouring island of Rum into a valley which had been hollowed out of the oldest basalt rock. And how was that discovered millions of years afterwards? Because geologists found that the Squrr rests on a layer of old river gravel.

On the beach in the Bay of Eigg are sometimes found, and the finder is held to be lucky, Our Lady's Snuffbox and Our Lady's Kidney. How these names arose is a mystery, but the objects to which they apply are a hard, flat, rounded seed and a smaller kidney-shaped seed, both of which when split open, hinged and fixed with a clasp, were made into snuff-boxes. These are the seeds of South American trees and are carried to the island by the Gulf Stream, and indeed this island is well served by the Stream for the climate is equable, and in winter the sea is warmer than in summer.

Of all these things were we talking when Father Campbell remarked: "It's going to rain," and as there were no obvious signs of rain, I asked how he knew.

"By the oyster catcher's cry. Did you not hear it: 'Kleep-kleep'? That foretells rain, just as the moaning of seals is heard twenty-four hours before a storm. The oyster catcher, once black all over, was St. Donnan's bird and rescued children at sea. So Michael said, 'I'll make him white all over.' 'No, no,' said St. Donnan, 'just give him a dash of white.' So Michael arranged the white in the plumage and now the oyster catcher when flying looks like a black and white cross."

"I don't see how they can catch oysters."

"They don't. When the tide is falling they run out over the sand to catch limpets, cockles, and winkles before they close."

Going back to Loch Boisdale the *Lochmor* called at

Rum, an island four miles long and four miles wide, which lies four miles north-west of Eigg. The two highest mountains, Askval and Askival at the southern end of the island, have sharp pointed peaks, which although lower are as bare, ragged, and inaccessible as the Coolins of Skye. Yet these peaks are not the only inaccessible things on the island, and when the *Lochmor* stopped at the entrance to Loch Scresort on the eastern side and a motor boat came out to bring cargo, mostly provisions, ashore, the first officer refused to allow me to get into the boat.

"But I wish to go ashore."

"Well, you can't go ashore."

"I'll ask the captain."

"It's no use asking the captain. No one is allowed to land on that island without permission in writing, signed by the proprietor himself."

The first officer was right, and in 1931 the population of the island was thirty-one, which may or may not have included the proprietor in addition to his servants. In 1826 the population was four hundred, and in that year they were all, save one family, evicted and sent to America in order that the island might be turned into a deer forest, which it remains to this day.

As the *Lochmor* left the island an old Highlandman who had overheard our conversation said: "Desolation, desolation! When I was a young boy I met an old man who once was there" (and from the way he spoke he might have been referring to a man who was once in Tibet), "and he told me there used to be good arable land along the shore, plenty of black-faced sheep, and fertile valleys between the ranges. Now it's only the deer and the estate servants."

The owner of the island is now the millionaire English ironmaster Sir George Bullough, who so far as I know did no active work in the interests of the people of Czechoslovakia.

Our last port of call was Cana, a small island four and a half miles long by three-quarters wide, which lies three and a half miles north-west of Rum, and to the north of the harbour at the eastern end is Compass Hill, of basaltic rock so rich in iron that compasses are deflected. The soil of this low-lying island produces fine pasture, and an experiment is now being tried to grow produce hitherto confined to regions much farther south. The owner of the island is not a millionaire but a Scottish laird who is also a practical farmer, Campbell of Inverneil.

At Loch Boisdale, reached after sunset when hills and moors were a dark purple, I realised that for several days I had not read a newspaper, but here the only one left was a popular illustrated news-sheet and I marvelled at the industry and ingenuity expended in the collection of so much drivel. Of a regular reader of that paper one might say with Lowell:

"A reading machine, ever wound up and going,
    He mastered whatever was not worth the knowing."

CHAPTER XVI

FLORA MACDONALD

THE Long Island is the popular name now given to three islands separated by fords—South Uist, Benbecula, and North Uist, and the length of all three together, including the fords, is just over forty-one miles. To the north of these three islands is Lewis and Harris, a single island sixty-one miles long, and in the time of Martin (*circa* 1695) this was called, and apparently with more reason, The Long Island. All these islands were formed from the fundamental rock—gneiss, traversed by veins of granite and trap, and their soil is peat bog varying in depth from a few inches up to twenty feet. On the western coasts blown shell sand, mixing with the peat bog, forms good pasture land, but with the exception of parts of North Lewis the eastern coasts are bleak and barren save for heather. Only in three places are trees to be seen, and in South Uist I cannot recall even one.

In South Uist all the mountains are on the east coast, and this island is best seen from the sea for a view of cliffs, with dark caves at their base, rising to heights of 700 and 800 feet, of steep ravines coming down to the rocky shore, and of heather-clad mountains. There is deep water at a cable's length from the shore (a cable being 608 feet, which is one-tenth of the nautical mile as fixed by the Admiralty), but despite the height of the cliffs and mountains this coast gives little shelter against westerly winds, and for small craft under sail the nearer the shore the greater is their danger, because from the ravines the most violent squalls blow down on the sea.

Having seen the Long Island from seawards, I decided to walk from Loch Boisdale to Loch Maddy, the port of North Uist, and set out at 8 a.m. As is natural, the road avoids the mountains, goes west of the Boisdale hills, of which Stulaval is the highest, and runs north in the centre of the flat western half of the island. There were no hills to climb, but around and ahead were bleak stretches of moorland with only lochs and inlets of the sea to break the monotony.

Three-quarters of a mile west of the road and five and a half miles from Loch Boisdale are the ruins of the farmhouse at Milton, the birthplace of Flora MacDonald, and where in 1746 she was staying with her brother Angus. In the neighbourhood was the sheiling (a roughly constructed hut on the pasture land where cattle are driven for grazing) of Alisary, where on the night of Friday, 20th June, she first met Prince Charles Edward Stuart, who was accompanied by Captain O'Neil and Neil MacEachen. They had been hiding in Glen Corodale, seven miles north-east of Milton as the crow flies, and it was Flora's stepfather, Hugh MacDonald of Armadale in Skye, but now stationed in Benbecula as captain of one of the independent companies seeking to capture the Prince, who planned the escape. The plan was that Flora, now aged twenty-four, should return to her mother who was at Armadale, and that the Prince disguised as a spinning maid about to enter her mother's service should also go to Skye, where he would be protected by Lady Margaret MacDonald of Sleat, now living at

Kingsburgh House in Trotternish. By this plan the safety of the Prince, for whose capture the English Government were offering £30,000, was to be entrusted to the wife of Captain Hugh MacDonald's superior officer, Sir Alexander MacDonald of Sleat, now serving at Fort Augustus, the headquarters of the Duke of Cumberland. Neil MacEachen would be in charge of the Prince and Flora on the journey to Skye.

At the sheiling the Prince was introduced to Flora, who was told of the plan and was asked if she would play the part assigned to her. Only four persons heard that conversation, but none of the three who afterwards recorded their recollections are in agreement as to what transpired. Flora, on whom the scene must have made a deep impression, states that only with difficulty was she persuaded to take part in the plan. Captain O'Neil says she refused on the ground that it would ruin her friend Sir Alexander Mac-Donald, but according to the faithful retainer Neil Mac-Eachen "she joyfully accepted of the offer without the least hesitation." For my part I take Flora at her word, because it is not incompatible with the evidence of Captain O'Neil, whereas Neil MacEachen's recollection has helped to weave a romantic story about one of the most practical and least romantic women in history.

Whatever happened at the interview, she set out next day, Saturday, 21st June, for Lord Clanranald's residence at Nunton in Benbecula, where the details of the plan were to be settled. After crossing the south ford she was arrested in Benbecula and detained for the night, but on the Sunday morning her stepfather Captain Hugh MacDonald had her released. As the two were having breakfast Neil MacEachen, who had also been arrested on the Benbecula shore, was brought before the Captain, who ordered his release. He had been sent by the Prince to find out how the plan for escape was progressing, and was now told to return to the hiding-place in Glen Corodale with instructions that the Prince should immediately make his way to Rossinish at the north-eastern corner of Benbecula. There Flora and the Clanranalds, with a boat and crew for the voyage to Skye, would meet the Prince and his two attendants.

From Glen Corodale to Rossinish is fifteen miles as the crow flies, but allowing for detours around lochs and inlets of the sea the distance must be nearer thirty miles, and yet the Prince with Captain O'Neil and Neil MacEachen were there late on the night of Tuesday, 24th June. Every day one or other of his companions walked the seven miles to Nunton to hurry the plan of escape, and on Friday evening, 27th June, Flora, accompanied by her brother Angus, Lady Clanranald, and her daughter Margaret, arrived at Rossinish. As the party were having supper news came that a large force under General Campbell had landed in the neighbourhood, and so supper was resumed at 5 a.m., Saturday, 28th June, on the southern shore of Loch Uskavagh, which they crossed by boat. At 8 a.m. Lady Clanranald learnt that General Campbell was at Nunton and had summoned her to meet him there, and so she and her daughter took leave of the Prince. Flora then persuaded Captain O'Neil to return with her brother to Milton, and as soon as they had gone she produced the clothes in which the Prince was to be disguised. At 8 p.m. that night Flora MacDonald, Betty Burke the maid, and Neil MacEachen entered the boat that was to take them to Skye.

At first the weather was good, but when about a league
(three miles) off the land the boat encountered a strong
breeze and a rough sea. On the Sunday morning, 29th June,
when sailing up the eastern coast of Skye the boat was fired
at by Militia men stationed at Ardmore Point in Vaternish,
but there is no authentic record that any damage was done.
At 2 p.m. they landed at the little bay of Kilbride in Trotternish, near Monkstadt, the residence of Sir Alexander Mac-
Donald, whose wife, Lady Margaret, was at home and was
at that moment entertaining some of the Militia officers to
dinner. Fortunately Flora left the Prince on the beach
whilst she and Neil MacEachen made their way to the
house, where at once she was questioned by one of the
Militia officers as to the whereabouts of the Prince, but so
calm were her answers that his suspicions were disarmed.
Amongst others present at Monkstadt House was Sir Alexander's chamberlain, Alexander MacDonald of Kingsburgh,
and to him she told the truth, which he in turn passed on to
Lady Margaret.

Immediate arrangements were made to get the Prince
away from the vicinity and Neil MacEachen was sent to
conduct him to a spot near Scudiburgh, a mile south of the
bay, where Alexander MacDonald would meet him between
eight and nine in the evening. MacDonald brought a
bottle of wine and some biscuits for the Prince, and they set
off on their ten-mile walk south to Kingsburgh House,
where they arrived at 11 p.m. They had gone a little over
two miles when at Uig they were overtaken by Flora on a
pony and accompanied by Neil MacEachen, as these two
were also on their way to Kingsburgh. Lady Margaret had
asked Flora to stay for a few days at Monkstadt, but she

declined as she wished to be with her mother at Armadale as soon as possible. The travellers did not arrive at Kingsburgh together, because Flora and Neil MacEachen kept to the road, whereas MacDonald took the Prince by a shorter path. At Kingsburgh the travellers had supper, and next morning before the Prince had risen Flora left for Portree to arrange with Captain Roy MacDonald, who had been wounded at Culloden and was lame in one leg, how to get the Prince out of Skye, now no safer than Benbecula, because the boatmen on their return to that island were arrested and had disclosed the identity of "Betty Burke." Later that day, 30th June, the Prince in a borrowed kilt and accompanied by a herd-boy, who did not know his companion's identity, walked eight miles to Portree in pouring rain. At the inn he was met by Flora and Captain Roy MacDonald, whom the Prince recognised and greeted with the words: "No ceremony here, Captain MacDonald."

The Prince was drenched to the skin and Captain MacDonald provided a change of clothing, but the Captain had considerable difficulty in persuading the Prince to adhere to the arrangements made for his escape, namely that he and the Captain should leave the inn after midnight and proceed to a place in Portree Bay where a boat was waiting to take the Prince to the island of Raasay four miles due east of Portree. Heavy rain continued, and when they were due to leave the inn the Prince wished to stay overnight, but the Captain insisted that it was unsafe to remain in a house which anyone might enter. One of the ironies of history is that in many cases it is the fugitive himself who wrecked the plans made for his escape, as witness the fifteen minutes' avoidable delay during the drive from Paris to

Varennes, but for which Louis XVI, Marie Antoinette, and their children would have escaped the worst horrors of the Revolution.

The Prince, having agreed to leave, said farewell to Flora at the inn, and their parting, according to Captain Mac-Donald, so far from being romantic was as follows: "The Prince, turning to Miss, said, 'I believe, Madam, I owe you a crown of borrowed money.' She told him it was only half a crown, which accordingly he paid her with thanks. He then saluted her, and expressed himself in these or like words, 'For all that has happened I hope, Madam, we shall meet in St. James' yet.'" Even in adversity the Stuarts had royal manners.

Such is the simple and noble story to which many fictitious and even ignoble additions have been made by imaginative writers. Thus the guide at Dunvegan Castle asked if I wished to see the lock of the Prince's hair which he gave to Flora MacDonald. Now thanks to Bishop Forbes, whose "Lyon in Mourning" was compiled from manuscripts, from the testimony of Flora herself, and of eye-witnesses, I knew that the Prince never gave a lock of his hair to Flora. The truth is that at Kingsburgh House in the afternoon of 30th June, when Flora was many hours on her way to Tiree, his hostess Mrs. MacDonald asked the Prince for a lock of his hair—"The Prince laid his head in her lap and bad [1] Mrs. MacAlister [a married daughter of his hostess] cut off some which the ladies divided into two parts, each taking one." One of these is now at Dunvegan.

Equally fictitious is the story that at Kingsburgh Mrs. MacDonald and Flora "went to the bedroom just left by

[1] Commanded.

the Prince, folded up the sheets in which he had slept, and took possession of one each, and there pledged themselves to preserve them folded up and unwashed until their dying day, when these relics would become their winding-sheets." As we know, Flora had left the house before the Prince was up, and indeed he slept that day until the early afternoon. Again it was Mrs. MacDonald and Mrs. MacAlister who folded the sheets, but in this case both relics were retained by Mrs. MacDonald, who wished them to be used as her winding-sheet. Only one of the sheets was thus used, and after her death the other was given to Flora.

On 6th November, 1750, Flora was married to Allan, eldest son of Alexander MacDonald of Kingsburgh, and from 1763 they were living at Kingsburgh House, where in 1773 they entertained Dr. Johnson and Boswell. There is a preposterous story that the Doctor "slept in the same sheets in which the Prince had slept." I say preposterous, because in the event of this having happened either Johnson or Boswell, probably both, would certainly have mentioned it.

Sir Harold Boulton, an Englishman, wrote one of our finest Highland songs to a Highland air—

> " Speed bonnie boat like a bird on the wing,
>   'Onward,' the sailors cry:
>   Carry the lad that's born to be King,
>   Over the sea to Skye."

To that song ever the Highland blood runs faster, but that is no reason why the Highland or any other imagination should run riot to the extent of suggesting that Flora Mac-Donald was a most beautiful girl in love with the Prince, or still worse that she was his mistress. There was an old Highland lady, somewhat hazy about history, who on hearing this gossip exclaimed: "What nonsense! Her maid Betty Burke was there all the time she was with the Prince." In point of fact the Prince was only in the direct care of Flora MacDonald for the space of thirty hours. Hyperbole arouses antipathy, and in an English paper I have seen her described as "a Highland hag with the face of a horse," although possibly the writer was merely exhibiting his sense of humour.

She was born in 1722 at Milton, where her father, Ranald MacDonald, a cadet of the Clanranalds, was Tacksman.[1] But he died during her infancy and at the age of six she was deprived of her mother who was abducted and married by Hugh MacDonald of Armadale. Flora remained at Milton with her brother Angus until she was thirteen, when Lady Clanranald took her to Benbecula to be educated with the Clanranald children by the family governess. The child showed musical tastes, played the spinet well, and sang Gaelic songs. When she was seventeen she was invited by Lady Margaret, wife of Sir Alexander MacDonald, to stay at Monkstadt, and soon afterwards she accompanied the family to Edinburgh, where she and the MacDonald children were to finish their education. For some time she was at a boarding-school in the Old Stamp Office near the High Street, and then continued her stay with the MacDonalds in Edinburgh until the fateful summer of 1745 when they all returned to Skye.

Before referring to her looks as described in 1747 by Mr. Dick, "one of His Majesty's Messengers in London," let us return to the inn at Portree. After the Prince had

---

[1] A middleman who leases directly from the proprietor of the estate a large piece of land which he sublets in small crofts.

left for Raasay, Flora, accompanied by Neil MacEachen, returned to her mother at Armadale,[1] and when staying there received a message to go to Castleton, four miles distant, where Captain MacLeod of Talisker wished to question her. On her way to Castleton she was captured by soldiers and taken on board the sloop-of-war *Furnace*, where General Campbell was in command of the troops on board. By his orders she was treated with greatest consideration and was even allowed to go ashore to say good-bye to her mother. The *Furnace* brought her to Dunstaffnage Castle on Loch Linnhe in Argyll. From Dunstaffnage she was taken overland via Glasgow to Leith, where the *Bridgewater* was at anchor, and in this ship, in which she was detained from the beginning of September to the 7th of November, Captain Knowler "used her with the utmost decency and politeness." On 6th December she sailed for the Thames in the *Eltham* and, as she afterwards told Bishop Forbes, Commander Smith "behaved like a father." The *Eltham* arrived at the Nore, and on 28th November Flora was transferred to the *Royal Sovereign*, which brought her to the Tower of London on the 6th December 1746. She was soon released and placed in "the custody of Mr. Dick," at whose house she and other prisoners of the '45 had full liberty except as to their domicile. In London Flora went into Society and Lady Primrose collected a fund of £1500 for her benefit, but in July 1747, after the Act of Indemnity, all the prisoners were released from "the custody of Mr. Dick," and soon afterwards Flora returned to Scotland.

Mr. Dick writes in 1747: "She is a young lady about

[1] Several passages in the article about Flora MacDonald in the *Dictionary of National Biography*, 1893, require revision.

twenty [actually she was 25], a graceful person, a good complexion, and regular features. She has a peculiar sweetness mixed with majesty in her countenance; her deportment is rather graver than is becoming her years; even under her confinement she betrays nothing of sullenness or discontent, and all her actions bespeak a mind full of conscious innocence, and incapable of being ruffled by the common accidents of life."[1] What a charming tribute, and what a charming gaoler!

At the age of fifty-one she is described by Dr. Johnson as "a woman of soft features, gentle manners, and elegant presence." She was now the mother of seven children, five sons and two daughters, and when Dr. Johnson wrote: "We were entertained with the usual hospitality by Mr. MacDonald and his lady, Flora MacDonald, a name that will be mentioned in history, and if courage and fidelity be virtues, with honour"—he little knew that her courage was to be tested higher, far higher, that his host and hostess were on the brink of financial disaster, that soon they were leaving Kingsburgh never to return, and that already they had decided to emigrate with their family to North Carolina in the following year.

In August 1774 they sailed from Campbeltown on the *Baliol*, and on the Atlantic their ship was attacked by a French privateer, which was eventually driven off, but during the engagement Flora remained on deck and broke her arm, which was set by a young Skye surgeon who happened to be on board. The family were not long settled

[1] *Some Particulars of the Life, Family, and Character of Miss Florence McDonald* (sic), *now in the Custody of one of his Maiesties Messengers in London*, 1747.

in North Carolina when the American War of Independence began in 1775, and Allan MacDonald received a Captain's commission in the 84th Loyal Highland Emigrants. In this regiment his eldest son Charles also served, and both were taken prisoner at the Battle of Moore's Creek on 27th February 1776, but were returned to the Loyalists during an exchange of prisoners in the following year. Flora and her two daughters returned to Skye in 1779, but it was not until five years later that her husband rejoined her. At the end of the war (1781) he received a Captain's grant of 3000 acres in Nova Scotia, but for lack of capital was forced to surrender this property, and came to London in the vain hope of obtaining compensation from the Government. In 1787 he became Tacksman of Peinduin, which is some miles from Kingsburgh, and here Flora MacDonald died in 1790, aged sixty-eight, after suffering, as her doctor wrote, "much distress for a long time." Her death was announced in the *Scots Magazine* as follows:

"4th March, 1790—at Isle of Skye, Flora MacDonald,
Spouse to Captain Allan MacDonald, late of Kingsburgh."

She was buried in the graveyard of Kilmuir, where two and a half years later her husband was laid beside her, and to-day a high Iona cross, a landmark for those at sea, stands over their graves.

CHAPTER XVII

MY LONGEST WALK

BEYOND Milton a man with a horse and cart came out of a croft and accompanied me for a short distance. He apologised for not offering me a lift, but his horse would have enough to do in bringing a load of peat from the moor. The season had been wet and only now were the peats dry, but the moor where he was going was still a morass. He told me that already I was twelve miles from Loch Boisdale and this I knew to be a lie, but in my experience the inaccuracies of the islanders are spoken with a wish to please rather than to deceive.

The scenery was now more interesting, because for four miles the road ran parallel to the Mountains of More and by the roadside were numerous lochs. Towards the middle of the island is the small War Memorial:

"In three Continents and in the Deep they lie,
But in our hearts their deeds for ever are remembered."

Further on was a small one-storied police station, and if the strategic position for a castle is on the shore, the strategic position for a policeman is in the middle of an island, where he is equidistant from all places where his services may be required. At that moment the policeman came out, mounted a motor cycle, and rode to the south, where he would probably supervise the dipping of sheep. It was not in this police station but in a similar station on another island that

justice tempered by thrift was dispensed to a man named
Tosh, whose story I shall now relate. In Scotland minor
offences are tried by the Sheriff-Substitute, and in days
when the salary of a Sheriff-Substitute included his travelling
expenses justice was sometimes administered in a homely
fashion. Thus a Sheriff-Substitute found that he had to
travel much too frequently from the mainland to one of the
inner islands for the sole purpose of trying a man named
Tosh, whose offence consisted of being drunk and disorderly
once a month. There was only one policeman on the island
and to him the Sheriff-Substitute confided that the conduct
of Tosh was making serious inroads on his salary. "What
is the use," he continued, "of sending for me? Could you
not lock the man up in your police station for a couple of
days, send him off with a kick in the pants, and tell him not
to do it again?"

The policeman agreed, and for a time the new arrangement was carried out to the contentment of all concerned.
After a time, however, the policeman began to think. It
was a very hot day in summer, and the policeman perspired
as he dug up the potatoes in his garden. The midges added
to his troubles. Here he was in his garden working like a
slave, and there in the cool of the only cell in the police
station rested the miserable Tosh. Moreover, he had to
feed the man. The new arrangement was unjust to the
police and ought to be modified. So when the time came
for the customary kick the policeman refrained and spoke
to Tosh in a friendly manner. "See here, Tosh, you and I
are well acquainted, and if I promise not to arrest you when
you are drunk and disorderly would you have any objection
to being arrested for the same thing when you are sober?"

"Not at all," said Tosh, and for some months justice was administered to the satisfaction of the Sheriff-Substitute and policeman, although not altogether to the satisfaction of Tosh. Finally he rebelled, and when the policeman next entered the local inn to send Tosh home he refused to leave. "Now, now, Tosh," said the policeman, "you mind our honourable agreement that when you are drunk and disorderly you go home when I tell you."

"I'm not going!" said Tosh.

"Now, now, Tosh, if you don't go I'll have to use my truncheon."

"Then use your truncheon," shouted Tosh, "and to justify your truncheon you'll have to charge me with assaulting the police. And if you do that I'll be sent to Dunoon Prison, where there'll be no two days of digging in your garden!"

I had walked eleven miles from Loch Boisdale when my feet began to tire, so I ate a lunch of chocolate on the bank of a small stream running into Loch Fada to the west, and bathed my feet in the cold running water. This was refreshing because cold water applied to the feet or hands stimulates the adrenal reflex, or in other words the stimulus to the skin is transmitted through the sympathetic nervous system to the adrenal glands above the kidneys and adrenalin is poured into the blood stream, where it raises blood pressure and promotes a feeling of well-being. These interactions between body and mind are often forgotten, but Disraeli recognised them when he said: "Dyspepsia always makes me wish for a civil war."

At the northern end of the island there are more lochs than moors, and for two-thirds of a mile the road crosses

Loch Bee on an embankment. At the hotel on the bank of the south ford between South Uist and Benbecula I ordered tea, and after a twenty-mile walk was disappointed to find that with the tea there was only white bread, butter, jam, and biscuits from Carlisle. Devastation of the Islands! During tea I asked the girl who served if it was possible to cross the ford dry-shod and she cheerfully assured me that the ford was now dry, albeit a moment later on looking out of the window I saw plenty of water. So I left the hotel bare-footed, and on the way down to the ford regretted this pre-mature removal of shoes because there was metal on the road.

The ford, here three-quarters of a mile wide, is only dry during low-water springs in fine weather, and a post on the opposite bank below the Creagorry Hotel gives the direction in which it is safe to walk, because the stretch of firm sand is limited. Thus when half-way across I saw a rock a few yards to the west and surrounded by a pool in which were anemones. To have a better look at the pool I left the straight and narrow path only to find that I was walking into quicksand. A horse and cart may cross until nearly half tide, and the dangerous part is on the Benbecula side, where at high-water springs there are depths of from six to eight feet. This was the ford crossed by Flora MacDonald and by Neil MacEachen, but Prince Charles probably crossed by boat further east, as he must have known that at Creagorry he would most likely have been arrested.

From Creagorry I set out to walk the four and a half miles across Benbecula to the North Ford, and in the scenery of Benbecula I was disappointed because the island belies its name and not one ben or hill is to be seen above the moors and lochs. When within half a mile of the ford I was overtaken by a car from the Creagorry Hotel and the driver gave me a lift. Moreover, he told me that I was in luck, as indeed I was, because at 7 p.m. he was to meet a gentleman who was crossing from North Uist in a trap from the inn at Carinish, and I could return in the trap. This ford, although only one and a half miles wide, is so encumbered with sandbanks, quicksands, rocks, and islands, that it must be crossed by a winding track four miles long and very dangerous. No stranger in his senses would attempt to cross on foot, but I had imagined for no reason at all that a horse and trap would be available on either side, whereas the trap from Carinish must be ordered in advance.

At the ford there was no sign of the trap, which was hidden by islands, and the driver asked me what I would have done had I arrived here by myself. There was a ruined cottage by the roadside, and I told him that I would have slept in the shelter of its walls. In the morning low water was at 7.30 a.m. when I would await the trap, but as he had explained, there might be no trap unless someone was crossing and I would have had to walk back to the telegraph office at Creagorry. Nevertheless, I would have enjoyed sleeping out, because in London if you sleep on a bench you may be arrested and sent to prison if you happen to have less than fourpence in your pocket. For some reason which I cannot fathom it is against the law of England to be found sleeping out of doors "without visible means of support." And yet why should I, who raised my voice against hikers who wished to sleep in a barn, now want to sleep out of doors, although I had more than four pennies in my pocket? Sheer inconsistency, and I am no better than my friend Angus Mackongas.

We are all more or less inconsistent, but only our major whim-whams, such as the doping of a Derby favourite by an Archimandrite, make front-page news and lead to long sentences of penal servitude. Yet many a promising career has been curtailed by a minor whim-wham. In the case of Angus Mackongas a whim-wham led to the missing of at least a knighthood—I say at least, because he was childless and for that reason a baronetcy might have been possible. Angus began on the lowest rung of the ladder, to be precise as a bricklayer's assistant, and by reason of bodily strength and forceful personality became the leading contractor in the Scottish town where he lived, prospered, and died. I regret the necessity of announcing his death so early in the story, but am advised that this is a good way of precluding actions for libel. If I said that this character was fictitious my readers might lose interest and, what is of greater importance, a jury might not believe it. Therefore I declare that the man is dead.

In subscription lists for charity no name was more prominent than that of Angus Mackongas. To the Christmas Appeal for Widows and Orphans he donated £50, and was likewise a stout supporter of the Society for the Prevention of Cruelty to Children, Quarriers' Homes, the Poor Sisters of Nazareth, and the Waifs and Strays. In the larger sphere of national politics his patriotism was unquestioned, and "Buy British" was the slogan with which in moments of relaxation he entertained his friends. "Take my tip, old man, and buy British," was his favourite saying, the advice being enforced by a friendly slap on his listener's thigh above the knee. A big-hearted man was Angus Mackongas, and to his credit be it noted that in business he bought

British in preference to inferior foreign materials, provided the latter were more expensive.

During infancy, childhood, adolescence, and early manhood Mr. Mackongas had never left his native town, even on holiday, but when at the age of fifty he became Angus Mackongas, Ltd., and secured contracts from overseas to build harbours, bridges, and other works of public utility, it was necessary that he should cross the oceans. Then, to the astonishment of his friends and to the annoyance of the local Travel Bureau, he insisted on booking passages in foreign liners. The old slogan of "Buy British" was still on his lips and this made his aversion to travelling on British ships the more remarkable.

It was the Provost of his native town who unravelled this little whim-wham on the night when Angus called to take those soundings which are so necessary a preliminary to wire-pulling. "I've been thinking," said Angus, "that our friends would take it as a compliment to the town if the Government were to give me a handle to my name. Not that I care two hoots aboot it."

"Aye," replied the Provost in a voice of non-committal, questioning affirmation.

"Weel, since we're both of the one opinion you might drop a hint to oor Member of Parliament."

"Aye, I might do that," said the Provost.

"Is there anything agin me?" demanded Mackongas, raising his eyebrows and eyeing the Provost.

"No, no, Angus," said the Provost, "there's nothing agin you. Yet folks do say that on your travels you avoid British ships, but that's your ain business, and maybe ye prefer the foreign cooking? Maybe on doctor's advice?

194

A statement from yourself to the local paper would clear things up."

"I've never had a doctor since the day I was born, and its got nothing to do with the cooking—cuisine, they call it."

"Well, Angus, it's most mysterious to all your friends."

"There's nothing mysterious aboot it. It's as plain as a pike-staff. Maybe I've heard wrong, but I've heard said that on foreign ships, in case of accidents—fires, mutinies, collisions, or suchlike—there's no damned nonsense about women and children first."

At 7.30 p.m. the trap arrived, and out there stepped a young, well-dressed, and cheerful Glasgow boot and shoe manufacturer, who in the summer travelled for his firm and so combined business with fishing. On seeing my fishing rod he hailed me as a brother angler and asked what the fishing was like in Benbecula. I told him the truth, that I had not yet set up my rod, but that from all accounts the fishing in Benbecula and South Uist was excellent.

Then I entered the trap and was driven by a short, dark-haired man, Mr. Hector Mackenzie of the Carinish Inn, on the four-mile journey across the ford. The track was marked by stone beacons on the rocks, but every few years the route has to be changed on account of the shifting sands. In fine weather this ford may be crossed on foot by those who know the way, except during the hour before and after high water, but in bad weather it is often impassable even at low-water springs. Some of the rocky islets are not submerged at high tide, and on these many a traveller overtaken by the incoming tide has been marooned for the night.

"Only two weeks ago," said Mr. Mackenzie, as the trap

195

lurched with one wheel axle-deep in water which had already reached the belly of the horse, "two hikers called at the inn and asked for directions to cross the ford. Now I knew they were poor and I didn't want their money. So I told them the way, but mind you" [here the trap lurched again and I wondered if we would all have to swim for an island] "I was not happy about them, and I was glad when an hour later a gentleman arrived in a car and asked to be taken across in the trap. All the way over I looked for the hikers, not a mixed couple but just two young lads. At last I saw them and they were walking due east straight into a quick-sand. I stopped the trap and shouted at the top of my voice until at last they heard me and turned back to follow the trap. Yes, you need to know this ford."

He himself had known the ford since childhood, for he was born at Carinish. As a youth he went to Canada, then served in France with the Canadian Highlanders, and after his father's death returned to Carinish to look after the inn with his mother and sister. His mother was still living but was now very ill, and they could not have me at the inn that night. "When I was a young boy," he said, "there were a hundred scholars at the Carinish school and two teachers. Now there are only twenty with one teacher. Mind you, I don't think what they call birth-control has anything to do with it, but the population is getting old."

Halfway across the ford is the island of Grimsay, a centre of lobster fishing at which two steamers call weekly in summer. The industry would be more prosperous if the fishermen built at the cost of a few pounds an open floating tank in which the lobsters could be kept alive and fed with white fish before being sent to Billingsgate. Lobsters only attack one another when starving, and as things are many die before reaching London, where dead lobsters are never sold. At Mallaig and at Oban are middlemen who buy boxes of lobsters from fishermen on the inner islands and keep the lobsters in open floating tanks so that they have a stock from which the demand of the London market may be supplied, but even these men are fortunate if one-third of their lobsters are alive on reaching the market.

At Carinish Mr. Mackenzie refused to accept the fare, which is ten shillings: "No, no, I had to come in any case, and I'm glad of having had a great talk. Aye, and many's the time I've taken your friend Doctor Gibson over the ford. A fine man, and he had known every one of my officers in France. Well, well, just give me what you like."

From Carinish I walked two and a half miles to the clachan, a few houses on the circular road running round the island, and in one of these I got a room for the night. The lady of the house was away and her daughter, on vacation from a Glasgow training college for teachers, was in charge. My supper would be ready in an hour, and afterwards I could have a hot bath. I told her my name and that having walked over twenty-eight miles I did not wish to be called in the morning, whereupon she shook hands and said that my supper would be ready in ten minutes. While awaiting supper I opened at random André Maurois on Disraeli, and read: "Men, in their long journey towards death, picture to themselves a variety of pleasant halts; a few steps more, the day's stage will be ended, and then will come the hour of repose round the fire. But in time's continuous flow there is neither repose nor halt. Every evening the past is a dream, the future a mystery."

That night I had twelve hours' continuous sleep, and next day walked ten miles along the west coast to Baleloch, where I got a room at the Old Manse on Loch Hosta, a fresh-water circular loch about half a mile across and a third of a mile from the sea. I was fortunate in getting a room, because from the following day the house had been let to shooting tenants, whose heavier luggage was already in the hall. On the way I stopped at a farmhouse to ask for butter-milk and was given fresh milk by the farmer's wife, who told me that her husband now aged thirty-six had decided to study medicine and had just graduated at Glasgow where he was taking up a hospital appointment.

In the evening I strolled round Loch Hosta, and after-wards read from the Lectures and Essays of Sir Stafford Henry Northcote, first Earl of Iddesleigh, whose works I commend to any reader who may be suffering from insomnia, as witness the following paragraph: "He has wonderfully ordained that increase of power and greatness shall always and of itself, as it were, bring with it unavoidable ruin to the state where it is found; and that the very success which is raising the nation in the eyes of the world shall be ever, in effect, working its destruction. It is not to the sea alone that He said 'Thus far shalt thou come, and no further'; human greatness, too, has its bounds which it can never pass."

At 6 a.m. I rose for a bathe in Loch Hosta, but had to walk out for over fifty yards before reaching a depth in which I could swim, and after breakfast I called on the Rev. Donald Macdonald, aged eighty-four, who had retired after his jubilee in the Church of Scotland and was now living in a neighbouring farmhouse. This tall old man in a dressing-gown received me in his library, and indeed he was a great reader of history, for every month he received a parcel of books from a lending library in the South and never purchased a book until he had read it. "Welcome, welcome," he said, holding my hand for a long time. "Your father and the other Commissioners in Lunacy always used to call on me," and then as we sat in chairs side by side he patted the shoe on my right foot, as I had one leg over the other: "And so you walked here. Well, well, well," and again the shoe was patted. He told me that he had been happy in North Uist—"There's no religious bitterness here. No, no, and many a Wee Free have I married and buried. In Harris you'll find bitterness, because at the Disruption in 1843 all the ministers came out and some of the old people will still tell you that the Church of Scotland is 'Christ denying, God defying.' But there's no bitterness in the southern islands, and there you'll even find Catholic and Protestant living in peace." At that I mentioned that I was a Catholic. "Well, well, that makes no difference to my welcome, no, no, no," and again the shoe was patted.

Of all dissensions those concerning religion may be the most bitter, but analysis will often show that this bitterness has a political rather than a religious basis. Thus some ten years ago when I visited Liverpool with the object of re-suscitating the Guild of St. Luke, a guild of Catholic doctors, I was astonished to find that English Catholic doctors would not consult with Irish Catholic doctors, and *vice versa*, and since both professed the same faith their differences were obviously purely political.

At noon I set off on a seventeen-mile walk to Loch Maddy on the east coast, where after midnight I would go on the *Lochmor* to East Tarbert, Harris. It was a warm day and

I was beginning to wonder whether there were not dis-advantages in walking over islands, when a private car over-took me and stopped. A lady was driving and it was obvi-ously a family car, because in front she had two children whilst in the back were her husband and the eldest daughter. The lady beckoned me and then asked: "Where are you going?"

"To Loch Maddy," said I.

'That settles it. Would you like a lift?"

"Most kind of you, but you haven't room."

"There's plenty of room. One of the children can sit on the back seat, and you can squeeze in in front."

Thus the seating arrangements were altered and I found myself being driven to Loch Maddy.

"It's providential that we met you," said the lady.

"It's I who should say that."

"No, the fact of the matter is that we were having a family discussion as to where we should go, and I said, 'Let us give that man a lift and go wherever he is going.'"

They were pleasant people, and all else I know about them is that their name was Stewart and that they came from Perthshire. If this ever meets their eyes they will know that I remember them gratefully.

Loch Maddy is the most remarkable sea loch in the Hebrides, because although only a mile wide at the entrance its ramifications into creeks and bays make a coastline of three hundred miles. Here I arrived, thanks to the kind-ness of the motorists, sooner than I had expected, and from 5 p.m. to 11.30 p.m. I was entertained by the local doctor, Dr. McLeod, and his wife who was also a doctor. I had never met them previously, but they explained that they were accustomed to friends waiting in the house until the *Lochmor* arrived. In their garden I saw the only tree that I can recall in North Uist.

The doctor, although he is a most competent general practitioner, favours what I would call rational dress, and in brown shoes, flannel trousers, a sweater, and Norfolk jacket, his appearance reminded me of those gentlemen who hold a towel for the Birmingham Bruiser or the Battersea Battler during their encounters in the ring. Indeed, the doctor tells with gusto the story of a smart commercial traveller who arrived at Loch Maddy in a car, and having cut his hand enquired for the doctor. The man of whom he enquired pointed to the doctor, who was looking over the sea wall, and instantly the commercial traveller came to a decision: "If that's your doctor, my hand can wait until I get to Inverness."

I found that the doctor had just returned from London, where he had been attending a post-graduate course. One of the lectures he heard was about pneumonia, and in the absence of the physician who was due to give the lecture it was given by a young doctor still in his twenties. Now any doctor must feel sure of his ground before lecturing to seasoned general practitioners about pneumonia, the Captain of the Men of Death or, as it has also been called, The Old Man's Friend, because of this disease many general practitioners have had more experience than some specialists. Nevertheless, Dr. McLeod enjoyed the lecture. "It was so up to date. The first thing to do with a pneumonia is to have an X-ray, so that you will know whether it's on the right or the left side. That means I'll have to send my pneumonias in the *Lochmor* to Stornoway, as we've no X-rays here. After the X-ray, if the disease is one-sided, you do an artificial pneumothorax to collapse the lung on the affected side, and as the general practitioner cannot do that himself he should send for a chest specialist."

"That treatment is merely on its trial," I interrupted.

"Never mind, it's up to date, and there was one thing I liked about that laddie who was teaching us. He was so well dressed."

CHAPTER XVIII

PILGRIM'S PROGRESS

EAST TARBERT, Harris, was reached by the *Lochmor* at 2 a.m. in darkness with a drizzle of rain, and I walked through the unlit village to the hotel, where no lights were showing. At the entrance I was passed by a car, out of which a man alighted with much luggage and a case of fishing rods. He rang the bell of the hotel, and we waited on the doorstep until a light appeared in the hall and the door was opened by the proprietor in trousers and shirt. There was a cordial greeting for the man with the luggage, but when I crossed the threshold the proprietor was surprised. "Have you booked? No, then I'm sorry but there's no room for you here. Every room is taken, and I've had to put beds into dressing-rooms. No room here at all."

"Good. It's not heavy rain, only a drizzle. I shall sleep out on the hillside in the heather," and I walked out.

"Stop!" called the proprietor, "are you daft? You'll get your death of cold. Come in here, and I'll give you a pillow and a rug on a couch in the lounge." This he did, and in the morning I was only charged for breakfast. After breakfast I found a lodging at Minch View, a small villa on the hillside above the post office, and after trying each of the three easy chairs in the sitting-room, I knew that Mrs. McCaskill provided comfortable lodging. Nor was I surprised to learn that her permanent lodgers were school teachers now on vacation. On the wall was a framed memorial of her only son—"Private D. W. McCaskill. Ypres. 22nd March 1918, aged 36 years." On the mantelshelf was a pokerwork text—"A clock helps us to remember the hours; a cheerful friend helps us to forget them"; and on the landing upstairs outside my bedroom door was a large coloured picture, calculated to inspire the most timid lodger with a sense of security, because it portrayed "Mr. Gladstone introducing the Home Rule Bill in the House of Commons, April 13th, 1886." The aged statesman wore a black frock coat, with silk lapels, brown waistcoat and trousers, a dark blue and white bow tie, a wing collar, and in his buttonhole a white rose.

Harris, which would be an island were it not joined to Lewis by a narrow stretch of land, is the wilderness of the Hebrides, consisting for the most part of bleak moorland broken by huge glacial polished boulders and hills of scoured archaic rocks. I went across and round the island, a distance of forty-eight miles, in a small motor bus for the modest fare of eight shillings, a journey recommended to those who like motoring thrills. The bus looked very old, and when the driver, behind whom I sat, asked me how old I thought it was, I said for the sake of politeness that it looked ten years old. "Only two years ago it was new," said he "but you'll understand its present condition when you see the road."

The surface of the road was rough, the sides unprotected, and it went up and down like a switchback with many a hairpin bend. Here and there, alongside and in other places far below the road, were mountain tarns whose water looked the blacker in contrast to the white water-lilies on the surface. On the west side by the shore was some pastureland,

and near some of the crofts small patches of corn were growing on virgin soil between boulders. Along the south-western shore is an eight-mile stretch of sand with little seaweed, and on this sunny day with a westerly breeze the colours of the sea from the depths to the shallows were indigo blue, olive and then apple green, and white were the waves breaking in sunlight on the level yellow sands.

At Rodel in the extreme south I found the place where I said good-bye to George Gibson at the end of *Arches of the Years* and where he prophesied that I would return to Obe when all the works of Lord Leverhulme had disappeared. At Obe there is now no industry, some of the houses built by Leverhulme have been bought by retired officials, others are occupied by squatters, and one of the half-built villas is used as a cow byre by a crofter living in a black house. It may be that my friend and I were too hard in our judgments, and no man has ever tried to benefit this island without losing a great deal of money. Lord Leverhulme bought the island from Sir James Matheson, himself a highlander, but who, nevertheless, was nearly ruined by an attempt to make tallow candles out of peat, and to-day the islanders show little interest in the experimental agricultural station founded by one of themselves, Mr. T. B. Macaulay, who made money in Canada.

At East Tarbert a spinning mill appeared to be flourishing and was in charge of a foreman, a pleasant, stout, middle-aged man, who came from Galashiels and was forthright in his opinions about snobbery: "That's the trouble with your black-coated worker, and how many bank clerks realise that most foremen earn more than they do? Of course to get on in industry you must be apprenticed to learn your trade.

At Galashiels I was apprenticed for seven years, and it cost my parents £20. That's not much considering the damage an apprentice may do. Only this morning a lad here did twenty-five shillings' worth of damage—that's what the repairs would have cost if we sent the part away, but as I'll do the repairs myself it will only cost five shillings. That's the best of being apprenticed in a big factory, you're qualified to do any job that may arise from a breakdown. Holidays? Well, I had a day last month in Glasgow to see the Exhibition, and I took my daughter aged twelve. I spent the time in the Machinery Hall, which was fine, and she spent her time in the Clachan, which they say is the most popular exhibit. But my daughter saw what was wrong with it. There were no hens or sheep, and where did you ever see a Highland village without a hen or a sheep wandering about?"

The mill buys wool from crofters, washes it, dyes it with chemical dyes, teases it, cards it, and then spins it into threads, which are then woven into Harris tweeds at the mills in Stornoway. I learnt that there are many qualities of wool, ranging from the fine curly wool under the neck of the sheep to the coarse straight hair that lies beneath the wool on its back. This explains the mystery of why the underclothing, marked "Pure Wool," which you may buy at sales in the great merchandising stores for 3s. 11½d. a garment, feels when worn next a sensitive skin about as comfortable as a hair shirt. It is of pure wool, but it is made from the straight hairs under the fleece. The finest wool is Merino, and that is expensive because the curly hairs are so short that forty per cent. is lost in the carding.

For the industry in hand-woven Harris tweeds, the mill

teases, cards, and spins wool that has already been washed and dyed by crofters who use the hand-loom for weaving. Wool is teased quicker by machinery than by hand combing, the carded threads are more even, and the spun threads are more uniform. Thus machine-spun threads may have anything from three to sixty twists per inch, seventy-one yards of thread weighing one ounce, and in every inch there will be the same number of twists, an accuracy which cannot be obtained by hand-spinning.

The crofters use natural dyes. From the heather bloom they obtain a brown dye, from the roots a green dye, and from seaweed a purple dye. All dyes need a "mordant," a substance which will fix the colour to the wool, and as a mordant the crofters use soot mixed with stale human urine, which contains ammonia, and it is this last which gives to home-made Harris tweeds their agreeable and distinctive odour. The hand-weaving of cloth is hard and continuous work, but a crofter engaged in this industry may earn from £3, 10s. to £4 a week.

From East Tarbert the road to Stornoway crosses the mountains of South Lewis, where winding sea lochs come far inland in the valleys and on the lochs are isles, some wooded. Having come to Stornoway by bus, I walked back on the loch road for two miles to see the Macaulay experimental farm, built on one of the wettest and most unfertile peat bogs on the island. Even with deep drains around every quarter acre, only the surface of the land is now dry, and by jumping upon it one can feel the spring of the wet, spongy peat beneath. It is as difficult to drain this peat as it would be to drain a dish of curds or junket, by reason of its gelatinous texture, and lack of frost had made the land unfertile because, where there are severe frosts, as in the Frisian islands, the peat cracks, sand enters, and the soil becomes more porous.

Nevertheless, some remarkable and successful experiments have been made, as witness the quarter acre that was ploughed, dressed with cow manure, sown with hay and clover, and is now good pastureland. A neighbouring half acre was also ploughed, dressed with artificial fertilisers, sown with hay and clover, and in place of pasture produced nothing except deer grass and moss. Here also I saw fifty varieties of grass being tested on treated peat soil, and the most successful was Timothy.

To encourage the crofters an acre of peat soil was ploughed, treated with sand and basic slag, sown with hay and clover and was now a field of pasture worth £5 a year, and would be worth £5 a year for three or four years, when another dressing of sand and basic slag would be required. I saw this acre in its second year when it was feeding one sheep and was only half cropped. And the cost? £2 for the sand and basic slag and £3 for fencing off the field. If forty crofters contributed £2 each they could have forty acres of pasture on which stirks could be raised in place of sheep, and once the improvement had paid for itself more and more of the common land could be brought into cultivation.

From the experimental farm the crofters could borrow a motor tractor plough, but in spite of this inducement none of the crofting communities would adopt the plan. There was always at least one crofter who held out and demanded that "the Government" should pay for the fencing, despite the demonstration that their capital expenditure of £5 a head would be recovered from the land in the following year.

Thus a philanthropic attempt to improve the land has met with no better response than Lord Leverhulme's efforts to make the island a centre of modern industry. Even with the existing crops many of the crofters are short-sighted in growing oats with a long straw, the latter to be used for bedding, whereas it would be more profitable to use a quicker growing oat and to take in more land, but to exhortations from agricultural experts the crofters reply: "We must take what the land gives us."

That evening I went to a Stornoway boarding-house recommended by a tall young man whom I had met two days previously at Rodel in the south of Harris. We had arrived at the same time at the door of St. Clement's, a pre-Reformation church, and had found it locked. "That settles it," said I, "we can't see the inside of the church."

"Yes, we can," replied the young man, "if you wait here while I run for the key." Off he ran, a distance of half a mile, for the key, and so we both saw the inside of the church and signed our names in the visitor's book. It is a very good idea to keep a visitor's book within ancient monuments, because if you are allowed to sign your name you are less tempted to carve your initials on venerable stones, and if you happen to be a criminal your signature might give you an alibi, provided you are really on holiday. Yet I have known a case where the signing of visitors' books led to a regrettable misunderstanding. A priest, the Rev. William Shakespeare now of Droitwich, was visiting Stratford-on-Avon, and after twice signing his name was taken aside by an irate guide who said: "That's enough of this nonsense. If you do it again you will stay outside the next place. In your cloth you should know better." In the churchyard at Rodel we also saw an interesting tombstone to one Donald Macleod of Berneray, whose claim to be remembered is that "in his 75th year he married his third wife, by whom he had nine children, and died in his ninetieth year, the 16th December, 1755." Truly, an Indian summer.

At supper in the boarding-house I was glad to see the young man, although he took little part in the general conversation, which was mostly between myself and an Aberdeen Doctor of Agriculture now in the Government service. The company included another Government official from one of the many Departments that administer our affairs, a nondescript married couple, and the inevitable homeless lady of uncertain age, with many rings on her fingers, who knows every boarding-house and *pension* from Stornoway to Mentone, including those on the Belgian coast.

Next morning the young man asked me if I would go with him on an excursion to the west of the island, to which I readily agreed, and it was he who made the arrangements, because at the bus office the girl said there would be no excursion unless ten people joined. He advised her to telephone the hotels for the other eight, and after an hour eight middle-aged ladies arrived to complete the party. Apparently they were attending a summer Gaelic school at Stornoway, and like all persons who attend such schools had become more Highland than the peat. Moreover, throughout the drive they waved their handkerchiefs to every man, woman, and child whom we passed on the road. For those reasons I was glad to sit at the back of the bus with the young man for company.

He was a school teacher in the South of Scotland, where his father was a miner, and every week-end during term this teacher cycled twenty miles from his lodgings near the school to his father's cottage, for such was his gratitude to the parents who had spared him from a life in the mine. His outlook on life was serious, and he neither smoked nor drank, but there was nothing priggish about him when he deplored the amount of alcohol consumed in Stornoway on Saturday nights. It was rather the remark of one who had observed all the implications of this aspect of life as accurately as Stacy Aumonier when he wrote that masterpiece in short stories—*The Two Friends*.

On the way to Carloway, seventeen miles west of Stornoway, I noticed that most of the "black houses," which I had seen in 1924, had been replaced by modern houses. For the building of these houses there is a Government subsidy of £240, which is given in materials and in the labour of one mason, all rough labour being done by the crofter and his friends, who receive a further subsidy of 3s. 6d. per cart load of lime or of shell sand. An annual rental of £4 repays capital and interest in sixty years. Many of these crofters have good bank balances, and those of their sons who are in the Mercantile Marine are generous, sending home from a quarter to one-half of their pay to the old people. Moreover in the Lews alone over 1700 men are in the Fleet Reserve.

At Carloway, on a hill in view of the loch, is a well-preserved broch or Pictish tower, a defensive structure peculiar to Scotland and the Western Isles. Most of the hundreds of brochs that once existed have been dismantled, their stones having been used for building houses, and only their outlines or earthworks survive as dunes. They were built after the Roman conquest of south Britain and

were in use until the end of the Viking period, and, therefore, date approximately from the sixth to the twelfth
century.

The Carloway broch consists of a dry built circular wall
fifteen feet thick and thirty-four feet high, enclosing an
open inner circle twenty-five feet in diameter. The outer
face of the wall has a slight set inwards, but the inner face
of the wall is perpendicular. On the ground level a
tunnel-like entrance six feet high and thirty-six inches wide,
easily barricaded, leads through the wall to the inner
courtyard which is open to the sky. The fifteen-foot wall
is solid for the first ten feet, and is then divided into
circular galleries three feet wide between the outer and
inner walls, the galleries being formed of paving stones
set from wall to wall, the roof of one gallery being the
floor of the next above. In the walls of the Carloway
broch are five galleries, each the height of a man, and
reached from the inner court by a stair in the wall,
and this stair crosses all the galleries at one slope, a flat
stone in each gallery forming a landing. Each gallery is
ventilated by a stone rectangular window opening on the
inner court, the flagstone forming the top of one window
serving as the sole of the one above.

These brochs were analogous to modern air raid shelters
in as much as they were intended to protect the civilian
during marauding raids. The object of the enemy was to
murder the people and to carry away their cattle and sheep
before local forces could be assembled, and this purpose
the broch defeated. Into the central court the people drove
their cattle and sheep, and found safety for themselves in
the galleries between the massive walls. A broch could

only be taken by a long siege, and that meant a risk which the enemy were not usually prepared to accept.

As we stood in the open court one of the most authoritative of the ladies who had joined the excursion announced that originally the centre of the broch consisted of a series of circular rooms with wooden floors from wall to wall; and when I asked her the source of the wood she replied, "From the forests that once grew here." There she was in error because, although it is known from trunks of trees found below the peat that there were forests here after the last glacial period, all large trees had disappeared before the time when these brochs were built.

From Carloway we went seven miles southwards to Callanish on East Loch Roag, where there is one of the most remarkable sets of standing stones in Britain, because it is cruciform in outline, and the area enclosed by these monoliths of unhewn gneiss is 408 feet long by 130 feet wide. From the north an avenue between two lines of standing stones—originally ten stones on each side, but one stone is now missing—leads to a circle forty-two feet in diameter and surrounded by twelve stones. In the centre of the circle is the largest stone, seventeen feet high and five and a half feet broad at the base. To the east and west of the circle are four stones in line, and to the south is a single line of five stones. The authoritative lady stood with her back to the large monolith in the centre of the circle, and spoke as follows: "Here the Chief Druid stood, and when the rising sun on Midsummer's Day was in line with these four stones to the east, he plunged his dagger into the heart of the white-robed human sacrifice who lay on the altar which once stood here." I said nothing, because I do not suppose

213

that anything I could say or write will ever convince the majority of people that there is no evidence of standing stones having anything whatsoever to do with the Druids, or that the Druids had human sacrifices.

In 1858 five feet of peat, the accumulation of many centuries, was removed from the base of the stones, and in the circle they found a small chambered cairn, in which the people of the Bronze Age used to bury the bones of their dead, usually after burning the corpse. Within sight of these standing stones are seven smaller stone circles.

Near the Callinish standing stones is a black house, preserved as a museum, to which the public are admitted by a crofter's wife who lives next door, and on entering this black house I knew that I had done enough sightseeing for one day. Everything about that black house was wrong. There were skylights in iron frames on the thatched roof, and the walls were cemented. The larger portion of the house, once partitioned into living-room and bedroom, contained a spinning wheel, a hand loom, chests, dressers, a cradle, dirks, and pottery. Worse still, the caretaker announced that this portion of the house had once been the byre, and she was by no means pleased when I told her that the smaller portion, which she had described as the living-room, had once been the byre. To clinch the matter I asked her where the bedroom was, and to this she answered: "Next year we're going to build a bedroom on behind."

"I hope you'll do nothing of the kind," said I, "because if you do you will be showing a black house such as never existed from the Butt of Lewis to Barra Head." The black houses are fast disappearing from the islands and will soon be forgotten unless one of the few remaining ones is removed, stone by stone, and re-erected under cover in one of our large museums. May this be read by a millionaire!

That evening after supper, when strolling round the quays of Stornoway, I heard singing to the strains of the accordion—

> "The Bible stands though the hills may shake,
> It will firmly stand though the earth may quake;
> I will plant my feet on its firm foundation,
> For the Bible stands."

Now the only occasion on which I had literally planted my feet on the Bible was when as a child I placed a large family Bible on a chair and stood upon it to reach a shelf; and for this I was chided. Nevertheless, I sought the singers and found four young men beside a small open motor van, which was placarded with exhortations in large red letters, "Prepare to meet thy God," and on the other side, "The Blood of Christ hath blotted out my sins." The audience consisted for the most part of school children and, in the background, well-tanned old shellbacks smoking pipes as they leant against the harbour wall.

After the hymn singing, the eldest evangelist, a clean-shaven man of between thirty and forty, mounted the back step of the van and smiled upon us. "This morning as I and my friends were coming in our van across the country, I saw a little bull calf tethered by the wayside, and so I stopped the van in order that I might pat the little bull calf. But the little bull did not like being patted. He ran round and round me until I was held fast in the rope twisted round my legs. [Laughter from the children.] The only thing I could do was to ask my friends to come from the van and set me free. How many of you here to-night are held in the chains of sin? Some years ago in Wales I saw a little lamb whose head was stuck between the bars of a gate. Its ears prevented it from withdrawing its head, and so I went to the assistance of the little lamb. But the mother sheep did not trust my assistance, and butted me as I was rescuing her lamb. [More children's laughter.] I was once sitting by the wayside in the middle of Egypt, preaching to ten Bedouin and an old brigand who had robbed and killed many people. I could not speak their language, but my interpreter told them what I was saying, and they were all converted. Many years after, I returned to the middle of Egypt, and this time it was so hot that I had to preach in a shed, and at the back of the shed I saw the old brigand. He had grown cold and had been robbing and murdering again. Practically every one of you here can read either English or Gaelic, but in Egypt they cannot read and you must tell them stories. When I was at college I thought theology a wonderful subject, but in the Mission field your theology will not help you, only the Bible stories will help. The East loves a story, and in the shed I could see that they loved my stories, and they knew the end of the story before my interpreter had finished translating. The old brigand was in tears. Has anyone here," and now the speaker raised his voice, "grown cold after accepting salvation? Memory is a wonderful thing. We remember what we don't want to remember, and forget what we should remember. I tell you," and his voice now carried the fifty yards I had drifted from the meeting, "that there is no Power in Heaven, on Earth, or in Hell than can undo the seal. You are sealed with the precious blood."

This remarkable speech caused me to meditate on the nature of oratory, an art now under a cloud since many speeches in the House of Commons, once the home of oratory, are read from typescripts prepared by private secretaries. One of the dictionary definitions of oratory is "eloquent speech," but to my mind it means more than that, and if you analyse a great oration you will note that every gesture and inflection of voice are in perfect harmony with the thoughts expressed, and that the speech, with which you may or may not agree, is hall-marked by sincerity.

Yet oratory is more than the gift of speaking sincerely. It is the art of giving spontaneity and vitality to thoughts and words already familiar to the speaker and to him alone, without the audience realising that his speech, either in thought or word, has been memorised; for if they perceive that the speech is a recitation, the speaker is an elocutionist and not an orator.

CHAPTER XIX

A HERRING FLEET

AT Stornoway I joined the Fishery Cruiser *Vigilant*, built to resemble a steam trawler, 131 feet by 23 feet beam, with real "gallows" fore and aft, and with a dummy wooden winch painted black on the foredeck. She has wireless telephony, and one afternoon Captain Murray, when listening in, overheard a conversation between two trawlers.

"I'm new to this coast. Can you tell me anything about this damned *Vigilant* that's supposed to be watching us?"

"You can spot her ten miles away; there's three things about her you can't mistake. There's no smoke because she's Diesel-engined; there's no gulls following her because she has no fish on board; and, lastly, she comes out of places where no self-respecting trawler would be seen."

Foreigners are less knowledgeable, and the *Vigilant's* last capture had been a large French sailing-boat, with a cargo of 1500 poached lobsters and crayfish in tanks. She was brought to Stornoway where the cargo was confiscated and sold, but her skipper stormed, wept, and shouted, "Assassins," when he was not allowed to buy his own cargo, for which he offered 8000 francs, approximately £24. Some of the mysteries of the law are as unfathomable as those of the sea, and the cargo was bought for £18 by a Stornoway dealer, who sent it to Billingsgate, thereby making a clear profit of £50 on the transaction.

In the afternoon we towed a 30-ton Zulu, the generic name for fishing-boats built on the Moray Firth, from Stornoway to the Port of Ness, two miles south of the Butt of Lewis, where her timbers would be used for fencing. Her engines had long since been sold for debt; it was many years since she had paid any harbour dues; and this was her last voyage. There was slight fog, a calm oily sea, and as we passed the promontory of Rudha Geall I saw the Braga rock three cables north-north-east of the promontory and two cables from the shore. This rock shows eleven feet at low tide, when there is nine feet of water in mid-channel between it and the shore. At high tide the rock is submerged, but with any sea there is swirling water around it. On this rock a trawler ran aground some years ago in the early hours of the dawn, and the crew abandoned ship, making their way along the coast to the Port of Ness, whence a motor bus brought the shipwrecked mariners to Stornoway, where they saw their ship at anchor in the harbour. Some crofters had seen the wreck, had rowed out in a boat, had found steam up with no water in the holds, and had brought her back to Stornoway. A curious story, and there must have been Hell's Bells ringing somewhere. Even stranger was the mystery of the wrecked fishing-boat reported to be drifting about the Minch with only the mast showing, which was most unusual because with any ballast a wrecked fishing boat would sink. Eventually one of the Fishery cruisers found the mast and towed it to Stornoway. It was the detached foremast of a large sailing ship and was floating upright by reason of the weight of the lower rigging. A Norwegian sailing ship had run ashore at St. Kilda, now a deserted island, and the crew had rowed to West Tarbert, a distance of over fifty miles. Their abandoned ship had then refloated herself and had followed them as far as the Sound of Harris, where she was finally wrecked and lost her foremast.

In Ness Bay the *Vigilant* anchored and launched her motor boat to tow the hulk into the little harbour, where about a hundred people were lining the quay. I was standing on the fo'castle deck when two boats came out from the harbour. "The Reception Committee!" said the second officer. "There's a hundred people on the shore, and I'll bet you not one of them will lend a hand, although we're doing this for their benefit. Just look at that harbour all silted up because they haven't the sense or energy to put an iron grid in one of the piers so that the sand would be washed out. They are lazy."

From Port of Ness we went round the Butt of Lewis, where vertical cliffs rise to a height of 94 feet, and on rising ground above the cliffs is the lighthouse 126 feet high. The sea was calm, but *Vigilant* rolled in the long Atlantic swell, and to the west were thunder clouds from which sheet and forked lightning fell on the sea. At sunset we turned and sailed through the night across the Minch, and through the Inner Sound of Skye to Mallaig. In Mallaig harbour was one of the few steam drifters that had made a profit out of the herring fishing that summer. Her skipper (and the men of Banff do not exaggerate) during the past nine weeks had made £300 and every man on board had made £60. He was an up-to-date skipper who had wireless telephony on board, and it was information gleaned from the air which had brought him to Mallaig, where his catch had sold for 55s. a cran (approxi-

mately 1000 herring) against a price of 25s. a cran in
Stornoway the same morning. Now that was an amazing
difference in the price of herrings at two ports some eighty-
five miles apart as the crow flies. Yet that is not the only
fishy thing about this business, because the lowest price at
which the consumer can buy a fresh herring from his
fishmonger is a penny and a half. Now if herring are sold
on the quay at 25s. per cran, which means ten for 3d.,
and retailed to you at 1½d. each, it means to my simple way
of thinking that the middlemen are making a profit of
400 per cent.

I say "to my simple way of thinking," because if I buy
shares for £100 and sell them for £200 I would reckon to
have doubled my capital and made 100 per cent. profit.
With that simple method of calculation our merchant
princes disagree, and, possibly for income tax purposes,
they reckon their profits on the selling price, so that my
profit would be reckoned at 50 per cent. This I learnt
from one of the great merchandising stores in London
when I asked them to stock *Sutherland's First Aid* to sell at
4d. net, which I was prepared to supply for 2d. per copy,
giving them a return of 100 per cent. In reply they pointed
out that their profit would be only 50 per cent. Only 50
per cent.! This means that no merchant can ever make
100 per cent. profit unless he obtains his stock for nothing!

Nevertheless, let us accept the rule of thumb as laid
down by our merchandisers, and then on the prices quoted
the middlemen of herring are making a profit of 80 per
cent. Moreover, even if herring are bought from the boats
at 55s. per cran, and sold at two and a half pennies in the
shops, the middlemen are making, to my way of thinking,

a profit of over 227 per cent., or according to their own method of calculation a profit of 56 per cent. And that is by no means the most fishy thing about the herring industry.

Near the harbour I saw a machine which removes the back-bone and guts from herrings before they are smoked into kippers over burning oak sawdust. This machine was invented, so I was told, by a Scotsman who, having received no encouragement for his invention in Britain, sold the patent rights to Germany, and four hundred of his machines are now leased to British curers. Each machine deals with fifty-two herrings per minute, and only one girl is needed to feed it. It was an ugly machine and I hated its inhuman precision. In the name of Progress what was it really doing? It was throwing a lot of girls out of work, was making profits for its manufacturers and users and was not reducing the price of kippers to the consumer. Incidentally, I learnt that consumers in Manchester and London will not buy kippers unless they are artificially dyed with what is said to be a harmless vegetable dye, but fortunately there are two curers in Stornoway who guarantee to supply undyed kippers by post. For their names and prices you must apply to the Town Clerk of Stornoway, because I have no financial interest in this business.

On returning to Stornoway the *Vigilant* lay one afternoon alongside a steam drifter the *Xmas Morn*, ninety feet by twenty feet in the beam, the two ships being separated by the latest and most effective type of fender—old motor tyres with which all drifters are now festooned when in harbour. I was walking round our deck and the skipper of the *Xmas Morn* was leaning on the side of his ship. On my first round of the deck I nodded to him, and when next I passed he took the pipe from his mouth, smiled, and said: "Hi, mister, a gull has been taking liberties with your back."

"Thank you," said I, "and it's a blessing that cows don't fly." A greaser cleaned my coat with a piece of cotton waste, and thereafter I had a talk with the skipper of the *Xmas Morn*.

The season had been a bad one for him, and he recalled the days when Russia was in the market and every man on board, for they shared profits and losses, had made as much as £300 in six weeks. He thought the fish curers might be responsible for bad markets, and from another reliable source I learnt that one day in Lerwick, after the first catches had been sold, the curers told the skippers of the other boats that the market was glutted and that they would pay 5s. for every cran of herring thrown overboard. The greatest uncertainty during this summer of 1938 was caused by the operations of the Herring Marketing Board. It was quite a usual experience after a night's fishing for boats to return to port only to find that by order of the Board no herrings could be sold, and consequently thousands of crans were thrown overboard. Some of the Clyde skippers were able to cross to Belfast and sell their catch, and one skipper defied the Board and sold his catch of Loch Fyne herring at Inveraray at so good a price that he treated himself to a long telegram to the Chairman of the Marketing Board, who was left in no doubt as to what that skipper thought about the Board.

All this was an example not only of a rotten economic system but also of grave social injustice, because whilst all this food was being wasted thousands of unemployed

families in Glasgow were living below the level of adequate
nutrition. In normal times it is sometimes necessary to
throw herring overboard, but these are "day-overs," fish
that have been on board for more than twenty-four hours
and are, therefore, unsuitable for curing and cannot be sold,
as the buyers can tell the freshness of herring by the brightness of the eyes. Indeed, things had reached such a pitch
of confusion that the Scottish Office appointed a Commission to enquire into the work of the Herring Marketing
Board. Meanwhile the German and some of the Aberdeen
boats were catching a lot of herring by trawling, but these
herring are not suitable for curing because the scales have
been rubbed off and the fish bruised in the trawl. "And
then there's the matter of luck," said the skipper of the
Xmas Morn, "for of two boats fishing side by side one
may get a heavy catch and the other nothing. I'm going
out to-night and if you see me back in the morning, come
on board and I'll give you enough herring for the *Vigilant*."

In the evening 135 steam drifters left the inner harbour
for a night's fishing. These vessels are called drifters
because they fish with drift nets, which form a perpendicular
barrier in the sea at a depth of two fathoms below the surface and extending for two or three miles. Pelagic fish,
such as mackerel and herring, which live near the surface,
are influenced by a change of light, and shoals begin to
move after sunset or before dawn, which are, therefore, the
best times for fishing. As a boy I have been out with the
fishing fleet on the Clyde in the days of sail, and then the
presence of herring was detected by striking the anchor
with a piece of iron, and if herring were alongside the noise
so startled them that they turned belly upwards for a mo-

ment and could be seen. The modern way is to tow a weighted piano wire astern and to note the change in vibrations when the wire is passing through a shoal, although this gives no indication of the direction in which the shoal is moving.

When the drifter reaches a likely fishing ground the long fleet of seventy or more nets, each fifty-five yards long and six yards deep, is "shot" by four men. The upper edge of each net is buoyed with corks, and as the nets are dragged on deck from the hold a canvas or a blue glass buoy is attached to the upper corners by twelve feet of rope. These buoys mark the position of the nets when shot and help to support them in the water. Another man looks after the netting, which has about thirty-four meshes per square yard, of a size which allows the head and gills to enter, but prevents the thicker bodies of mature fish from passing through the net. A third man passes the "seizings," short ropes from each of the two lower corners of the net, to the mate, who makes them fast to the "messenger rope," two to three miles of warp to which the lower edge of each net is attached. Once the fleet of nets has been "shot," twenty fathoms of messenger rope are let out to act as a "swing-rope," a mizzen sail is hoisted to keep the drifter into the wind, and then with her fleet of nets ahead the vessel drifts with the tide.

At night you can tell when a drifter is fishing because she must show two white lights so placed "that the vertical distance between them shall be not less than six feet and not more than fifteen feet, and so that the horizontal distance between them, measured on a line with the keel, shall be not less than five feet and not more than ten feet. The lower of these two lights shall be in the direction of the nets and both of them shall be of such a character as to show all round the horizon, and be visible at a distance of not less than three miles."

From time to time the messenger rope is hauled in, so that any fish in the nearest net may be seen, and after three or four hours the fleet of nets is taken on board. The messenger rope is hauled in on the capstan and passed down to the rope room, a dark cubby-hole seven or eight feet square, where a boy coils two or three miles of wet rope. One of the hands unties the nets from the messenger rope, two others remove and stow the buoys, and the remainder shake fish out of the nets into the hold. In the event of a heavy catch this means several hours of hard work, and once the last net is on board the drifter returns to port at full speed with the added help of jib and mizzen if the wind be favourable. The nets are drawn from the hold and piled on the foredeck, and on these wet nets I have seen tired men sleeping in the early hours of the morning.

Next morning I was up early, but there was no sign of the *Xmas Morn*, and the first boat to arrive was the *Ellen Girl*, who entered the inner harbour at 5.20 a.m. As each boat comes alongside, two of the crew carry a basket with a random sample of the catch to the auction market, where they leave it outside the door, so that each catch is dealt with in rotation, first come first served. The sample must be a random sample, because the buyers judge by the sample when bidding for the entire catch. If a buyer afterwards thinks the catch was not up to the sample displayed, he goes on board the boat with two referees who have power to alter the price at which the catch was auctioned.

226

The auction began at 7 a.m., and it was an auction in which no novice could have taken part. Two auctioneers, standing side by side on the rostrum, were selling different catches at the same time; in front of them were a score of buyers, and I was unable to detect the signs by which the latter were bidding. Yet there was never a dispute as to the identity of the buyer who bought the catch or as to the price, which varied that morning from 34s. to 36s 6d. a cran. After the main auction everybody rushed outside to bid for baskets of herring which were called "scum," and I did not understand why the "scum" often fetched a better price than the main catch, until I learnt that the "scum" was the perquisite of the engineers, who when nets are being hauled on board use a large landing net to recapture some of the fish, and often the large ones, that have fallen out of the net into the sea.

Afterwards I watched the fisher "lassies" gutting and packing herring in the curing yards around the quays in Stornoway harbour. The "lassies," aged from twenty to forty, are mostly dark-haired and bareheaded, although some wear a kerchief or a sou'-wester, and their costume of blue serge, short-sleeved blouse, and wide skirt to below the knees, where it covers the tops of their gumboots, is more practical than attractive. They form their own teams of three, and as each woman, in addition to a subsistence wage of 25s. a week, is paid 1s. per barrel of salted herring, it is difficult for a slacker or a weakling to find work in the yards. The team I am watching are putting on full, black, waterproof aprons hung round the neck and tied round the waist. One of the team has bandaged the palm of her left hand with coarse linen, and is standing beside a shallow wooden trough, four feet wide and raised some three feet from the ground. A man in a blue jersey pours a basket full of fresh herrings into the trough and freely sprinkles them with hard coarse salt, because the salt and the bandage will enable the girl to grasp the slippery fish. She picks up a herring in her left hand, inserts the point of a sharp knife into the belly behind the gills, and with one upward thrust the fish is gutted, the guts falling into a shallow tub at her feet. They will be sold to manure manufacturers. She then throws the fish, according to its size and quality, into one of three tubs behind her. She never looks back at the tubs but her aim is unerring and her speed is amazing. Thus in one operation the herring are both gutted and classified, in order that every barrel may contain fish of the same size and quality.

As soon as a tub is full, the two other girls carry it to a line of barrels in the background, but before the herring are packed they are thrown into "rousing tubs," in which there is no water but a large quantity of coarse salt in which the fish are stirred by hand so that each is well coated. A packer then picks up from the "rousing tub" an armful of herring and drops them into her barrel, the bottom of which is covered by a layer of salt, on which she packs the fishes bellies upwards. Over each layer of fish she throws another layer of salt until the barrel is filled with layers of herring separated by layers of salt. The barrel now contains about 750 herrings, and a good worker will pack three barrels every hour. The barrel when full is covered and allowed to stand for eight days, so that the salt may extract water from the herring and become saturated brine. In this process the herring shrink and the barrel is no longer full. A one-inch hole is now drilled in the bilge of the barrel, a third from the top, so that the supernatant brine may be run off, and more layers of herring and salt added until approximately 1000 herrings have been packed in one hundredweight of salt. The lid is permanently fastened and the barrel turned on its side to be filled to capacity with saturated brine through the bung hole, which is then corked. Russians and Poles, the largest consumers of salt herrings, eat them raw and also dip their bread in the brine, which has some nutritive value as it contains proteins and amino bases, extracted from the fish, but "for thy stomach's sake" I would not advise readers to follow their example.

Of all fish the herring is the cheapest and most nutritious, its food value at the time of writing being as follows:

Fish.	Calories per lb.	Price per lb.		Food value per shilling.
		s.	d.	
Halibut . .	258	2	6	103
Fresh Herring .	709	0	6	1418
Salt Herring .	1129	0	5	2709

In Germany salt herrings are boiled for twenty minutes and then steeped overnight in equal parts of vinegar and water, which bleaches them white. For British palates salt herrings should be rinsed in running water for twenty minutes and soaked overnight in sweet milk, which removes most of the salt, so much indeed that you may have to add salt to your herring in the morning. The fresh herring is best boiled or fried ungutted, to obtain the added flavour of the liver, and gutted before serving. Herring, be it noted, are clean feeders and live on a microscopic organism called "plankton."

I learnt more about plankton on the research ship of the Scottish Fishery Board, the *Explorer*, which happened to be in Stornoway harbour. As she cruises over the fishing grounds samples of the micro-organisms in the sea are collected every few hours in a muslin net. There are two kinds of plankton, pink and green, and when the pink variety is found it means that this area of the sea is a likely feeding ground for herring, whereas herring are not attracted by the green plankton, and the information thus gleaned is of value to the herring fleets. The scientist in charge, Dr. Rait of Aberdeen, also showed me how under the microscope the age of the haddock and the lemon sole may be told by markings on their scales. In the case of the plaice and cod age is told by the ear bones. Thus the plaice has two circular cartilaginous ear bones, which when cut across show concentric rings, one for each year of life like the ring marks on the cross section of a tree.

Most remarkable of all, I learnt both from Captain Murray and from the laboratory attendant on the *Explorer* that it is most dangerous to prick your finger with the sharp breast bone of the flounder, plaice, turbot, or of any flat fish. After an interval of from seven to ten days there is a sensation of heat in the injured finger, followed by suppuration, swelling of the glands at the elbow and armpit, and then by necrosis of the finger. A laboratory attendant in the *Gold Seeker*, another research ship, had lost all the fingers and the thumb of his right hand as a result of these wounds. On the *Vigilant*, Captain Murray had warned a boy to be careful when cleaning a flounder, but despite the warning the boy pricked his right forefinger. After ten days he lost the top of the finger, and later the whole finger. Now it seems to me, by reason of the interval, that the necrosis is not due to germs but to fish protein, and that raises the speculation as to whether it might not be possible to immunise the victim by minute injections of fish protein before the consequences of the injury developed. At all events, I cannot recall ever having read of this variety of wound in any textbook of surgery.

CHAPTER XX

THE DUNGEON AT DUNVEGAN

THE *Vigilant* landed me on the pier at the end of Loch Dunvegan and near the Castle which, so far from being gloomy, as I had anticipated from my reading, recalled a line from Shakespeare—"This castle hath a pleasant seat" —and overlooked the sea from a background of pine trees, azaleas, hydrangeas, and heather in bloom. For centuries the Castle has been the ancestral home of the chiefs of the MacLeods of Skye, the oldest family in Britain. Leod, the progenitor of the clan, was a son of Olaf the Black, King of Man and the Isles, whose father, Harold Hardrada, the Norse King, died fighting against King Harold of England at the battle of Stamford Bridge. In folk-lore the Castle is famous for its Fairy Flag, now a tattered oblong remnant of yellow silk with some red stitching and preserved under glass in the drawing-room, with the following inscription: "Given by the fairies to Ian, 4th Chief, about 1380. It brought victory to the Clan at the battle of Glendale in 1490, and at the battle of the Wall, Trumpan (Waternish) in 1580."

According to one legend this Ian was married to a fairy wife who after twenty years was recalled to her own people and left this magic flag, which if waved when the clan was in danger would save the MacLeods on three occasions. Twice it was waved in battle, and once to ensure the safe delivery of a son and heir. Another version is that during a banquet to celebrate the birth of this heir his nurse left him and joined in the festivities. The child became uncovered, awoke and cried. No humans heard his cries, but a host of fairies appeared and wrapped him in the magic flag. Most assuredly this flag is very old and unlike any other flag in Scotland. The late Sir Reginald MacLeod took it to the Textile Department of the Victoria and Albert Museum, where an expert said that it had been woven in Syria or in Rhodes, and suggested that possibly the flag had been brought from the east by Harold Hardrada, who is known to have visited Constantinople. "It was woven by the fairies," said Sir Reginald, and the tactful expert replied: "As Chief of the Clan, you know best."

The most circumstantial evidence that there is magic in this flag is the testimony cf the Rev. Norman MacLeod, D.D., a minister of the Church of Scotland and Chaplain to Queen Victoria. When sixteen years old he stayed at Dunvegan Castle, where he witnessed the fulfilment of a prophecy made by Coinneach Odhar, the Brahan seer, who was put to death over two centuries before the prophecy was fulfilled. This seer made many prophecies about the ruling families in the Highlands, and by reason of his forecast about the end of the Seaforths he was hanged or burnt alive by the wife of the chief of that clan. Long afterwards the Seaforth prophecy proved to be true in every one of its five pathological details, and even at the present time his prophecy about the Sutherland estates is being fulfilled. As regards the strange happenings at Dunvegan Castle, the man who was Moderator of the Church of Scotland and Chaplain to Queen Victoria wrote as follows:[1]

[1] *Memoir of Norman MacLeod*, D.D., London, 1876. Appendix, pp. 333-335.

"In the summer of 1799 the late General Norman Macleod . . . came to the manse of Morven, on his way to the
Isle of Skye. My father had been for some time tutor to
this brave and talented man, who was a distinguished soldier
in the American War, and obtained great renown afterwards
in India during conflicts with Tippoo Sahib and other chiefs.
He was frequently and severely wounded. Macleod insisted
that my father should allow me to go along with him to
Dunvegan; and I was delighted at the prospect of visiting
the place of which I had heard so many traditionary legends.
There were no steamers at that time, and we took our passage
in a small wherry from Oban. . . . We arrived at Loch
Brachandale . . . where we found horses and carts, with
crowds of people waiting our arrival; we reached the old
Castle of Dunvegan, where many of the gentlemen tacksmen
of the Macleod estates were waiting to receive us. . . .

"Dinner was laid in the great dining-room; the keys or
the cellar were procured, and a pipe of claret was broached,
and also a cask of Madeira wine of choice quality, brought
from India by Macleod; the wine was carried up in flagons
to the dining-room, and certainly they were very amply used
in the course of the evening. A bed was provided for me in
a small closet off Macleod's room, and I can never forget
the affectionate kindness which my greatly beloved chie
showed me while for three months I remained in his
castle. . . .

"One circumstance took place at the Castle on this
occasion which I think worth recording, especially as I am
the only person now living who can attest the truth of it.
There had been a traditionary prophecy, couched in Gaelic
verse, regarding the family of Macleod, which, on this

occasion, received the most extraordinary fulfilment. . . .
In the prophecy to which I allude it was foretold that when
Norman, the third Norman ('Tormaid nan' tri Tormaid'),
the son of the hard-boned English lady ('Mac na mnatha
Caoile cruaidh Shassanaich'), would perish by accidental
death; that when the 'Maidens' of Macleod (certain well-
known rocks on the coast of Macleod's country) became the
property of a Campbell; when a fox had young ones in one
of the turrets of the Castle, and, particularly, when the
Fairy enchanted banner should be for the last time exhibited,
then the glory of the Macleod family should depart—a
great part of the estate should be sold to others, so that a small
'curragh,' or boat, would carry all gentlemen of the name
of Macleod across Loch Dunvegan; but that in times far
distant another John Breac should arise, who should redeem
those estates, and raise the powers and honours of the house
to a higher pitch than ever. Such in general terms was the
prophecy. And now as to the curious coincidence of its
fulfilment. There was, at that time, at Dunvegan, an English smith, with whom I became a favourite, and who told
me, in solemn secrecy, that the iron chest which contained
the 'fairy flag' was to be forced open next morning; that he
had arranged with Mr. Hector Macdonald Buchanan to be
there with his tools for that purpose.

"I was most anxious to be present, and asked permission
to that effect of Mr. Buchanan, who granted me leave on
condition that I should not inform anyone of the name of
Macleod that such was intended, and should keep it a pro-
found secret from the chief. This I promised, and most
faithfully acted upon. Next morning we proceeded to the
chamber in the East Turret, where was the iron chest that

contained the famous flag, about which there is an interesting tradition.

"With great violence the smith tore open the lid of this iron chest, but in doing so a key was found, under part of the covering, which would have opened the chest, had it been found in time. There was an inner case, in which was found the flag, enclosed in a wooden box of strongly scented wood. [Probably cedar wood.] The flag consisted of a square piece of very rich silk, with crosses wrought with gold thread, and several elf-spots stitched with great care on different parts of it.

"On this occasion, the melancholy news of the death of the young and promising heir of Macleod reached the Castle. 'Norman, the third Norman,' was a lieutenant of H.M.S. the *Queen Charlotte*, which was blown up at sea, and he and the rest perished. At the same time the rocks called 'Macleod's Maidens' were sold, in the course of that very week, to Angus Campbell of Ensay, and they are still in possession of his grandson. A fox in possession of a Lieutenant Maclean, residing in the West Turret of the Castle, had young ones, which I handled, and thus all that was said in the prophecy alluded to was so far fulfilled, although I am glad the family of my chief still enjoy their ancestral possessions, and the worst part of the prophecy accordingly remains unverified. I merely state the facts of the case as they occurred, without expressing any opinion whatever as to the nature of these traditionary legends with which they were connected."

At the Castle I was received by the chief, Mrs. Flora MacLeod of MacLeod, daughter of Sir Reginald, in the library, and although my visit was unexpected and we had never met before, she gave me a Highland welcome: "So you have found your way to Dunvegan at last! I am glad to see you, and you are just in time for tea."

We talked of my walk through the islands, of their depopulation, and of the need of Government subsidies, and then I said, somewhat thoughtlessly, "Of course it's a question if the islands are worth subsidising as they export so little." Instantly the grey eyes of the chief, a tall, handsome woman of middle age, met mine. "We export brains. I don't know whether you think it worth while to preserve a race that has done so much for the Empire."

She was right, but before I could frame a reply the door opened and half a dozen people entered the library —Mr. John Colville, Secretary of State for Scotland, and members of the staff from the Scottish Office in Whitehall and Edinburgh, all of whom I had met before, and I do not know whether they were more surprised to see me than I was to see them. It was an official visit, and as the Secretary of State sat talking to Mrs. MacLeod the rest of us stood around a table where more tea and cakes were being served. Be it admitted that I felt an unholy joy in thinking that the Secretary of State, who had been most kind to me, was now hearing all about the export of brains and of the need for further Government subsidies.

When the official visitors had left I asked Mrs. MacLeod if I might see over the Castle, and as this was the weekly visiting day, when the Castle is open to the public on payment of a small charge in aid of charity, I went round with a guide. I told him that I did not wish to see the lock of Prince Charlie's hair, but that I would like to see the Fairy Flag, the portrait of that Norman MacLeod who perished in the *Queen Charlotte*, the autograph letters from Dr. Johnson and Sir Walter Scott, and the dungeon. To see the dungeon he led me along a passage and opened a massive oak door through which I entered, although at that moment one of the servants had called the guide away. I found myself in a vaulted stone chamber with no windows, but on the floor an electric bulb at the end of a flex gave a certain amount of light, and the only other furnishing appeared to be an oblong black mat on the flagstones. The place looked more like a cell than a dungeon, and I was walking around looking up at the vaulted roof when the guide entered. "This is a curious sort of dungeon," said I.

"This is not the dungeon," he answered.

"Then where is it?"

"At your feet."

I looked down and saw that what I had taken to be a black mat was an open trap-door in the flagstones and that I was standing on its brink. My first reaction was not fear but anger as I asked the guide the depth of the dungeon.

"Eighteen feet deep, sir."

"Then it's a damned good thing for you that I'm not at the bottom of it now." Upon reflection I realised that it was an even better thing for me that I had not stepped into it.

When saying good-bye to Mrs. MacLeod I told her of my experience, because I thought it was my duty to do so, and she closed her eyes as do many Highland women when seeking to shut out an unpleasant mental picture. "He had no right to let you in there alone."

"It's all right, Mrs. MacLeod, my Guardian Angel was with me."

"Well, I'm very glad he was functioning."

I went for an hour's walk and on returning to the hotel at Dunvegan found an invitation to dine at the Castle at eight o'clock and a message that there was no need to dress for dinner as it would be only a small party of friends. This was most considerate of my hostess, because the only clothes I had were those I was wearing.

At eight o'clock I was in the drawing-room looking again at the Fairy Flag and awaiting my hostess, when the door opened and there entered in evening dress the Lord Chancellor of England and Lady Maugham. There were three other visitors, and we had an excellent dinner and conversation at the same candle-lit table where Boswell and Johnson had dined, and on leaving Dunvegan Castle I realised what the doctor meant when he wrote about being "entertained with all the elegance of lettered hospitality."

At Portree, the largest town and port in Skye, there were three days of rain and no excursions to Loch Coruisk, because I was the only visitor who wished to go there. In good weather a motor-bus goes from Portree to Elgol, a distance of forty-two miles, and from Elgol a motor-boat crosses Loch Scavaig, a sea loch which is often rough and at whose head Loch Coruisk, a fresh-water loch, lies amongst the Coolins. This loch may also be reached from the steamer *Lochnevis*, which anchors for half an hour in Loch Scavaig daily during the summer season.

I took my seat every morning at 9 a.m. in a bus on whose bonnet was a placard, "Loch Coruisk," and at 9.30 every morning the driver told me there would be no excursion as I was the only passenger. Apparently the majority of visitors stay in their hotels or lodgings during wet weather, which means a waste of time and money, and the best advice to those visiting the west of Scotland is to be prepared for rain. With a sou'-wester, light oilskins, and goloshes you can be out and about on wet days, and I once spent a pleasant holiday in Argyllshire, although it rained for four weeks without stopping. On the third morning the driver told me that I could see Loch Coruisk for £4, 10s., which meant hiring a motor-car and boat. I told him that I would see the loch for 2s. by taking a bus to Sligachan Inn and by walking up the glen of that name to a ridge on the Coolins. In point of fact it is well to see Loch Coruisk both from its shore and from the mountains, because each of those viewpoints gives a different impression.

Sligachan Inn is at the entrance of a glen running south between the Red Coolins to the east and the Black Coolins to the west, thus distinguished by the colour of their rocks. The inn is really a first-class modern hotel whose proprietor Mr. Campbell directed me to keep to the path on the east side of the glen, until at the end of three miles two small lochs were reached. Beyond these lochs the path crosses the glen and ascends to a height of over a thousand feet on a ridge of the Black Coolins.

"I suppose it's perfectly safe, no mountaineering necessary?"

"Perfectly safe, but the last mile and a half is a climb all the way. Where the rock is bare small cairns of stone mark the track. Only last week a couple of English schoolgirls, aged fourteen and fifteen, walked from Loch Scavaig across the ridge and down the glen to this hotel. All the same, it's better for people not to be alone on the Coolins."

The news about the schoolgirls was disappointing, because I had looked forward to this walk as likely to be something of an adventure, and I knew that H. V. Morton, whose pleasant footsteps are increasingly difficult to avoid, had also walked from Loch Scavaig to the hotel.

It was raining, and the narrow path at the foot of the mountains became a rivulet at every incline and decline. These mountain paths are very old, and when Prince Charles Stuart returned to Skye from the Island of Raasay this was the route he followed when he walked with Captain MacLeod from Portree to Elgol, a distance of nineteen miles as the crow flies. He also had walked in drenching rain. On each side of this comparatively narrow glen the Coolins, Red and Black, rise almost vertically, and mountain streams, foaming white, fall from heights of over a thousand feet. I cannot understand why Dr. Johnson called the Coolins "inferior mountains" unless he was using the adjective in the sense of "infernal."

The hotel was out of sight and I had not yet come to the two small lochs when I lost the path and reached a large burn over which there were no stepping-stones. I walked for half a mile up its course, seeking a place where I could cross dry-shod, and finally waded across. There was no sense in trying to be dry-shod, because my raincoat, which might have withstood an April shower, was now permeated with rain and from my panama hat water was trickling down my back. Indeed at the end of this walk I was drenched to the skin, and on returning to Portree at 8 p.m. I went to bed in order that my clothes might be dried over night in the hotel kitchen. Yet there is no risk to health from wet clothes, or even from sleeping out all night in wet clothes, provided the moisture does not evaporate too quickly. It is not the moisture but its evaporation that lowers the body temperature, produces a chill, and may induce pneumonia.

Thus after the '45 when loyal Highlanders were driven to the mountains by the Duke of Cumberland's troops, it was their custom when sleeping in the open to soak their plaids in a burn or loch before using them as blankets. The wet plaid kept the body warm, and even to-day this is done by Highland shepherds when sleeping on the hills.

Having crossed the burn my problem was to find the path, and it was now comforting to reflect that two school-girls had passed this way. Soon afterwards I heard voices and saw a couple eating their lunch on the side of a hillock half a mile off. Indeed so curious are the accoustics of mountains that despite the distance I distinctly heard the woman remark, "He seems to have lost his way." Thereafter the three of us continued the walk together, and I took them to be brother and sister, she aged twenty-five and he about eighteen. Their names I do not know, nor they mine. They were English people, and the boy had done some mountaineering in the Pyrenees, so that when it came to climbing he easily outdistanced his sister and myself. She was attempting to keep her feet dry and so I helped her across stepping-stones in the burns until the burns became so swollen that we both had to wade. When wading she removed her shoes but not her stockings, and incidentally she had dainty feet.

"Forgive my curiosity," said I, "but why have dry shoes and wet stockings?"

"Because my rubber shoes would slip on the wet boulders."

"You should have leather shoes like mine with studs. This pair is thirteen years old, resoled, of course."

She laughed. "I wonder if thirteen years from now you will be walking on the Coolins in the same shoes."

"Most unlikely, unless my ghost walks."

"You shouldn't say that."

Once she slipped, and when I held her from falling: "What would you do if I sprained my ankle?"

"I'd stay with you, and send your brother back to the hotel for a stretcher party because he's the quicker walker. The last person to be injured here was a lady doctor. She was climbing one of the peaks with a party, fell twenty feet from a ledge and fractured her thigh. One of the party went back to the hotel and Mr. Campbell called for volunteers. Fortunately his guests included some first-class climbers, members of the Alpine Club, but even so it took them twelve hours to get her back to the hotel at three in the morning. The strange thing is that nobody has ever been killed on the Coolins." [1]

After a stiff climb we found ourselves on a ridge which we took to be the place from which Loch Coruisk could be seen on a fine day, but now everything was enveloped in mist.

"This must be the place," she said, "because of these two cairns so close together."

Visibility was not more than twelve yards, and neither of us realised that the two cairns when in line pointed the way up the smooth, steep, black basaltic rock, rock so rich in iron as to make the compass useless. I thought that we were at the base of one of the pinnacles of the Coolins, and

[1] A climber was killed in 1939.

from above in the mist the occasional sound of a dislodged stone told us that the boy was climbing higher.

"Where are you?" she called.

"Up here," he shouted.

"Excelsior," said I, and then: "Are you staying at Sligachan?"

"No, at Broadford. We'll get a bus from Sligachan to Broadford."

"I'm sorry, but you'll get no bus. The last bus to Broadford has left. You see for two days I've been making a careful study of the Portree buses, those that go and those that don't go."

"Then we'll have to walk, but it's only twelve miles from the inn."

Finally the boy descended out of the mist and told us that we had not yet reached the end of the climb.

"How much farther?" I asked.

"Well, I did it in ten minutes, and I daresay you two could do it in twenty."

"I'd like to finish the climb," she said.

"Of course," I agreed. "Having come all this way it's ridiculous to turn back without seeing Coruisk."

With great good humour he guided us to the summit of the ridge and over the steepest part of the climb. Indeed, he was so good-natured in this matter that I began to wonder if he was really a brother or a son. Yet she looked no more than twenty-five. On the summit we were surrounded by clouds of whirling mists, and then for a moment at the foot of a vortex of vapour Loch Coruisk appeared. The view was worth the climb, and I realised why a would-be suicide had turned back when he saw the dark water of that loch, more forlorn than his mind. Soon the mist partly cleared on our left, and I felt the shock that comes when you suddenly realise that all unbeknown a stranger has been standing beside you, because only a few yards away and towering above us was the black pinnacle of Sgurr na Eidhn. Here then was a place that would have suited Milton's mood when he wrote:

> "Hence, loathed Melancholy,
> Of Cerberus and blackest Midnight born,
> In Stygian cave forlorn,
> 'Mongst horrid shapes, and shrieks, and sights unholy,
> Find out some uncouth cell,
> Where brooding Darkness spreads his jealous wings,
> And the night raven sings."

CHAPTER XXI

H.M.S. *CHAMPAGNE*

"YOU'LL always find," said the Captain, "that twin-screw ships are slower on the helm than a ship with one propeller, that is—if they're going ahead. Going astern they answer much quicker."

"The steering that scared me," remarked the Second Officer, "was the first time I went through the Suez Canal."

"Yes," agreed the First Officer, "everything is different in canals."

"I was Fourth at the time," continued the Second, a lad in his twenties, "and on the bridge with the French pilot, a bearded johnny, who kept walking up and down. Suddenly I saw our bow turning towards the starboard bank. The pilot saw it too, and told the steersman—hard a-starboard. I thought he'd made a mistake and I wanted to shout 'hard a-port'—but no, the ship moved from the bank towards the centre of the canal, and the pilot told me afterwards that if he had ported the helm she would have gone over the bank on to the railway line."

"It works like this," said the Captain, "there's a limited amount of water between the ship and the bank. When he put the rudder to starboard that increased the pressure in the water between the ship and the bank, and pushed the ship away from the bank."

"Aye," added the Chief Engineer, "water pressure is a queer thing. Do you remember what happened to the

Normandie on her first voyage? Well, as she neared New
York she came into shoal water of twenty or thirty fathoms
and stopped. She's got electric-driven turbines and had
blown her fuses. It took them a long time to find out why
all the fuses should have blown when she came to that
particular place. Finally they found that in comparatively
shallow water the bottom of the sea acted as a drag on the
ship, put an extra strain on the turbines and blew the fuses.
After that, they put in stronger fuses for use in shoal water."

"I can understand how that works out," said the Captain,
"and surely you've all noticed that if you push a floating
plank across a pond—one did it as a boy—it will raise mud
from the bottom even if there's several inches of water
between the plank and the bottom."

So talked the officers of the Fishery Cruiser *Rona*, then in
Stornoway harbour, as I sat with them at high tea in their
messroom on Wednesday, 2nd November 1938. The *Rona*,
a new cruiser of 151 tons gross, painted leaden grey, looked
like a trawler, 115 feet long, 20½ foot beam and 8 feet
draught. She has a whale-back fo'cs'le, a well deck, two
masts, one funnel, and twin-screw Diesel engines with a
speed from eight to fourteen knots. In her long deck-house
is the chartroom, top of the engine-room, messroom, galley,
and entrance to the crew's quarters in the hull astern.
For'ard on top of the deckhouse is a covered bridge surrounded by a verandah, and reached by vertical iron ladders
with six steps against the bulkhead on either side. Officers'
quarters are in the hull ahead of the engine room, with a
bathroom in the bows, and such comparatively ample
accommodation in so small a ship is a tribute to the architect.

On the previous day in a westerly gale we had crossed

from Mallaig, and in the Sound of Sleat were overtaken by a hail-storm, which came across the sea in a great cloud, white above and black below. Snow clouds are the same, rain clouds are grey and fog is fluffy. The sky was overcast, but in front of an approaching hail or snow storm the atmosphere is strangely clear, and the outline of the mountains on either side of the Sound was as defined as it would have been in the light of the setting sun. When the hail-storm reached us I was in the wireless room listening to the Captain calling the *Minnow*, an old steam yacht and flagship of the cruisers. It was an intriguing talk, since many of the words were in code: "G.L.X., G.L.X., calling C.K.H., C.K.H., are you getting me? Over to you." The Captain moved a switch and the sending set became a receiving wireless telephone.

"G.L.X., G.L.X., you're coming in fine. Owing to the gale, I had to shift last night, and am now in Milford Haven —Milford Haven. Has the party I spoke about yesterday arrived? What are your movements? Over to you."

"C.K.H., C.K.H., you might be in the next room. Yes, the party arrived safe and is beside me now. Well, this morning at 6 a.m. I left Gosport, Gosport, on my way to Leith, Leith. I tried the southern route, but it was no use. I was doing eight and only making four. Full gale and a heavy sea. It would have taken me thirty hours at that rate. So I turned back at Holy Isle, Holy Isle, and am coming up the Sound of Plymouth, Plymouth. When I turned back I asked how the party you mentioned was liking it, and was told he was in the bath. At breakfast he said it was the most exciting bath he'd ever had, so you see he's enjoying it. The way I'm going will reduce the sea crossing, and I expect to make Leith, Leith, about 6 p.m. We've got to go there for our cheques, but the bank will be shut to-night. North of the island I expect we'll get a proper dusting, but she's splendid in a sea. You're very wise, C.K.H., C.K.H., to stay where you are. This is no weather for you to be at sea! Over to you."

"G.L.X., G.L.X., no need to insult me. I'm only staying in here because of a slight breakdown in the engine room. When that's put right I'm going south to Madeira, Madeira. I got Malin Head this morning, but there were no messages. You're right to go to Leith, Leith, but it's your wives who want the cheques. I'm glad to know the doctor enjoyed his bath. I hope he's not putting cleanliness before godliness. . . ." Then came a noise like a railway engine whistling in a covered station.

"That's the hail hitting our aerial," said the Captain, "and we won't hear another word."

"Then hailstones must be charged with electricity?"

"No, I think it's just the amplification of the mechanical noise made by the stones hitting wire, because I've noticed that it never interferes with 'sending.' "

Anyone who knew the wave length could have listened to that talk, and I wonder what they would have made of it. Both Captains were speaking straightforward English, but often for their own amusement and for the further bewilderment of eavesdroppers they practice talking in the Welsh, Cockney, and Lancashire dialects. Indeed, the next time I heard the Captain of the *Minnow* speaking on the air I was completely deceived by his: "Look you, G.L.X., G.L.X., there is one little thing that I would like for you to do for me, sure to goodness, yes."

Be it said that the code I have given here is not the real code, and that the time when the cruisers telephone to each other changes every day.

At 7 p.m. on the Wednesday evening I was reading in the chartroom, the ship was rolling and the wind pressure on the bridge caused the whistle of the speaking-tube beside me to give a long faint whistle every now and then. All ports were shut and darkened, as we were steaming without lights. The way to catch poaching trawlers at night is to sail either without lights or with such a blaze of light that they take you for a small tramp. A seaman in oilskins came into the chartroom to say, "The Captain would like you on the bridge." I was about to open the iron door giving access to the deck on the port side, when the messenger said: "Not that way, sir. That's the weather side and you'll get drenched. Best go by the engine-room door to starboard."

"Very good," said I, "if you'll watch the door."

"Aye, aye, sir, I'll watch it." For that iron door from the upper part of the engine room to the deck had an evil reputation. It moved too easily on its hinges, and if the rolling of the ship caused it to close before you were clear its weight and sharp edge were capable of breaking, if not of amputating, a limb. On the darkened deck I found the iron ladder, and when the ship next rolled to port I climbed up as quickly as possible. On the covered bridge were the Captain, his two officers, and the steersman.

"I thought you'd be interested, Doctor. I've never seen anything as big as this in Broad Bay."

We had passed Tiumpan Head, and in Broad Bay and on our port bow were the lights of what appeared to be an enormous ship at anchor.

"What is she?"

The Captain was using binoculars. "I don't know—
port a little—steady—I think there's two of them—we're
going in to see—yes, there's two of them—see these lights
opening out, Mr. Mitchell—fair-sized ships—shows what
the Atlantic is like round the Butt to-night. The nearest
one has a list to port—probably deck cargo. Get a man to
stand by the searchlight."

From the shadow of the land the *Rona* approached the
nearest ship. "Light," and the great beam of light shot
across the sea. "Put that light on her stern," and to me:
"It's difficult to keep a searchlight steady in a sea." She
was *Lysakery V.*, of Oslo, with a deck cargo of wood, and a
fairly heavy list to port. The light was shut off until we
neared the next ship—*Corona*, Helsingfors, 2439 tons according to Lloyds, and now in ballast. "Run the light along
her decks." She was a beautiful ship with two upper decks,
but the only person who appeared in the searchlight was the
lady cook.

"How are you liking it, Doctor?"

"Very much, and for the moment that searchlight took
me back to 1914."

"Yes, I can understand that."

The silence that followed meant mutual understanding,
for he also had sailed in more perilous seas, in darkened ships
with searchlights and guns. One of the greatest pleasures in
life is to recapture, if only for a moment, the thrill of high
adventure first encountered, and if you know the way almost
everything may be recaptured, save youth and love.

It was glorious to be standing once more on the bridge of
a ship in a gale, in the company of resourceful men, and to

be watching the Furies unchained on the sea. Strange, too, that only a week ago Captain P. G. Brown, R.N., had told me an epic of the Northern Patrol in 1917. Of all stories the most interesting are these of men who in full consciousness have escaped from the clutches of death, and are able to analyse their sensations when in the valley of the shadow. This was his story.

In 1917 I was appointed to command H.M.S. *Champagne*, an armed merchant cruiser of 10,000 tons, with ten 6-inch guns and a complement of 20 officers and 350 men. She had belonged to the Pacific Steam Navigation Company, and was a strong ship, built to go round the Horn. I forget her original name, but the Admiralty had lent her to the French when the U.S.A. were making themselves extremely unpleasant about the blockade, the idea being that France should share the onus. It was the French who rechristened her *Champagne* and when the U.S.A. came into the war we took her back to join the Xth Cruiser Squadron on the Northern blockade. The Admiralty asked if I wished to change the name, and I replied that it was a nice expensive name and that we'd better stick to it.

We were due to leave Liverpool on the evening of Sunday, 15th October, but it was blowing so hard from the southwest that the dockyard authorities would not take the responsibility of shifting us until 9 p.m. on the Monday. On the Sunday evening as we were lying alongside the quay the sentry reported to the Officer of the Watch that a lot of rats were coming out of the ship. The Officer of the Watch verified this and reported to me that there was a regular procession of rats, some carrying young ones in their mouths, going over the bow on a hawser to the shore. Of course, I'd often heard about rats leaving a sinking ship, but took it to mean that water in the bottom of a ship drove them out of their nests. I don't know why these rats left us, and it seems incredible that they could possibly know that Fritz was waiting for us somewhere off Belfast.

At 6 a.m. on Tuesday morning, after a night on the bridge, I said to the Navigating Officer: "We're out of the danger zone. I'm going down to have a nap, and you'd better turn the ship over to the Officer of the Watch and get some sleep." On those cruises I never got into pyjamas. It was uniform by day, and after dark—shirt, trousers, thick stockings, a duffle coat, and sea boots. In this kit I turned in, minus coat and boots, and at 6.30 a.m. there was the devil of an explosion that threw me out of the bunk. I knew at once what had happened and slipped on my coat and boots. One of the doors to my cabin had jammed but luckily the other opened and I got out on deck. It was just breaking daylight, typical north-westerly weather after a south-west blow, bright intervals with heavy showers, wind north-west, force about six but reaching gale strength in squalls. Sea rough.

We had been hit in the after engine room, putting the wireless out of action and stopping the engines. The man on the lookout in the crow's nest on the foremast had all his front teeth knocked out by being thrown against an iron rail. It was a proper explosion.

There was no panic and the ship's company automatically went to their stations. Soon afterwards there was another explosion, probably a boiler, and as we were settling down very rapidly, I gave the order to abandon ship. This went off without a hitch and we got the ship's company away. A Petty Officer who was my coxswain came up and said: "What about some of us waiting to see if he comes up, and give him a shot?" I thought this was quite a good idea, and so four men and myself went to a six-inch gun on the port side and loaded it. When the submarine came up the water on the upper deck was up to my knees, and consequently it wasn't a steady gun platform. We just missed him, the shell passing over his head. I suppose this annoyed him. Anyhow, he dived and gave us another torpedo, which struck the ship under where we were standing. As the effective life of a submarine ends for a time when all her torpedoes have been fired, I thought it quite useful drawing another tooth, as in any case we couldn't have remained afloat another fifteen minutes.

The explosion was terrific. I went up in the air, how far I don't know, but it seemed a long time. When I came down the ship had broken her back, the planks on the upper deck were splitting, the ship was in two pieces and I slid down between the bow and the stern. Before sailing my wife had given me a Gieves Patent Life Belt and I'd promised to wear it night and day. It was a rubber contraption that lay flat under your coat, and if you pulled a string two fluids mixed like a seidlitz powder and made gas. I remember slipping down through the broken deck, pulling the string, and saying to myself: "I'll bet a bob this damned thing won't work," but it did work, blew up into a great sort of balloon and undoubtedly saved my life.

I was sucked down and down and when I opened my eyes everything was pitch dark. There didn't seem to be any possible chance and I didn't struggle much. I was considering things in a rather impersonal way and with a certain feeling of gratification that I'd done my job. I remember saying to myself: "I've often wondered what the next world is like, and I'll know in about five minutes." Then I came up only to be sucked down again, and I expected nothing except to die. To my surprise I came up again and saw a glint of sun through the clouds. Strange the difference a glint of sunlight can make. Instead of being resigned, I now began to fight like a madman—anything for more life.

I got my arms on an air vessel that must have got out of a lifeboat, found my coxswain and got him to put his arms on to it. He and I were the only survivors of the five who had remained on board. All sorts of wreckage came to the surface and a great derrick shot up about six feet away which would have killed us had it been nearer. After that a dead man kept bumping into us and we shoved him off, but the water was breaking over our heads and half-drowning us. I tried to keep calm so as to keep the Petty Officer calm, and said, "Dash it, I gave up sea bathing some years ago," to which he replied, "You've had a good dose of it this morning, sir."

We didn't know if the boats knew we were there or if they could get up to windward on account of the sea and of their being full of men. I was about done, my arms were aching, I felt I couldn't last much longer, and the boats seemed no closer. All the same I said to the Petty Officer, "Never give in while there's a shot in the locker," and he answered, "Aye, aye, sir." After that I just clenched my teeth and neither of us spoke.

Then, thank God, a boat, very well handled by an R.N.R. lieutenant, name of Bingham, came up and hauled us in. I told Bingham to put some sail on her, run before the wind and signal to the other boats to follow. Then I fainted. Next thing I remember was being undressed in the boat and someone dressing me in a pair of bluejacket's trousers and a singlet. After that I was just lying quiet with my eyes shut. It was about 8.30 a.m. when they picked us up. I had a dim sense of being annoyed about something—a fat Cockney boy, who was my messenger, was saying: "A fine turn-out this is, on my birthday too."

I opened one eye, and said: "Are you eighteen to-day, my lad?"

"No, sir, seventeen."

"Then put out that cigarette," and the men realised that the Old Man was beginning to sit up and take notice.

At noon we sighted land ahead, so I had to buck up. I didn't know what the land was, but there was a heavy surf, and I thought we should have to come up into the wind until I could see a landing place. Then one of the crew said, "I think that's the Isle of Man, and that's my home." It was, and he being a local fisherman piloted us in. We got into smooth water about 12.30 p.m., and landed. The people treated us with great kindness, and one man told me he was the agent for the Shipwrecked Mariners Society. I said that I came under that heading, and he gave me a good pair of boots which I needed badly. They opened up hotels and bedded us for the night. Next day we all went to Liverpool and were sent to our homes. I borrowed £5 from the Senior Naval Officer, bought a suit off the peg and wired to my wife. Remembering the censor, I wired, "Have had a puncture, am returning home." Consequently her greeting was: "I thought you were out fighting the Germans, and then you go motoring round the country enjoying your-self, and in that disgraceful suit." The first night she didn't tumble to it, but the next night she heard me talking in my sleep—telling her the water was now up to the edge but that if she remained still and held on to me there was no danger. She then woke me up, and began to realise that there had been some dirty work going on.

I*

CHAPTER XXII

THE SEA PATROL

LEAVING the Scandinavian steamers anchored in Broad Bay, the *Rona* went out in a north-westerly direction towards two trawlers whose lights were visible in the distance twelve miles away. The wind had shifted to the north-west and was of gale force, which means a velocity of over thirty-eight land miles an hour. As we passed Tolsta Head the sea increased, for there was added the spent force of enormous waves coming from the Atlantic round the Butt of Lewis, albeit we were still within the comparative shelter of land. There was a moon that shone from time to time through racing clouds and lit up a confused tumult of white-crested masses of water through which the *Rona* rolled and pitched.

"How high are these waves?"

The Captain looked out for a moment. "From ten to fifteen feet. You'll never get them much bigger about here, but in the Atlantic they can reach twenty-five to thirty feet. I don't think they're ever bigger than that, although people talk about mountainous seas. The danger is not the height of waves but their periodicity, the distance between crest and crest in relation to the size of the ship. If bow and stern are resting on the crests of two waves, and amidships she's suspended over the trough, then she may break her back. Or if amidships she's held up on the crest of a wave with bow and stern over troughs, she may 'hog' her back, which comes to the

258

same thing. One or other is the most likely cause of those disappearances of ships at sea, about which nothing is discovered. The ship suddenly breaks in two. In some cases strained deck plates may have given the owners fair warning that the ship was not fit to meet the seas to which they were sending her. I've known that to happen, and met men who left a ship which afterwards disappeared with all hands. With 'hogging' she may just broach-to, fall into a trough in the sea and be out of control for a moment or two until the propellers get a grip on the water."

"Isn't this rough weather for trawlers to be out? '

"Well, they're a bit bigger than we are—these ones are from 125 to 130 feet long, and those that go to Iceland are larger—150 feet long, 25 beam and 13 draught. It takes a lot to stop a trawler. Trawling is their bread and butter, and if the skipper says the trawl is to be down three or five hours, down it stays. I think it's daft, but they'll hang on to the last minute. You'll see what it's like when we get up to them.

"Poaching? There's very little poaching. Most of these skippers have no wish to lose their job, and remember that on the second conviction the owners are fined as well. That makes a difference. Of course, there are a few exceptions, dare-devils who don't care a damn, and we know who they are. Even they are not such fools as to come inshore in daylight when anyone on the beach can read their number unless it's concealed or falsified. No, these lads come in at night to places where they know every foot of the ground, and they come without lights. The bright lights of the ordinary trawler make people ashore think that she's much nearer than she is. Now test it for yourself. How far off would you say are these two on the starboard bow?"

"I'd say two miles."

"Well, they're at least five miles off, and they're well outside the three-mile limit. I'd say they're at least four miles from the shore. But we'll fix the exact position when we get up to them."

"I suppose that explains some of the complaints about trawling?"

"It explains a few, but you've no idea of some of the complaints we have to investigate. The First Officer and I have walked three miles across bog and hills to get particulars of the complaint sent by an old crofter who had seen a trawler within half a mile of the shore. This was the kind of talk we had:

"'Did you take his number?'

"'No, I could not read his number.'

"'Can you read the numbers on those fishing boats on the shore?

"'Yes, I can read them.'

"'Well, they're half a mile away, so if the trawler was half a mile away you could have read his number. And how do you know he was trawling? Had he his gear out?'

"'I did not see his gear out.'

"'Then how do you know he was trawling? Perhaps he came in for shelter.'

"'No, no, he was trawling.'

"'But had you any reason to know he was trawling?'

"'Yes, yes, I could tell he was trawling.'

"'How could you tell he was trawling?'

"'I could tell that he was trawling by the colour of the smoke coming from his funnel.'"

Of a truth the officers of the sea patrol have to be a combination of navigator, fisherman, policeman, and lawyer. Nor was that by any means the most ridiculous complaint. A Fishery cruiser on a Saturday night sailed sixty miles to investigate a telegram that trawlers were working near a certain island. On the Sunday morning the Captain and First Officer waited until the complainant returned from church, when he frankly admitted that he himself had not seen the trawlers but had been told about them by the minister. It was a three-mile walk to the manse, where the minister was most apologetic. He had mentioned about the trawling in the course of a general conversation with the complainant, but had omitted to mention that the events to which he referred had occurred eighteen months previously. Now zeal is an excellent attribute, but if in your zeal you were to set the English police on a wild goose chase you might be prosecuted for doing "a public mischief," in that you had caused a needless expenditure of public time and money.

Trawling inshore involves great destruction of spawn, and so helped to destroy the line-fishing that once was one of the staple industries of the Western Isles. A greater economic factor was the introduction of steam fishing vessels with a cruising range of 2000 miles, whereby fish from distant grounds could be brought rapidly to the great fishing ports. With these no sailing fishing boat could compete, and yet a sailing boat might partly enable her owner to make a living if the fish were sold locally. These thoughts arise by reason of what an old man in one of the islands said about trawlers.

"Trawlers! Let them come in and poach as much as they like. In the old days I agitated as much as anyone for fast

Fishery cruisers, but now that we've given up line-fishing how are we going to get fish? I'll tell you. Whenever we see a trawler near shore we send out two men in a boat with a bottle of whisky as a present for the skipper. They never ask for money, and the boat comes back full of fish."

The Captain of the *Rona* turned to the Second Officer. "You might go on top and take a 'fix' of Tiumpan Head and the Butt as soon as we open the light." [You "open" a light or any other landmark as soon as you see it, and you "close" the same as soon as it is out of sight. Of two lights or landmarks in the same direction the nearest may be either opening or closing on the more distant.]

"Would you give me the course from Cellar Head, sir?"

"Certainly, I'll put her in line from Cellar Head to the nearest trawler—starboard a little—steady." He looked astern and then at the compass: "Cellar Head is North 75 West, True," and with the parallel rulers he drew a line on the chart, lit by a shaded lamp over the long table that ran the length of the bridge below the glass windows in front.

"True" is the direction in relation to the fixed geographical North Pole as distinct from the movable North Magnetic Pole which at present is in North America to the north-west of Hudson Bay. When Amundsen passed over the latter in the *Gjoa*, when drifting round the North American coast, he records that his compasses tried to stand upright and became useless. For that reason around Great Britain the north end of the compass is deflected several degrees to the west of true north. So far as I remember, the westerly deflection at this time in the Minch was 15 degrees, and, therefore, from a westerly compass bearing you subtracted 15, and from an easterly bearing you added

15 degrees in order to get the true geographical position. In this instance the compass bearing would have been— Cellar Head, North 90 West, which is due west.

The Second Officer's footsteps were heard on the deck above the bridge, and then he shouted something.

"In this wind," said the Captain, "I can't hear what he's saying. Mr. Mitchell, would you go on to the verandah and hear what it is."

The First stepped out of the open door on the lee side, and reported: "He says the thermometer has been blown overboard, sir."

"Tell him not to bother about the thermometer but to look out for the Butt light."

"Yes, sir." [Thermometer was returned half an hour later by the seaman who had been cleaning it. Be it also said that the Second Officer, a deep sea man used to ocean liners, had joined the *Rona* on the same day as myself.]

"There's the light," said the Captain. "What does he make it?"

More shouting outside, and then: "North 45 West, True."

Another line was drawn on the chart. "Aye, and Tiumpan Head?"

"Tiumpan Head light, South 21 West, True."

"Thank you, Mr. Mitchell," and a third line was drawn.

"Now you see, Doctor," and I clutched the edge of the chart table to steady myself as I looked, "where these three lines intersect was our position a moment ago, and with the dividers you can measure our distance from three points. We were 10 miles from the Butt, 11½ miles from Tiumpan Head and 4½ miles from Cellar Head. Now that nearest trawler is at least half a mile ahead of us, so he's well outside the three-mile limit, and he's steaming farther out."

The trawler was well lit. Beneath the white navigation light on the foremast was the tricoloured lantern "so constructed and fixed as to show a white light from right ahead to two points on each bow, and a green light and a red light over an arc of the horizon from two points abaft the beam, on the starboard and port sides respectively." Six feet below the tricoloured lantern was "a white light in a lantern, so constructed as to show a clear, uniform and unbroken light all round the horizon." By these signs you know that a steam trawler is fishing. The foredeck was illuminated by four powerful acetylene gas lights swung overhead so that the crew may have light when gutting the fish. "He's not rolling as much as we are," I said.

"No, the trawl keeps him steady. He's dragging maybe five tons of gear and fish along the bottom of the sea."

The gear of an otter trawl includes two almost rectangular "boards" or "doors," measuring nine by five feet, made of deal planks three inches thick, heavily clamped edge to edge with iron brackets. As the "doors" move through the water on the bottom of the sea their short edges are vertical and their long edges are horizontal. The lower of the long edges is shod with an iron shoe, the front bottom corner being rounded like a sleigh runner, so that the shoe or keel may glide over obstructions on the bottom. Each "door" weighs half a ton and is attached to a two and a half inch wire warp, whose breaking point is twenty-three tons, by four short chains from one of the sides. These chains are fixed to the side of the "door" on the same principle as the rigging of a kite, so that the moving "door" is subject to two forces. It is being pulled forward by the hawser and pushed outwards by the pressure of the water which it meets at an oblique angle. When the two "doors" are on the bottom their chained sides are opposite each other and, consequently, the "doors" diverge one from the other.

The ropes to which the mouth of the net is attached, namely, the head-rope and the ground-rope, are fastened to eyes at the top and bottom respectively of the after end of each "door." Thus as the "doors" diverge the mouth of the net is pulled right and left and so held open. The head-rope, a three-inch hawser, by reason of resistance of the net to the water, takes the form of an arch whose centre is from ten to fifteen feet above the bottom. It is estimated that a ninety-foot head-rope when arched will give the mouth of the net a width of sixty feet. The ground-rope is longer than the head-rope and drags along the bottom in a deep curve, this curve being known as the "bosom" of the net. The ground-rope is made of old iron hawser covered with small rope to prevent chafing the seizings of the net. Old iron hawser is used in order that the ground-rope may break if it encounters an immovable object, as otherwise the whole net might be lost. On smooth ground loops of chain are attached to the ground-rope, these loops being known as "danglers" or "ticklers," and their purpose being to stir up all fish lying on the bottom. When the ground is rough, a rope fitted with heavy cylindrical wooden rollers is used in order that the rope may be drawn over rocks. These rollers are alternately large and small, the large ones being a foot in diameter, and to the small ones the bottom of the net is attached by seizings.

The net, in shape a flattened cone, 120 to 140 feet long,

tapers from its mouth to the 10-foot "cod-end," where the fish are trapped by an open pocket projecting from the "belly" of the net. The mesh, measured from knot to knot, varies from $5\frac{1}{2}$ inches at the mouth to $2\frac{1}{2}$ inches at the cod-end, and be it noted that it would be impossible to drag nets of this length through the water if the mesh was too small. Moreover, if the mesh be too small, immature and therefore unwanted fish would be captured. Before the net is shot, the cod-end is closed by a line that is loosed when the catch is taken on board, and once the trawl is down the two wire hawsers are shackled to the stern of the ship.

In the days of wooden steamships many a trawler was lost in a heavy sea when the trawl stuck fast on the bottom. If the steam winches and wire warps could not move it, then, provided the warps did not break, the vessel was held rigid in the sea to meet the full force of tons of water breaking against the side and on deck whereby the timbers were strained, for it is the pitch and roll of a ship that saves her from the force of waves which, when large enough, are capable of smashing a concrete breakwater. The truth about rolling and pitching is no comfort to those who suffer the miseries of seasickness, but should be remembered by passengers who clamour for a ship that will not roll. Such a liner could be constructed, and at the centre of gravity would have a heavy and powerful gyroscope, but the strain on the framework of the ship would be enormous, and if the gyroscope came adrift I would not like to be anywhere about in that floating hotel.

We overtook the trawler on her port side, and by searchlight read the letters and number on her stern—F.D. 33, a Fleetwood number. Apart from a man in the wheelhouse there was no one on deck, and the crew were probably trying to snatch an hour or two of sleep. A few moments later the same number was read on the port bow, and I judged the distance between ourselves and the trawler to be a hundred yards, which seemed little enough in such a sea. As soon as the bow number was read, the Captain, still watching the trawler, said, "Hard a-port."

The steersman put the wheel over and answered, "Hard a-port, sir."

I was watching the compass card, and for a moment or so there was no change in direction.

The Captain turned sharply. "I said hard a-port."

"Hard a-port it is, sir."

"She's rather slow on the helm," said I, speaking out of my turn.

At that moment the *Rona* begun turning away from the trawler, and the Captain answered, "Yes, when she's turning against a full gale."

Afterwards he told me that if the delay had lasted another second he would have ordered full speed astern. "And then you'd have seen her back off at once in a circle. I know what this ship can do. We could go round the Butt to-night, if there was any reason for doing so. Remember, every ship has her limits and a ship's like a woman. There's no sense in trying her too hard."

Trawlers, like other fishing vessels, must have the letters of the "port of registry" and the number painted "in oil colour" on the stern and on the bows, the size of the lettering being ruled by the size of the boat. Before the new fast Fishery cruisers were built a modern trawler when caught poaching within the three-mile limit could escape capture, and if the registration marks had been altered could not be identified. The British marks are comparatively easy to remember as they bear some resemblance to the port of registry, thus B.C.K. stands for Buckie, and B.E. for Barnstable, but the lettering on foreign boats is more complicated, and without a *Mariner's Almanac* no one could tell that A.X. stands for Borkum. No trawler, British or foreign, may use the otter trawl within three miles of the shore, nor have they a right to come within the three-mile limit unless the otter doors are on board and the net is stowed. In Scotland cases of illegal trawling are tried before the sheriffs, and if convicted the skipper is fined from £50 to £100 and the gear is confiscated. In Iceland the penalties are heavier, and a British skipper was recently fined £500 with confiscation of gear. Yet in Scotland there are anomalies, such as the law about the Moray Firth. No British boats are allowed to use the otter trawl in this Firth, but any foreigner may do so provided he keeps outside three miles of its shores. The middle of the Firth is, therefore, preserved for foreign trawlers. The foreigner is only subject to an international convention which decided that three miles from shore marked the limit of "territorial" waters, this decision having been made at a time when effective fire from naval guns was limited to a range of three miles. The range of effective gunfire is now twelve miles, and already Russia, Norway, and Portugal have extended the area of their territorial waters in regard to trawling.

When the second trawler, F.D. 75, came under the searchlight the scene resembled the Arctic, for all round the ship were snow-white mounds rising and falling like pack ice. These white mounds were thousands of seagulls, close-packed, riding on the waves and waiting for the unwanted fish and for the gutting of the others. The gulls knew that the trawl was coming up.

Seagulls are intelligent birds and if taken early may be partly tamed. During a hard winter at Lerwick the crew of the Fishery drifter *Veila* befriended a young gull whom they named Jock. When they went ashore the bird would walk beside them, and when they said, "Hullo, Jock," would answer, "Haak, haak." The engineer taught him to ask for food by raising and dropping with his beak a hinged bolt on the hatchway above the Captain's quarters. This trick became a nuisance, for whenever the *Veila* was in Lerwick the Captain was awakened at break of dawn by a persistent tapping which continued until someone got out of his bunk to give the gull a fish. On hearing this, I understood the frenzy of Donald Duck when his leisure was disturbed by the woodpecker who tapped overhead on the corrugated iron roof. When the *Veila* left Lerwick, Jock stayed on board until five miles out, and, what is more remarkable, whenever the ship was coming in the gull met her ten miles out at sea. A tapping on the hatch proved his identity. Jock regarded the *Veila* as his property and fought off any other gulls who attempted to settle on the ship. He would walk around the deck and on the bridge, but nothing would induce him to go below, and all gulls probably suffer from acute claustrophobia. Moreover, except on ships, they might be somewhat expensive pets, for on Mallaig pier I watched a large gull swallow, entire and tail first, a discarded mackerel about as long as himself. Oh! for the digestive juices of a gull!

The second trawler, rolling heavily, was broadside on

to wind and sea, for the gear must be hauled up from the weather side lest the hawsers, doors, or net foul the propeller. To raise the trawl the wire hawsers are unshackled and wound in on two separate drums of the steam winch for'ard, each drum holding 1000 fathoms of hawser, since trawling is possible up to a depth of 200 fathoms. Each hawser first passes over a pulley at the top of a gallows, a large iron structure shaped like a horseshoe and rising above the bulwarks. There is a gallows fore and aft on each side of the ship, because two trawls are carried, and to these gallows the doors are made fast when not in use. Only one trawl is down at a time, but the "doors" on the gallows on the other side are ready for use if the net of the first trawl is found to need mending. There are no delays in trawling, even if the crew must go without sleep.

Once the "doors" are secured to the gallows, the mate and all deck hands, usually four in a small trawler, haul the head-rope and then the net foot by foot over the bulwarks. To protect their hands they may wear mittens or woollen gloves. The rolling of the ship eases their work, for with each upward roll the net is held taut so that the movement of the ship draws more net out of the water, and then as she rolls seawards the slack of the net is pulled on board. Heart-breaking work on a cold and dirty night, and if they lose control of the net so that it slips back into the sea, then the man who happens to be entangled goes overboard and another life is lost. When the "cod-end" appears on the surface a rope is passed round the net and by block and tackle the "cod-end" with its load of fish, and dripping like a huge sponge, is hoisted gunwale high and swung over the fore-deck.

The foredeck has been divided into four temporary divisions or "pounds" by boards two feet high, so that the fish when released from the net may not scatter all over the deck. The mate unties the cod-line at the end of the net, now ballooned by its contents, and jumps aside to escape the slithering mass of fish, mussels, and seaweed pouring and spreading into the "pounds." Again the net is shot. The "pounds" are alive with wriggling fish and creeping things, of which hundreds of little crabs, yellow and brown, are the first to emerge and escape to the scuppers. Hermit crabs are too slow. The crew now sort out the saleable fish into baskets, throwing the grey haddocks into one and the dull grey-green whitings into another. Sole and plaice, turbot and skate, cod and hake, each has its basket. Then coarse fishes, starfish, hermit crabs, mussels, all sorts of shell fish, immature fishes and spawn, living things useless to man, are swept up with the seaweed and thrown overboard to the feeding, fighting, screaming gulls. Other things are sometimes found in the "pounds," a sea-boot, an oilskin, or a sou'-wester.

Now the crew settle down to gutting the fish, the cod's livers being thrown into a barrel. For this work no gloves may be worn, however cold the wind. No one wearing gloves could hold a live fish, and these men are gutting living fish, including large cod and turbot. Think of it. The fish are then washed with a hose and in baskets are passed down to the fish-hold where, packed in ice, they are laid out on shelves. Nor is gutting the hardest work on a trawler, for repair of a badly torn net, frozen stiff, may keep the crew at work for thirty hours or more without sleep, and with meals as their only respite. And of what are these men thinking as they work all night in dirty weather?

Had there been steam trawlers in the first half of the last century when Mrs. Sherwood wrote *The Fairchild Family: a Collection of Stories calculated to show the Importance and Effects of a Religious Education*,[1] we might have read something like the following:

"What do the trawler men think about, mamma?" asked the children.

"My dear children, they think about the nice sole, fried in egg and bread crumbs, you will have at breakfast to-morrow if you are good and are grateful for all the blessings bestowed upon us."

"Is that all they think about, mamma?" asked Henry.

"No, Henry, they also think how noble a thing is work and that working for shareholders brings its own reward."

"What are shareholders, mamma?" asked Lucy.

"My dear children, shareholders are the kind ladies and gentlemen who provide the money to build the trawler and so enable these men to earn an honest living by going down to the sea in ships."

"Were the men drowned, mamma?" asked Emily.

"No, my dear child, the words 'going down to the sea in ships' are scriptural."

Now, if any child, or adult for that matter, asked me what the trawler men in their misery were thinking about, I would answer that they were thinking about their next

[1] This book was much read to British children as late as 1887, thirty-six years after its author's death. As a child I did not like the book except for the "Story of the Gibbet." That remains a masterpiece of prose, and an example to any writer of how to build up a cumulative effect when writing about the macabre. Unfortunately for *moral* (!) reasons it is usually omitted in modern reprints, which proves what a topsy-turvy world this is.

two or three nights on shore, of the warmth of a pub and of the glamorous dope of the films. And how are these men rewarded?

I am now writing about the largest trawlers, built at a cost of £25,000, that go on a three weeks' trip from Grimsby, Swansea, or Lowestoft as far as Iceland. The running expenses are £150 a week or £450 for the voyage. Deck hands are paid, in addition to their keep, a wage of £2 a week, plus two pennies on every £1 net profit earned by the ship, and a share of the "liver money," which per man averages £3 per trip. These extras bring up the wages of a deck hand to an average of £4, 10s. per week.

The skipper and the mate have no wages and they pay for their keep. In place of salary they receive respectively 10 per cent. and 7 per cent. of the net profits on each trip. If the catch for a three weeks' trip is sold for less than £450 the skipper and the mate get nothing and are in debt for their food to the owners. When that happens it is known as "Settling under the Red Line," and if there be many such settlements the skipper hears the dreaded order, "Get your clogs on," which means a job on shore, grading and packing fish, and this may happen to a skipper in his forties. In our great and free democracy no system is more calculated to make a skipper work like a slave and to act like a slave-driver. And what of the glittering prizes! If the catch is sold at a net profit of £1400 then the skipper receives £140 and the mate £98 for three weeks afloat. Their ambition is, therefore, to earn and save as much money as will enable them to retire as soon as possible; and on the outskirts of English fishing ports many comfortable little houses are owned by ex-skippers.

A trawler is no place for a slacker, and the deck hand who does not turn out of his bunk and jump to his work on the first word of command will soon be cursing the day on which he was born. The skipper will neither curse him nor hurt him, since the other deck hands will do all that is necessary to convince the slacker that on a trawler the only law is the Law of the Wild. All the skipper has to do is to give orders whose meaning is understood by the other hands or "rats," so called because they are over the bulwarks and away as soon as the ship is in port. The "rats" know why the net is being hauled in every hour instead of every three hours. They know why when once the net is on board the order is given to shoot the net on the opposite side. They understand what it means when an experienced skipper gives a wrong turn to the wheel, so that the net is torn by the propeller and they are kept working all night at repairs. Aching in body and mind, yearning for sleep, they seek their bunks only to be awakened in a few minutes by another order: "Stand by, all hands! Stow both nets! We're steaming." Their lives are being made a perfect hell, and the "rats" know how to deal with the culprit.

Under these conditions and with changing crews anything like *esprit de corps* is a moral impossibility, and to one and all a trawler is only a means of making money. No one is proud of a trawler, and of all ships they alone are called "He" by other seafaring men. No paint or polish is wasted on trawlers and their crews have no time to keep them clean.

Life on a trawler is mostly sustained by strong sweet tea made with condensed milk—of which a mug is to be had at almost any time. Even in the *Rona* and in the *Vigilant* I had tea six times a day, and very good it was. For that reason I am astonished when I read in *The Fishing News*[1] that Mr. Scott Hewett, "trawler owner, the chairman of the Port of London Health Committee," is reported *inter alia* to have said: "Even where men are well-found by the owners they will drink tea with their meat. If only they would eat eggs or fish with their tea and drink lime juice and water or some other cordial with their meat they would be much healthier." For all I know, Mr. Scott, as a dietician, may be right or he may be wrong, but as one who, albeit a doctor, loves the sea, I rejoiced in the editorial comment entitled, "Yo! Ho! Ho! . . . and a Mug of Tea. . . . We can hardly describe the trawler man as effeminate or degenerate; his is probably the toughest job in the world. Unearthly hours, incessant toil, and appalling sea conditions are his normal outlook, but he sticks it with a stout heart and a determination which no shore job anywhere can possibly call for. If he finds solace in that tea, can we blame him? . . . If a craving for tea is the weakness of the trawlerman we may be sure there is foundation for it, just as a distaste for lime juice and soda water indicates exactly the same thing. Healthy men consume, naturally and automatically, exactly what is best suited to their requirements and reject what they find, consciously or unconsciously, to be alien to their needs. The gastric troubles of seamen, we imagine, are the least of their many afflictions."

A most excellent editorial and my sentiments expressed to a T! The juice of the lime is excellent to drink with water or even with soda water, in the heat of summer. It may also help the playboys and the playgirls of Mayfair, who drink it at 3 a.m. to escape a well-deserved morning headache.

[1] 13th August, 1938, p. 9.

With these few parasites I am not concerned. All that I know is that tea, and strong sweet tea, also coffee, are the only beverages to keep a man awake and alert during the hours when Nature intended that he should sleep; and every doctor can remember those long watches of the night, when a nurse made tea every two hours in order that he and she might be awake and alert when a new inhabitant of this planet chose to make his or her first appearance.

Having inspected the two trawlers the *Rona* turned south, and Captain Stout said: "You may want to turn in, Doctor, because we'll be cruising all night."

"Yes, but if you don't mind I'd rather stay on the bridge until there's less of a roll," for *Rona* was rolling heavily and I thought of the iron ladder to the deck in darkness. I was not ashamed to make this request, but I remembered the day long ago when, to the cheers of a Norwegian crew, I had climbed the rigging to the Crow's Nest of a whaler rolling in a swell on the cold grey northern sea[1]; and now I was sharing the sadness that inspired R. L. S. when he wrote:

> "Give me again all that was there.
> Give me the sun that shone!
> Give me the eyes, give me the soul,
> Give me the lad that's gone."

"That's all right, Doctor," said Captain Stout, "I'll put her head to sea for a couple of minutes and then she'll only be pitching. Starboard—steady."

"Thanks very much. Good-night, Captain."

"Good-night, Doctor."

Two days later we were rounding the north-western coast

[1] *The Arches of the Years*, p. 78.

of Skye and across the grey sea were black cliffs, and hills on which the bracken was now a reddish brown and the grass a pale yellow, a beautiful seascape of desolation; and next morning when the *Rona* left me at Kyle of Lochalsh I stood alone on the pier which in summer is crowded with visitors. The *Lochnevis* with a few passengers on deck arrived from Portree, two pier hands caught her mooring lines, but no one either landed or went on board, and in a few minutes she was on her way to Mallaig. The islands were asleep.